I'm a Day Late
and a Dollar
Short...
and It's Okay!

I'm a Day Late and a Dollar Short... and It's Okay!

Jo Ann Larsen

Deseret Book Company
Salt Lake City, Utah

Library of Congress Cataloging-in-Publication Data

Larsen, Jo Ann.
    I'm a day late and a dollar short—and it's okay! : a woman's
survival guide for the '90s / Jo Ann Larsen.
      p. cm.
    Includes index.
    ISBN 0-87579-480-7
    1. Women—United States—Life skills guides. I. Title.
HQ1221.L36 1991
305.4'0973—dc20   91-16535
                                                                      CIP

Printed in the United States of America

10   9   8   7   6   5   4   3   2   1

Contents

Preface   vii

Introduction   1

1   The Caretaker   12

2   The Juggler   27

3   The Guilt Sponge   53

4   The Pleaser   80

5   The Perfectionist   117

6   The Depleted Woman   150

7   The Woman and Her House   177

8   Women, Husbands, Kids, and Houses   201

9   Filling in the Woman   242

10   Investing in Your "Self"   268

11   The Woman and Work   289

Notes   309

Index   319

Preface

This is a picture of me—a woman of the '90s—snapped as I was deeply engrossed in writing this book. As you might have noticed, the picture looks somewhat like the frazzled woman on the cover. In writing this book, in fact, at times I was just hanging on by my nails—sometimes by my broken nails—as I juggled my wifing, mothering, writing, and "therapizing" roles. However, as I now look back on that experience, I realize I was actually doing fairly well overall in keeping myself intact. I was able to do so because, as I increasingly contemplated the profound stresses on the '90s woman and thus on me, I also became increasingly aware of the need, under the additional stress of writing a book, to apply my own motto: "You're a day late and a dollar short...and it's okay!" Not having a particularly ordered life during that time period *had* to be okay. Otherwise, I would have just come apart at the seams.

But even without a book-writing project in my life, I've realized that in today's world it simply isn't possible for me — or for any woman — to always have her bases covered. That, in fact, is the core message of my book. As women of the '90s, we're living in a transitional era that offers bewildering choices, with accompanying intense stresses. In no other era have the promises to women been more abundant, the messages more confusing, or the pressures more acute. And, under such conditions, there's absolutely no way for us to "have it all" or "do it all." If we're going to maintain any semblance of emotional equilibrium, that *does* need to be okay.

As women of the '90s, we're taking the same trek in discovering our issues and finding creative solutions to them. This book is an expression of what I've learned about myself — and other women — in a five-year quest to piece together the effects on us all of living for several decades in a swiftly changing culture that has blurred the traditional roles of both men and women and offered mushrooming new options, particularly for women. The five-year mark was the beginning of a glimmering and growing consciousness of myself as a woman shaped by the culture in which I lived, often tugged at by conflicting societal forces that I little understood.

In my new "consciousness," I realized I had many more optional ways of thinking and feeling as a woman than I had ever understood before. I also realized I generated much of my overextended scheduling, my own stress, and my own guilt!

Listening to the women around me, I could hear their voices, in concert, speaking repeatedly to the same issues I experienced: too much to do, too little time to do it, a sense of personal failure in not having their lives under control. Ironically, each woman seemed to feel alone in her struggles, unaware of the multitudes of other women who were also beset by similar frustration and exhaustion.

As I presented to women's groups my growing awareness of issues facing the '90s woman and experienced the relief of women in recognizing they were dealing with cultural, not individual, flaws, I recognized the need for a book expressing this reality. In conceiving the book, I decided to capture the themes I was hearing from women through their own voices. Thus, I have incorporated several hundred messages of women speaking in the first person about their stresses. Intertwined with these personal voices are the voices of many female authors who, often through humorous scenarios, have articulately described their own dilemmas. I've also added a view of the stresses of the '90s woman depicted through the eyes of cartoonists whose drawings have appeared in national magazines. They bring to life the old adage that "one picture is worth a thousand words," capturing the awesome and often exasperating dilemmas of the woman who is taking today's cultural roller-coaster ride.

To the chorus of women's voices, I've also mingled my own voice—and a hard-earned personal knowledge of women's struggles that I've gained through frontline experience as a wife and employed mother of five children. Too, I've added my professional experience—twenty-five years of listening intently to women in counseling and, paralleling that, fourteen years of teaching at the University of Utah Graduate School of Social Work, an experience that has enabled me to view women's issues from a broader perspective than I might have otherwise.

Finally, I've mixed in portions of many articles particularly applicable to women that I've published the past seven years as a weekly columnist for the *Deseret News* in Salt Lake City and the *Times News* in Twin Falls, Idaho.

This book would not have been possible without all the women who have so trustingly shared their inner lives with me, including my clients, those women who agreed to personal interviews for this book, those who attended my women's seminars, and those to whom I have spoken in community groups. I give special thanks to these women—their penetrating voices in unison—who have added to the depth of my knowledge of today's woman and her issues and my own understanding of myself.

My thanks also to Eleanor Knowles, vice president and executive editor at Deseret Book, who gave me maximum freedom to develop the book as I envisioned it. Though I created the book's character, it was Eleanor who brought it to life.

In addition, my heartfelt appreciation goes to five special women in my life:

• To Barbara Sandberg, my designated miracle worker, who has offered backdrop support, arranged and taped my seminars, and gathered and organized most of the written material on women I've incorporated into the book. It is to Barbara that credit goes for the book's title after she said to me one day, "I have this great idea. In naming your book, why don't you use your own motto—'I'm a day late and a dollar short . . . and it's okay.' " It didn't take me long to decide that was a good idea. Barbara *does* have good ideas!

• To Kim Turner, who transcribed my seminar tapes with a flair, offered valued editorial assistance, and manned my telephone so I could retain a mind uncluttered enough to work on this manuscript. Kim has embarked on the journey to "conscious caretaking" discussed in Chapter One and has been a willing and fascinating subject whose own personal success stories have been interlaced throughout the book. In more than one instance she provided just the right quotation for a bare space.

• To Colleen Burt and Joy Morse, who weekly have cleaned

my house, raked the clutter aside, and saved us all from utter ruin. Despite all I know and have described in Chapter Seven about women needing to separate their houses from their self-esteem, I still feel better with a clean house. Colleen, in a pinch, has also been a willing chauffeur of children and a rescuer of both children and mother in crisis situations.

• And to Alice E. Jackson—my mother, friend, confidant, educator, consultant, proofreader, critic, chef, nurse, model, nutrition and health expert, procurer of supplies, and forager in charge of unusual requests—I offer my deepest love and appreciation. She is the Ultimate Caretaker, endowed with the most exquisite of caretaking characteristics. Through her generosity, sensitivity, empathy, intelligence, and writing skill I have learned much. Sharing our life experiences as caretakers through the medium of this book's development has increased our knowledge of each other and brought us even closer as women and friends.

Add to this indomitable support system my father, Ivin M. Jackson, a retired veterinarian. I have often marveled how I could be so fortunate as to have two such nurturing parents. I periodically traveled from Salt Lake City to Kimberly, Idaho, taking refuge with my parents for a week at a time while I struggled over this manuscript. My father was always there, quietly worrying about me, loving me, cheering me on, bringing me drinks and snacks, and offering well-deserved advice concerning my health and well-being—an elegant caretaker in his own right.

Finally, my thanks to my family:

• To my husband, Larry, for his love, support, and understanding; his bedmaking and dishdoing; his patience in spending many late nights alone; and his many trips to the corner convenience store for some timely refreshment to propel me through a mind-numbing episode with my manuscript.

• And to my children — Shelly, Jared, Brian, Rani, and Erin — who collectively provided much of my lab experience for the chapter on surviving with kids, and who individually cheered and encouraged me many times. My thanks for their patience concerning my time away; my sporadic "brain cramps," mental "check-outs," and ozone trips; and frequent pizza dinners.

I love you all.

Introduction

The Woman of the '90s

Every now and then I have a fleeting feeling I can actually make it all work, but then something happens and I realize it's a delusion."[1]

These words come from a woman — by nature, a caretaker of others — whose job it is to keep her world and the world of all those around her tidy and in order. These are also the words of a woman who concludes she is not succeeding.

Do this woman's words sound familiar? Are you, like her, juggling an impossible number of tasks, always straining to do your best but never quite feeling you can "make it all work"? If so, this book is for you. It is dedicated to the many women who believe they are alone in experiencing the guilt and frustration that emanate from never having everybody or everything in their jurisdiction attended to or taken care of. The woman, of course, knows whose fault that is!

In today's world, the acute stress many women typically experience does not occur without significant reason. Such stress, in fact, results largely from living within a rapidly changing culture that is constantly being transfigured by such forces as the advent of new knowledge and technology and changing economic and social conditions.

Such forces have significantly transformed the roles of women, leaving them with myriad new options and few guidelines by which to measure their competency. As Nicholas von Hoffman, in an article titled "American Woman of the '90s," observes, "The story of American women from the founding of the Republic to now is the transition from social role to role model. Women were born into a social role in Martha Washington's day; choices were few and traditional duties were many." Today, traditional social roles have been largely abandoned, replaced by a staggering array of role models from which a woman may choose. As a result, messages concerning her role are often inconsistent, confusing, and confounding. "We search for rules to live by," Hoffman points out, "but the ground is unstable; no sooner does a person think she has it straight than an announcement comes of a new norm, a new truth."[2]

The many choices women face today, particularly with respect to marriage, family, and career, are aptly described in this analogy: "For many, life on the cusp of the '90s is a little like eating dinner at a five-star restaurant. Everything on the menu is tempting — just about any combination is possible. But what you choose for the main dish is likely to affect your decision about dessert, so it's worth taking time to decide."[3]

Though each woman has choices, she also suffers from penetrating guilt accompanying those choices. "Like a burr, guilt attaches itself to working mothers' lives, making it all but impossible for them to derive satisfaction from *any* decision or action they take," observes Barbara J. Berg, the author of an article entitled "Working Mother Overload." She sees this guilt as emanating primarily from a woman's sense that she has betrayed her personal past. Today's women were raised by traditional mothers who dedicated their lives to home-making and childrearing, a model that remains fixed in a woman's subconscious. Thus, she says, "No matter how far we may have moved away from our mother — socially, intellectually, professionally or geographically — she continues to be our most important and persistent role model. And when we find ourselves not measuring up to this model or behaving in ways that depart from it — deciding to take a job, for example, instead of staying at home — the response is automatic and immediate: guilt."[4]

Ironically, even today's "stay-at-home" mother (who is supposedly emulating her own mother and thus should be off the hook!) suffers intense guilt, which arises partly from her experiencing in today's achievement-oriented culture much higher performance expectations (and performance anxiety!) than her mother experienced in an earlier era. Today's homemaker constantly absorbs, without discrimination, never-ending messages in the media detailing what a woman might do to increase her family's well-being, thereby ever-extending her role description and her "job."

In addition, the woman at home usually assumes she should be the ideal homemaker — and she also usually assumes she isn't. This conclusion, which generates guilt, originates in part from the fact that a homemaker's responsibilities are not well defined, as in a paid job, so it is difficult for her to assess how she is doing. As a result, she is likely to infer that her performance isn't up to snuff. Researcher Janet Murphy reached this conclusion in a 1984 study of guilt in women who worked outside the home and those who did not. Says Murphy: "My sense from the women I interviewed is that they are second-guessing their every move; no matter which choice they make, it won't be right."[5]

The issues described thus far barely scratch the surface of

those over which women may feel guilt. Today's woman typically suffers epidemic bouts of guilt — over just about everything — almost all the time. She is, in fact, a *Guilt Sponge*. Observes one author: "The circumstances that can set off a woman's defense mechanism range from ridiculously trivial to overwhelmingly important matters. A sloppy house. Ten extra pounds. Dirty hair. Working. Not working. Marrying a younger man. Marrying an older man. Not marrying at all. Too many children. Too few children. No children at all."[6]

Today's woman is also ordinarily a *Juggler*. Absorbing — with little screening — the nonstop messages from an overheated culture about all the things she ought to do, she races to get those things done. She can become particularly overwrought if she is juggling responsibilities both at home and at the workplace. Says author Maggie Strong, "It's impossible to be two places at once and that's exactly what's demanded of a working mother. She's supposed to be at the office but the baby's sick. Or she's on a crowded subway, late to the day care center, and the center's about to shut its doors for the day. These are frantic situations."[7]

And, today's woman is often a *Pleaser*. A large portion of her "self" is devoted to appeasing others, and that self is diminished when the approval is not forthcoming. Says one woman who has organized her life in the quest of pleasing others: "I realize now I've retarded my own growth by giving people power over me. I kept trying to read their cues and do what they wanted. I thought that if I was only good enough long enough, that I would gain the approval I've always sought from others."

To the above characteristics, add the tendency of today's woman to be a *Perfectionist*. Many a woman ties her performance to her worth and, therefore, tacitly assumes that the more she accomplishes and the better the job, the better she will feel about herself. However, her perfectionism prods her to achieve impossible goals—and thus prevents her from ever achieving those goals or feeling good about herself. There is always something undone ahead, some step she has missed, some contingency she didn't count on, something not done well enough, that brings her down and calls her worth into question.

Finally, today's woman is usually a *Depleted Woman*. Many can identify with the remark of one overworked woman who, in passing a cemetery, was surprised to hear an inner voice whispering, "Now that looks like an easy job—just lying around."[8] The depleted woman takes care of everybody but herself. When push comes to shove, she gives up the activities that could keep her "self" in good repair—sleep, exercising, eating nutritionally sound meals, even relaxing.

Described thus far are five typical characteristics of today's woman. She is a juggler, a guilt sponge, a pleaser, a perfectionist, and a depleted woman. Add to these her most basic characteristic—that of *Caretaker*. These characteristics, featured in upcoming chapters, are manifestations of traditional cultural conditioning that has inadvertently shaped the perceptions and attitudes of women, often to their disadvantage, in an era that requires more flexible responses. These characteristics particularly emanate from the 1950s concept of the traditional family—"a concept," says Berg, "that places men in the workforce as the breadwinner and Mom at home baking cookies."[9]

Traditionally—since the 1840s, when men began going off the farm to work each day and women became general managers of the home—the sexes have shaken out into two categories: he the breadwinner, she the caretaker of people and the home. While men were culturally trained to be dominant, aggressive, competitive, and focused on work, women were trained to deliver emotional support to all within their purview twenty-four hours a day. Thus, while a man's identity emanated from his work, a woman's identity emanated from pleasing others and making them happy.

Eroding and transforming these traditional roles over the past several decades have been immense social changes: in new technology; in inflation; in housing; in medical and tuition costs; in consciousness-raising with respect to equality issues; in education for women; in divorced and single mothers heading and supporting one-parent families; in women entering the workplace; in industry, in recognizing and acknowledging women's contributions; in new career openings for women.

As a result of these dramatic cultural changes, both women and men are affected by immense reverberations in sex roles, many reeling from emotional collisions, their marriages shaken to the core, as traditional responses no longer fit changing family circumstances. Lacking are creative new responses to insure the family's basic survival.

Largely unrecognized in this cultural shift in gender roles is the impact of men and women changing, but not at the same rate. Arlie Hochschild, in her book *The Second Shift,* calls this the "stalled revolution." "There is a 'his' and a 'hers' to economic development of the United States," she explains. "In the latter part of the nineteenth century, it was mainly men who were drawn off the farm into paid industrial work and who changed their way of life and their identity. At that point in history, men became more different from their fathers than women became from their mothers. Today the economic arrow points to women; it is women who are being drawn into wage work, and women who are undergoing changes in their way of life and identity. Women are departing more from their mothers' and grandmothers' way of life, men are doing so less."

The cultural shift in women's roles has created significant

stress for both men and women and has been unaccompanied by a cultural understanding of marriage and work that would make this transition smooth. As Hochschild observes: "Each marriage bears the footprints of economic trends which originate far outside marriage. . . . Problems between husbands and wives, problems which seem 'individual' and 'marital,' are often individual experiences of powerful economic and cultural shock waves.

"Many of today's marital clashes reflect a broader social tension—between faster changing women and slower changing men," she continues. "The 'female culture' has shifted more rapidly than the 'male culture'; the image of the go-get-'em woman has yet to be fully matched by the image of the let's-take-care-of-the-kids-together man. More important, over the last thirty years, men's underlying feelings about taking responsibility at home have changed much less than women's feelings have changed about forging some kind of identity at work."[10]

And so, what happens to men and women who are changing at different rates, especially when they understand so little about the dramatic cultural shift in roles over the past two decades and the personal impact on themselves?

They fight. And argue. And get angry and hurt over the issue of who does what. And they become emotionally estranged. And sometimes they divorce, often because they personalize issues caused by cultural forces that are quietly transforming their marriages.

The cultural impact on marriages and on men's roles is addressed in this book. The book's broader purpose, however, is to delineate cultural shifts in women's roles and the manner in which these changes may impinge on a woman's well-being. Despite cultural redefinitions of roles, women are still primarily caretakers at heart. And they are caught in "unconscious

"Would you mind sending me to Law School instead?"

caretaking"—driven by traditional cultural conditioning operating at an unconscious level to achieve far beyond what it
is humanly possible to accomplish. This tacit programming is
creating in women today epidemic stress, depression, and low
self-esteem.

The cultural programming that drives women—programming that dovetailed with social conditions in the '50s—does
not work carte blanche in the '90s. Yet most women are judging
their performance using outmoded programming and standards from an earlier era; and, despite the fact that they invest
100 percent of themselves in discharging their "duties," they
consider themselves as flawed and failing.

Why is it that the self-esteem of a woman—who gives all
she's got—is likely to take a tumble when she opens her refrigerator and sees new life forms? Or when an outsider sees
her house when it is not put together perfectly? Or when her
kids look scruffy and the neighbor's kids don't? Or when . . .

The "when's" are endless. There are few events in a woman's life that don't indict her, don't call her worth into question.

This is a book that addresses a woman's self-esteem, moment by moment. It will aid you, as a reader, in divesting your worth from the hundreds of events that happen to you each day. And, hopefully, there will come a time when you can view those life forms in the refrigerator, or invite someone into your less-than-perfect house, or allow the fact your kids look scruffy, all unemotionally and without getting a crimp in your self-esteem!

In addition, this book will help you in moving from unconscious to conscious caretaking — to make conscious choices, in view of your priorities, about how you allocate your limited time, energy, and resources. It will also help you to ask for help, to say no, or to even get a no, without batting an eye — and to realize that there is an end to you and that it is okay not to be all things to all people all the time.

Another aim of this book is to encourage you to slow down — for your sake. If you're like most women, you're going a hundred miles an hour down the track — and you may not even know why or where you're going. Today's woman tends to be on automatic pilot — a flurry of frenzied motion, achieving activity for activity's sake. And today's woman tends to lead the unexamined life, expending all her energy and her "self" without assessing how her efforts relate to her basic underlying priorities.

As a result of pressing herself to perform nonstop, today's woman is likely depleted and on her way to burnout and even depression. Thus, still another aim is to aid you in assessing if you are a woman who is wearing herself down and out and not taking care of that self. And if you are, you are encouraged to take immediate steps to institute a self-enhancement, repair, and maintenance program. No one else can do it for you! And you are the person who will incur the penalties if you wear your emotional and physical self to the bone.

Yet another aim is to help you to take charge of your own self-esteem. Most women gather data about their worth by carefully scrutinizing the cues of others. If the perceived re-action in the environment is positive, a woman's self-esteem goes up—temporarily. If the perceived reaction is negative, her self-esteem plunges—and is likely to stay bottomed out for some time. Thus, her self-esteem rests with the whims of others rather than in her own hands and head.

You are encouraged to invest in yourself. You are the guardian of yourself. And you are all you have. This is the only mortal life you will experience. You and all those you love will be better off for the investments you make in yourself.

A final aim is to encourage you to celebrate the temporary: to take time today to feel, to experience, to be happy, and to savor your significant relationships with others—today! So often, says one author, women are "like the gardener who will water and weed but forgets about smelling the rose. Smelling roses is hard to fit into our schedule."[11]

With that introduction, you're ready to begin making con-scious and deliberate decisions about your self-esteem, your commitments, and your priorities. Your trek will take you through the following content:

Chapters One through Six describe typical culturally de-termined responses in women that exhaust their energy and resources.

Chapter Seven describes another characteristic response of women—that of entangling their self-worth with their houses. A chaotic house often signals a chaotic woman.

Chapter Eight gets to issues that occur when women, whose self-esteem depends on the orderliness of their houses, inter-mingle with kids and husbands who are oblivious to that fact.

Chapters Nine and Ten address the growth, maintenance, and repair of women and the firming up of the self. Many women, who are used to meeting everyone's needs but their own, have trouble investing in their own development—and in considering that they are worth the time, energy, and resources such an investment would take.

Finally, Chapter Eleven addresses work issues, a subject that applies to every woman because, as you well know, there is no such thing as a nonworking woman.

Chapter 1

The Caretaker

Of a woman's characteristics, the most notable and noble of all is that she was designed to be a caretaker—a dispenser of all emotional supplies—who dutifully stretches to nurture and to meet the needs of everyone in her space all the time. If caretaking is a woman's foremost strength, it may also become her Achilles' heel, causing her unending stress if the caring for others goes unchecked. Depleting her resources and over-whelming her capacity to give, her nonstop caretaking may finally cause a woman to use up her "self" and collapse into burnout or depression.

A woman who drives herself repeatedly to exhaustion is driven by *unconscious* caretaking. She simply responds to her cultural programming. She isn't thinking about what she's doing or making deliberate choices. Neither is she looking ahead at the consequences of her runaway behavior. She's on a treadmill that is moving faster and faster, and she'll be there until, sooner or later, she crashes. And she will crash if she doesn't pay attention—for, as one woman who knows, put it: "If you don't take care of yourself gracefully, you will take care of yourself ungracefully."

You are a caretaker. This chapter is about whether you are engaging in unconscious or conscious caretaking. In *unconscious caretaking,* you simply respond, without thought, to internal and external signals. In *conscious caretaking,* you take charge of your life and your choices. You become acutely aware of the internal programming that constantly pushes you to always give, give, give, and to only reluctantly receive. You learn to act rather than react. You realize you have limited capacity to give, and therefore you make decisions — without guilt — about how to allocate your limited time, energy, and resources. You give amply to others but you also allocate time to nurture yourself. You know that if you take care of *you,* there will be enough of you to take care of *them.*

How do I know this? Because I am a caretaker — and because I am taking the journey from unconscious to conscious caretaking. We are of the same kind!

To launch a discussion of the impacts of caretaking, consider a personal example drawn from my own life several years ago. Though this example is one from my mother role, my stress level in this situation was affected by acute and accumulating stress coming from juggling a number of different roles, including full-time work as a therapist and the author of a weekly newspaper column. I present this example because I believe it illustrates in general the conflicting and overwhelming feelings most women experience — whether they are married or single, young or old, with or without children — as they struggle to perform perfectly in all aspects of their lives. Women in the '90s are juggling a multitude of roles. No matter what their position, women today usually take on too much, and the stress they place upon themselves exacts a terrible price. The single mother suffers most intensively because she is juggling all the multiple roles and also doing the jobs of two people.

Turning to my story, it was Monday evening, and the weekly newspaper column I write was due early the next morning. I had been home all day, giving to four of my five children, and I was brain-dead. There was nothing left of me to choose a subject or to do the preparatory work to meet that deadline. *I'm not going to make it,* I thought. *I'm just too stressed.* And that's when an idea hit. I would write about my stress. I would capture a grueling half-an-hour scenario with my children. Here is an excerpt from the article I wrote:

"No, Jill, you can't make a hopscotch in the kitchen. It will be in the way."

"But Mommmmmmmmm, I'll clean it up soon and I'll use masking tape — it won't hurt anything."

"No — you'll have to make the hopscotch outside. I'm trying to clean the house."

"But Mommmmmmmmm, it's cold outside. I have to have someplace to play right now."

"No, Jill! Jamie, watch out! You're going to spill your milk. Push it back . . . well, get a rag and clean it up. No, never mind, I'll clean it up."

"Mom, can I make the hopscotch in the . . . "

"No! I said No! Here's another glass of milk, Jamie."

"Mom, can I have four dollars?"

"What do you need four dollars for, Debbie?"

"I have to pay back the money I borrowed from Cary."

"I'm not sure you answered my question but, all right. Where's my purse? I don't know where my purse is."

"Where's my permission slip, Mom? I HAVE to have my permission slip signed or I can't go to the garbage dump tomorrow."

"I don't know, Michael. You said garbage — look in the garbage. Maybe I threw it away."

"Mom, I HAVE to have my four dollars right now. Cary's outside waiting for me."

"I'm still looking for my purse, Debbie. Maybe I left it in the car. Look in the car."

"Well, Mommmmmmmmm, where *could* I put the hopscotch?"

"I don't know, Jill—let me think for a minute...Jamie, you're going to spill your...where's the rag? Has anyone seen the rag?!!!"

"Mom, here's my permission slip—it *was* in the garbage and it has ketchup on it. What will I doooooo?"

"Here, don't cry, Michael—it will still work. Give it to me!"

"Mom, I need some more milk."

At this point, mother is in a daze—blitzed by four innocent children who have nothing more on their minds than meeting their own needs—right now. She wipes the ketchup on her dress and signs the permission slip, finds her purse in the car (where she told Debbie it was) and shells out her last four dollars, cleans up what is now the third milk spill, and then goes to Jill's bedroom, where she discovers Jill and two of her friends playing hopscotch.

With a glazed look in her eyes, mother turns and walks away—too distraught to even comment on the hopscotch. "My mother never told me it was going to be like this," she thinks, staggering to a chair.

Mother has temporarily equalized the situation by responding to everyone's needs, but another onslaught is in the offing. Debbie will be back to talk about the dress she needs for the dance this weekend, Jill will show her mother the patches that need to be sewn on her Brownie blouse *right now,* Michael will report he has to have a treat for his school class party tomorrow, and Jamie will come screaming that the dog has chewed up his favorite whoopie—all life-threatening emergencies as far as the kids are concerned.

Stress—that is what mother is under. And by the time she has experienced a number of such offensives throughout the day (with demands that can come four or five times a minute), she may have full-blown symptoms of battle fatigue: headaches, exhaustion, withdrawal, crying, and difficulty concentrating.

What feelings does this stressed-out caretaker experience as she staggers to her chair? When asked this question, various women from all walks of life have inferred that she feels—

—exhausted. She thinks, "How am I ever going to be strong enough to accomplish everything?"

—overwhelmed, frustrated, and out of control. She feels she can't handle a simple day like everyone else in the world does.

—disillusioned. She wonders, "Is this all there is?"

—guilty. She simply can't get everything accomplished. Or she just plain might not like her kids at that moment. That puts a whammy on a mom, because aren't moms always supposed to like their kids at *all* times?

—like giving up. She wants to turn in her mother's card. But no one will take it. She's tried to give it away before.

—resentful. It seems as though she's the only one on the defensive team. Everyone else is on the offensive team.

—inadequate. She asks herself, "What's wrong with me? I should be able to do this."

—a sense of failure. She berates herself for not being able to keep her life ordered and organized.

—a sense of being alone. Sometimes she feels as though she's the only one going through this.

—trapped. She wonders, "How did I ever get myself into this?" and "Who assigned me to this duty anyway? I'd like to have a word with that person."

Besides experiencing a multitude of awful feelings toward herself, our caretaker is likely to review all her "sins of omission." I could get control of my life, she concludes, if I would just—

—work harder
—sleep less
—organize better
—make better use of my time
—cook and clean more
—exercise more
—spend more quality time with my children
—make more money (and spend less)
—be more patient . . . kind . . . cheerful
—train my children better
—lose ten pounds (especially lose ten pounds!)

The relentless self-recriminations are painful and over-whelming—the anger toward herself for failing, unbearable. Moving to a self-preservation mode, our caretaker ponders, "How could this just be *my* fault?" She knows she can't be completely responsible all the time. Look at how hard she's working—how hard she's pushing—nonstop. She feels over-burdened, unappreciated, and overworked. It's not fair.

So she looks around. If she is not entirely to blame, there are only two categories of people who are likely candidates to take the rap—husband (if she has one) and kids (if she has any).

Now she's angry at *them*. She zeros in on her hapless husband. "It's your fault. (Look what you did to me!) (If you really cared, you'd help more!) (You don't appreciate me!) (Your socks are always on the floor!) (You're never home to take responsibility!)"

And the kids (who are demanding, of course) get their share. She yells and screams at them. They're to blame because they (are ungrateful) (are lazy) (are spoiled) (don't give her the respect she deserves) (don't love her).

One woman says about her anger: "I've only just realized how angry I was at people for expecting things from me. But I never said anything. I would just mumble and grumble. Iron-ically, I was the one teaching them to expect everything I was doing for them. It wasn't their fault."

Another woman says: "I was carrying all of these people on my back, like an opossum, and these attachments were always there. My anger came from feeling like I never had any time to myself."

These reports are from overburdened women who are moving toward *conscious* caretaking—who are acknowledging their anger and beginning to take charge of it. Many women, however, given to *unconscious* caretaking, just simply expe-

rience anger without any introspection—and feel tremen-
dously guilty about it. They resent the onslaught of demands
that are coming in on them, and are doing their best to contain
their anger. But it won't stay put!

The caretaker caught in this bind knows she is supposed
to be sweet, to have a smile on her face, and to be patient with
the people she loves most while they're seemingly making
horrendous demands on her. But she isn't making it and it's
her fault. There must be something terribly wrong with her
because the monster inside keeps coming out.

Does the description of the caretaker given thus far strike
uncomfortably close to home? Are you involved in unconscious
caretaking? And, if so, are you ready for a change? You're stuck
if you repeatedly play out your old program. There is only
more exhaustion, more stress, more distress ahead. We're talking major wipeout!

If you want to start the journey toward conscious caretaking
that others have taken, you'll need to challenge several deeply
ingrained—but erroneous—beliefs that constantly cause you
to indict yourself or others for the fact you don't have your
life together.

One false belief is that it is your fault when you can't
accomplish everything; the flaw is in you. Rather, the flaw is in
a culture that floods a caretaker at a multitude of levels with
overwhelming messages about what she needs to do in order
to be adequate: "Are your glasses sparkling clean?" "Have you
flossed your children's teeth today?" "Does your husband have
ring-around-the collar?" The shoulds are staggering and endless.

Another false belief is that it is *someone's* fault. As you'll
see throughout this book, caretaking issues are not "fault"
issues. There are simply tacit cultural forces at work that you
need to understand. With this knowledge, you can make con-

scious choices to control your life (and to free others from your wrath).

Yet another false belief is that the solutions to your problems lie outside yourself, perhaps through a change in someone else's behavior or actions. Instead, *you* are responsible for your choices. You are responsible for any runaway caretaking—for having too much to do, for not having control of your schedule or your time. You are your own taskmaster. The bad news is that you may need to change. The good news is that you can.

Toward Conscious Caretaking

Perhaps you've had the experience of rolling out dough too thin and getting holes in the dough. And when you try to patch one hole, often you just get another.

That's the way it usually is with the caretaker. She stretches too far, too often, too many ways, and she gets holes—or, as one woman put it, "stretch holes" (to go with our stretch marks).

Caretakers will continue to get "stretch holes" until they truly grasp that they are finite or limited, that there is only so much of them to give to others.

Consider, if you will, the Boundary Box (see illustration 1, p. 20) and put in that box all the time, energy, and resources you have. There is nothing left of you outside of that box. Notice, however, that the box has dotted rather than firm lines because you probably have very unclear boundaries.

Though you are finite and limited, at any one moment you may be operating outside of your boundaries. You may stretch to take care of "just one more little thing." You can do it, you know. You've done it before. No problem.

You are, without thinking about it, viewing yourself as invincible. You *can* do this job, no matter how far you have

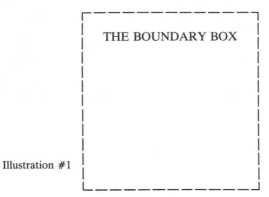

THE BOUNDARY BOX

Illustration #1

to stretch past your boundaries or how many holes you get. Consider these ways of stretching past realistic boundaries:

• Someone calls from work requesting you take another shift and, although you're staggering from overload, you agree.

• Somebody from a school committee asks you to run for PTA president and you've already said yes to the Heart Fund, the Cancer Fund, and the Blood Drive. You nod again.

• You meet an old friend you haven't seen in five years and learn that her husband recently died of cancer. You tell yourself, "Oh, I ought to take dinner to her." Never mind that you're so exhausted you wish someone would bring dinner to your house.

• A friend of yours calls who needs to talk. But she needed to talk yesterday and the day before, and several times last week. Talking to her repeatedly is eating into the time you spend with your kids in the evening. But you continue to be available because you feel so bad for her.

• Halloween is only two days away. Earlier you bought the material for your children's costumes, which you're firm about making, although now it means you'll have to work completely through at least one night.

• Your grown daughter phones and asks you to make costumes two days before Halloween because she doesn't have time to make them—and you say yes.

• Your neighbor calls to tell you that her grown daughter called her to make the Halloween costumes because she didn't have time, and she (the neighbor) said she would but she doesn't have time, and would you make them because you're single and you probably do have time—and, bless you, you say yes.

By themselves, none of these discrete events might be a problem to you. The real rub comes when you constantly say yes to things that stretch your capacity to give and that cause you to operate consistently on the fringes of your boundaries. Consider the effect of your repeated yeses on your Boundary Box (see illustration 2, p. 22).

Each of the assignments a caretaker accepts extends and stretches her further out and further into overload. Her basic schedule (the box) is already full—nothing more can be jammed in there. If this pattern sounds familiar, you may want to assess whether you're stretched too far by comparing yourself against these typical characteristics of the stretched-out caretaker:

• You're well organized, efficient, somewhat compulsive, always planning ahead to anticipate every contingency so everything will be perfect.

• Your mind whirls nonstop with all the things you have to do.

• You're typically rushing and late for appointments.

• You feel constant pressure—too much to do and too little time to do it.

• You feel tense, frazzled, or anxious much of the time.

• You become angry at people who ask you to do things (though you just quietly swallow your feelings and say yes).

• At times you don't have the energy to give any more (but you still keep moving your weary bones to take care of others).

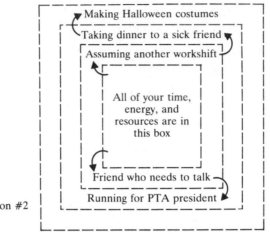

Illustration #2

• You find yourself constantly on edge and snapping at your kids or other people.

• You have difficulty relaxing. Even when you slow down, you feel impelled to do several things at once.

• At times you find it difficult to concentrate or focus on the tasks you must get done.

• You feel that not getting everything done somehow has to do with your inability to measure up.

If you answered a resounding yes to the majority of these items, you're a likely candidate for "stretch-hole" repair. If that's in order, consider adopting the following guidelines, which will mark the beginning of your journey toward conscious caretaking:

1. You are in charge of firming up your own boundaries — nobody can do it for you. No one else is at fault if you stretch yourself paper-thin.

2. You have a right — even an obligation — to protect your limited time, energy, and resources. As one author aptly put it, you "can't respond to every public, personal, and professional cry for help."[1] That means being comfortable with saying no.

3. You also have a right to make your own choices about how to allocate those assets without defending your choices to anyone. It's vital that you trust your own judgment about what works best for you and yours.

4. You have an obligation to yourself to identify priorities and to weed out of your schedule time-drainers that sap your strength.

The key to ridding yourself of "stretch-holes" lies in giving up doing so many things or giving up doing them perfectly. You can't have it all or do it all without devastating personal cost.

5. You also have an obligation to clear a space for yourself in your boundary box and to take care of that self as dutifully as you do other people.

Are you ready to start tending to yourself? Take a deep breath. This is your first big test: Consider clearing a space in the boundary box for *you*.

When a caretaker hears she needs to take care of herself, she often perceives it as someone telling her to be selfish. "Who, me? Selfish? Never!" says this indignant woman, who would rather be caught dragging an extra pair of pantyhose from one leg of her slacks than being viewed as having a selfish bone in her body. So things that have to do with taking care of herself default to automatic reject when they go through her brain.

Why does a caretaker have such a tough time considering that *she* is important too? Because she is designed to be other-centered—to feel guilty if she *isn't* taking care of others and to feel guilty if she *is* taking care of herself.

It takes some pretty fancy talking to get most caretakers to hear what's coming next, but here goes: *You aren't being selfish if you take care of yourself. You aren't even being self-centered. You are essentially being centered-in-self!*

There is a quantitative difference between being selfish or self-centered (tending to the self to the exclusion of others) and being centered-in-self (tending to the self in the context of relationships).

To center-in-self is to say, "You count and I count. I need to take care of me so there is enough of me to take care of you." It is also to value your own personal development simply because a foremost task in *being* is to *become.* You exist, as Martin Buber has said, to actualize your "unique, unprecedented and ever recurring potentialities." For that mission, there need not be any defense, any apology. You are entitled to develop your uniqueness simply because you are.

Another way of putting it is that you are ultimately your own guardian, in charge of your own life and outcome. There is no one else to assume that task.

When you chronically deplete your resources, you draw against yourself until there may not be a self left. In several studies on self-esteem, in fact, women typically describe themselves as "shot full of holes," "full of gaps," "a big blank." As they look inward, pondering who and what they are, the report is often the same: "There's not much of a self there."[2]

So if you are convinced you need to invest in you — that you are important too — what then? What does it mean to clear a space for yourself? One practical woman who knows said it this way: "If I'm not on my list of things to do every day, then I put myself there because I realize I need to take care of me, too." What this woman has done is plan a way of systematically revitalizing herself each day. She counts. She's on her list. She accepts that she is deserving of the same kind of benevolent, nurturing treatment she gives to everyone else.

So what can you do? There are tons of options, but let's push this discussion a little with a radical idea. What if you took a day off? I can hear a "sputter, sputter" somewhere and

By James Estes. Courtesy *Good Housekeeping*

someone protesting, "I can't do that!" I just suggested a day off to test your tolerance level. I know *you* can't take a day off, or think you can't, but consider a woman who really did. This woman, who happens to be a homemaker, says:

"Tuesday became my day off. To me, a day off meant doing anything I wanted to do. Anything. If I felt like scrubbing the floor, I could. But if I wanted to sleep in or to go shopping, I could do that.

"At first I felt awkward taking 'my day,' and my husband was uncomfortable with it, too. We'd go through this conversation: (Him) 'What are you doing?' (Me) 'It's my day off.' (Him) 'What do you mean, your day off?' (Me) 'Well, I just decided to take my own day off because no one ever gives me one. I have seven-day-a-week, twenty-four-hour-a-day duty, and I just need a day off.'

"At first he would make sarcastic remarks like, 'Oh, that's right! It's your day off,' as I would sleep in or go off somewhere. But after several weeks he started asking me, 'What are you going to do today?' It became a fun thing. He could see that I was happier, and that pleased him. He just had to get used to the idea. Nobody likes change."

As this story illustrates, to "clear a space" means taking responsibility for what you want. It also means getting reacquainted with yourself. Quite frankly, the busyness of caretaking is often a way of avoiding responsibility for who you are and what you need. You don't have to think. Or go on record. Or represent your needs or feelings to anyone. Or examine the substance of your life. Or take responsibility for your sense of self, an issue we work on throughout the book.

Now take a look at the boundary box. It should be a box that has firm boundaries and a firm space for you (see illustration 3, below).

That seems fair, doesn't it—your having a small portion of the box? Say yes. Nod your head. That's right. It's not only fair, it's smart. As underscored previously, if you take care of *you*, there'll be enough of you to take care of *them*!

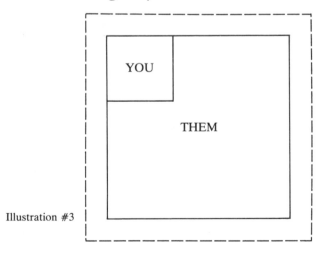

Illustration #3

Chapter 2

The Juggler

You've seen jugglers on TV who juggle an impossible number of plates and you say to yourself, "Nobody can do that!" Many caretakers do similarly as they try to balance innumerable details—many more than they can possibly manage effectively. And they become intensely preoccupied with their own balancing act as they try to coordinate and accomplish all those details. In that sense, they, too, are jugglers.

Describing her ability to juggle, one woman relates: "I consciously try to keep five things going at once. For example, I'll be doing the washing, preparing dinner, overseeing a child setting the table, wiping prints off the wall, and RSVPing a birthday party all at the same time. I'm always trying to synchronize the events and people in my life. The best thing that ever happened was when I got a portable phone. Now I'm not tied down. I can go everywhere—upstairs, downstairs—and do the laundry, fix dinner, check on the kids, and still have time to socialize without feeling guilty."

Another woman says: "In my planner I have lists of all the things I have to do. I have birthday invitations to get. I have to call the clown and order the cake. I have to get the carpets cleaned. I have to call the insurance man and the roofer. I have to take the dog to the vet. I have to pick out the kids' school clothes. Oh, and I have to call the prison tomorrow because I have to go there for a work-related TV story on Saturday. So, calling the prison comes between buying birthday invitations and shopping for the kids' school clothes!"

Perhaps the biggest reason women juggle is that burned in their brains are thousands of things they need to accomplish — implicit messages absorbed from the modeling of their mothers and from years of tacit cultural programming dictating to them their "woman's role." Women are also like sponges, soaking up from the media and from other women an ever-growing list of new things to do. ("Oh, that's wonderful! I'll have to try that!") As their families expand and they take on more employment-related responsibilities, their conception of what they should do continues to expand, too. There is little sifting or sorting through their shoulds, little setting of priorities, little contemplation of the unspoken, unaccomplished, and often unnecessary tasks that drive them.

Another reason women juggle is that they are likely to notice every detail in their charge that isn't done and to feel keenly responsible for it. No matter how minor, that detail nags at a woman, indicts her, says she's a slug. There is no forgiveness for tasks left undone. She must hurry. She must do more. She must take care of her "job" — no matter that three women couldn't accomplish all she has assigned herself to do.

Still another reason for juggling is that many women tend to tie activity and production level to self-esteem. The more they accomplish, the better they feel; the less they accomplish, the more likely they are to experience feelings of failure and inadequacy. For many, to stop or to rest equates with "not doing my job" and that, in turn, means facing feelings of being flawed because *job* and *worth* are inextricably linked. For these reasons, and the fact that their definition of a good caretaker resides in always meeting the needs of others—which are never-ending—such women have extreme difficulty in just *being*.

By nature and by training, caretakers are also programmed to be extremely intuitive and to meet other people's needs— immediately! A caretaker carries around a twenty-four-hour beeper that constantly alerts her to the needs of anyone (even strangers) who come into her space. She is on call. She will respond—speedily! She has even been trained to anticipate needs and will often zip in to meet a need before someone knows he or she has one. "Oh, you'll want that shirt tomorrow. It's already washed and ironed and in your closet." "Here—I already cut your corn off the cob." Never mind that, in some instances, people want to take care of their own needs!

Because new needs and new contingencies are constantly emerging, caretakers are easily derailed from one task to an- other. Referring to the fragmentation she experiences, one woman observes: "On Tuesday I had only three things to deal with but they were major—but I don't know what happened to Tuesday. Yesterday I got up and just crossed out Tuesday and wrote Wednesday on my list. Tuesday just kind of disin- tegrated."

The Juggler and the Workplace

Take the caretaker who is unconsciously programmed to take care of thousands of details—a woman who, without being aware of it, indiscriminately adds new details to her already overflowing list and then indicts herself for not having them done; a woman who focuses intensely on instantly meeting any need. Now add part- or full-time employment without any real release from full-time domestic duties, and you really get a frantic woman. Observes such a woman: "I make lists. I've got lists everywhere. I will put one in my purse, and when I pull it out there are still undone things on it from two months ago, so I start a new list. It gets to the point where I need to make lists of my lists."

Another says, "I just live from day to day and I always feel like I'm trying to catch my breath. Between trying to be the perfect mom and perfect worker, there's always something I need to do, and half the time I can't even keep track of what I'm behind on."[1]

One juggler describes the intense competition between work and at-home commitments: "The other day, on my day off, I called the head of the Immigration and Naturalization Service about this Soviet dancer who defected—and at the same time I am washing dishes and trying to help Julie get dressed and Dan to set up his Nintendo. Trying to juggle can get downright embarrassing. I remember when Dukakis came to town. My family went to the airport while I was there covering the story. My daughter saw me, ran over, and started to cry. So there I am, with this four-year-old on my knee, while I am asking the possible future president of the United States a question. It was incredible."

Time, in terms of seconds and minutes, becomes an issue to a juggler in the workplace. "I'm producing every minute," says the woman above. "The clock will say 8:25 or 8:26 and I have four minutes to put my lipstick on, pack my bags, finish getting the kids ready, and leave for work. Every minute counts. I live by minutes. I will look at the clock and say, 'Okay, I have four minutes. Can I do everything in four minutes?' If I lose a minute or two here or there, I'm late for work. But though I'm late, I am usually pretty reliable as to how late I am!"

The single parent—the working woman who has two jobs—feels inordinate pressure to perform. Observes one such woman: "I feel bad because I'm divorced so I have to make sure I do it all. I make my kids' Halloween costumes because all those mothers at home have made their kids' costumes. I take time off work to go to the school programs because I don't want people to say, 'Jill's mom couldn't be here because she's working.' And I push hard at work because I don't want to be treated any differently because I'm a mom—to have anyone say, 'Well, she *could* do the job, but she has kids.'"

No Time to Relax

It's no wonder, given the way the caretaker is constructed, that she can't relax. Most caretakers report that they can't relax unless they're also doing something else—any creatively engineered task that will give them "permission" to stop for a moment.

"I do what I call multiple relaxing," says one. "Even when I'm relaxing I have to do two or three things at once—like masking my face, painting my nails, or writing a note—and that causes a lot of stress!"

What happens to the caretaker who does stop momentarily—without something in her hand? Admits one woman: "It's unnerving. If there happens to be a little time, I don't know what to do with myself. I begin to feel guilty." Another admits, "I don't feel like I deserve the right to relax. My job is still undone."

The pressure to perform and to produce takes its toll on the caretaker. As the immense number of details she has absorbed buzz around her head, and as she drives herself every minute to accomplish tasks, she may become numb. "It might be my age," says one juggler, "but sometimes I can't remember what I'm doing. I'll run around doing three or four things and then, all of a sudden, I realize I'm sitting down and reading the paper, with no recollection of how I came to be there."

*"It's so nice to just sit down and relax for a moment and forget
that in five minutes I have to get up, do the dishes,
do the laundry, put the kids to bed, clean up this mess,
and lay some clothes out for work tomorrow."*

In her numbness, a juggler can begin to make mistakes. "I can't believe what I did," confesses a woman. "My aunt called me from California to say goodbye—that she was going to commit suicide. All the time she's telling me her troubles, I'm doing dishes! She finally said to me, in an incredulous tone of voice, 'Are you doing dishes while I'm talking to you?' I felt incredibly bad, but there I was, getting my dishes done while she was pouring her heart out."

The intense pressure a juggler experiences may totally exhaust her, resulting in resentment over her circumstances. Says one: "Sometimes I hate the idea of going to work. Then, when I leave work, I hate the idea of going home. I know each place I go is going to be a whole new nightmare starting over. Each place is another job, and there is no place for me to rest in-between."

The description thus far of the typical caretaker fits the description of a closet workaholic—or, as one woman put it, a "broom-closet workaholic." Numerous studies of workaholics have been conducted in the workplace, particularly of men, but no one has looked at home—at the woman cleaning the closet. A caretaker's workaholism is masked or hidden. But, in comparing herself to any list of workaholic symptoms, a caretaker stands a good chance of knocking the socks off the list. She is compulsive. She is driven. She is obsessed by her "job." She works sixteen to eighteen hours a day. And she doesn't stop—until she collapses in bed.

No artificial line signals that the caretaker can stop on the other side, or says that she doesn't have to do the dishes until tomorrow. No rule book says, "You can have a break at two-thirty." So, to avoid the guilt, she doesn't take time out. She just keeps pushing. She has just a dozen or more details on her list—but it's a revolving list, and so she's always looking to the future. Tomorrow she'll be done. Or the next day. Or the next. But, because of the way the caretaker is constructed, the truth is, she'll never be done. She is headed toward burnout, and all lights are green!

What is plaguing the caretaker is "traditional programming"—programming that served her grandmother and great-grandmother very well. She is attempting to respond to contemporary—and drastically changed—conditions in the western culture with programming that no longer directly applies. The fact is, twenty-five years ago a woman could do it herself. Her job was hard but limited in scope and well defined. She was not beset with literally dozens of messages a day coming from all directions about what she should be doing to be an adequate woman. She knew. But today's woman doesn't. She is a pioneer about the business of changing her core roles under unprecedented conditions.

Among the extraordinary conditions the juggler faces today is that of performing in a society that besets her with unrelenting time pressures.

If you sense an acceleration in the pace of your life — if you seem to have a more frantic schedule — it isn't your imagination. You're living on the frontier of monumental societal changes that are gearing life up to high speed and sending us all into overdrive. "We're all in the fast track," says one woman. "Life is spinning too fast and we don't seem to know how to hit the pause button."

As a juggler, you can't keep up in a society that is changing so fast. In order not to personalize many of the problems you have with schedules and routines and just getting through a day, it's vital to comprehend that, over the past few decades, profound societal changes have created forces that are pushing and pressing you. These changes, which are having an equally profound effect on your life, have created harried lifestyles and have made time perhaps "the most precious commodity in the land."[2]

You've probably experienced the time famine, saying to yourself repeatedly: "I don't have enough time in the day to get everything done." The sense of "no time" can contribute to your feeling distraught and overwrought and to a feeling that you always need to hurry. Life *is* spinning fast. But when you realize that you don't have to spin too, you can then step off the treadmill and gain greater control over your life.

The big question is: How do you decelerate? Take life in the slow lane? Find the pause button? Even live the unhurried life? Thinking about slowing down is probably enough to wear you out. It's just one more thing to do. But it may be worth it. While you're emitting a deep sigh, we'll forge ahead with time makeovers, strategies to help you get a grip on your frenzied pace.

1. Make a "hassles" list. Write down the things that make you feel hassled, arrange them in the order of their urgency, and decide on several you will either delegate or just not do.

2. Put a red dot on your phone, watch, hand—anything that is connected with urgency—to remind you to slow down.

3. Take power naps. Break up your most stressful days with a few moments of total relaxation for your body. Close your eyes and, as you count down from ten, let yourself be completely relaxed by the time you reach zero.

4. Get up fifteen minutes earlier in the morning and use the extra time to pamper yourself, read the newspaper, or simply avoid having to push so hard to make morning deadlines.

5. Ignore advice urging you to always make every minute count. One magazine article recommends, "Never walk upstairs empty handed. Carry something that has to be put away." It's fine to be efficient part or most of the time, but not all the time—not to the point that you can never relax because there is always one more thing you can get done if, say, you work harder, sleep less, or organize better.

6. Consider working easier, organizing less, and sleeping more as a way of reducing chronic exhaustion and that evening brain-cluttered feeling that comes from never-ending juggling.

7. Be prepared to wait gracefully. Plan ahead for a long wait anywhere—haircuts, appointments, grocery lines—by carrying a book to read or a project you would enjoy doing. Consider waiting as a gift that was inadvertently handed to you, and decide you have no good choice but to enjoy the time out.

8. Set time limits on housework, deciding, say, to devote thirty minutes to a cleaning task and then be done with it.

9. When you find yourself hurried and harried, take long, deep breaths from the abdomen and give yourself instructions to relax.

10. Practice downshifting. Don't always do two or three

things at once. Give yourself opportunities to focus on one thing and completely relax.

11. Leave open time on your schedule. Refrain from scheduling every minute with activities and appointments, and give yourself room to maneuver with respect to deadlines by saying, for example, "Expect me somewhere between noon and one o'clock" rather than "I'll be there right at noon."

12. Build into your schedule time for having fun and just relaxing.

13. Create uninterrupted time for important tasks by taking the phone off the hook or retiring to a place where you can't be reached.

14. Create an intermission between work day and evening (whether you're coming from the workplace or not). Take a walk in the park, sit in your car and meditate, take a hot bath, retire to your bedroom for fifteen minutes to read or contemplate the ceiling, or in some other form take a temporary mental check-out.

15. Use tension relievers at the office. Periodically take time out, even when you're pushing against a deadline, to look out a window, chat with a neighbor, or put your feet up on your desk.

16. Consider living with less. Acquiring possessions often generates many stressful hassles, including the upkeep of any objects you attain.

17. Give up "tryna." "The word 'tryna,'" says A. Hamer Reiser, Jr., a physician, "is a contraction of the expression 'trying to do too much,' which evolved over time to 'tryna'ta do too much,' then to 'tryna do too much,' and finally to 'tryna.'"

"Tryna" is accompanied by a long list of variable and nonspecific symptoms, including fatigue, irritability, insomnia, lassitude, exhaustion, headache, indecision, and depression, he explains. Persons with "tryna" are usually overcommitted and overextended. Management of the condition consists of helping a patient learn to set priorities, to realize that there are limits to what she can do comfortably and effectively, and to recognize that everything she does has a price. Although no medication has been helpful in treating "tryna," one prescription has been found effective — "Saying no!" Dr. Reiser recommends that the patient keep the prescription in a wallet or purse and take it out as a reminder whenever symptoms of tryna appear.[3]

The Juggler, Kids, and Time

The juggler — that whirlwind of a woman who hurries and scurries to beat the clock while she gets things done — often has kids who are affected by time.

How so? First, many children these days are beset with the same pressures of time as their parents. The reason, say experts, is that the full-speed-ahead lifestyle of the parents is now being visited on the children. Ambitious for their children, parents overbook them with appointments, classes, activities. As a consequence, kids leave the ways of childhood too early.[4]

Aside from being overscheduled at times, another way children are affected by time is that they are being reared in an atmosphere of stress, hurry, and anxiety, which is exacting a tremendous toll on their physical and emotional well-being. Suicide rates among young children are increasing at an alarming rate, more children are experiencing physical problems, such as ulcers or migraine headaches, and more are becoming psychiatric casualties. Many more children today are acquiring at a very young age "Type A" patterns, including intense striving, extreme competitiveness, deadline urgency, chronic impatience, and excessive organization. Finally, children are being reared in this fast-forward age by parents who are pressed by their own schedules and, as a result, very preoccupied.

Describing the effect of parents' fast pace on their children, author Carolyn Jabs observes: "Many of us have entire weeks or even months when our lives are so tightly scheduled that we almost have to pencil in the calendar 'Tickle Tommy at bedtime' or 'Play This Little Piggy when putting on Jennifer's socks.'" Under this pressure, parents are irritable. Jabs continues: "You've got a presssure-cooker deadline at work, your husband forgot to pick up milk for dinner, you just noticed that the car's inspection sticker is about to expire, and the phone won't stop ringing. Under these conditions, it's almost impossible to respond calmly when your third-grader asks for help with his homework or your toddler dumps a box of crackers on the floor."[5]

How do you, as a parent, reduce some of the insidious stresses of time on a child? Consider these possibilities:

1. Leave children some time for themselves. Children need time for experiences that allow them to explore their world at their own leisure and to experience a sense of inner peace or tranquillity. Children need to develop at their own pace. Allow them to enjoy their young years, and develop the capacity to be *with* them rather than *at* them all the time.

2. Create "peak experiences" — the once-in-a-lifetime experiences that can happen every day of a lifetime. Settling down on your child's bed to talk, bringing a treat home from work, or having a spontaneous picnic in the backyard, for example, can all imprint permanently on relationships and self-concepts.[6]

3. Connect with your child. Connecting describes those special times when you and your child join momentarily and link like meshed gears. When you click, good feelings flow — and you experience love and warmth that simply don't surface at other times.

How do you connect with kids? First, by entering their world and looking at life momentarily through their eyes.

Sherod Miller and other authors of a book titled *Straight Talk* explain: "Share your children's anger over a lost intramural game, their delight with a compliment from a teacher, their conflict over whether to wear the green slacks or jeans to a school dance, their hysteria because their nose has a pimple or their current love hasn't called, their desire to be left alone, their doubts about whether God hears their prayers." Increase your chances of connecting by joining your children wherever they happen to be and savoring the moment with them. When you do this, your behavior and actions say, "I, as an adult, take you seriously. What you are doing or saying matters to me. I like you and I want to be with you." Kids blossom in the glow of such messages, which have a high likelihood of increasing self-esteem and self-respect.[7]

Putting It All Together

If you're one of those frantic women afflicted with runaway caretaking, admit it! Most women are startled when they realize the extent they're stressing themselves out. One woman said, "I didn't realize I was one of *them* until my boss gave me a cup that said, 'Please, I can only do 12 things at once.'"

If you're a juggler experiencing unconscious caretaking, you're going to be fighting your programming all the way. Your tendency may be to get off your treadmill—take a deep breath—and hop right back on. To make permanent lifestyle changes, you must truly believe that you are responsible (but not at fault) for your stress level and that you can control it. You also must truly believe that other people are not responsible for your stress level and that they can't control it.

You'll need to be good to yourself on the journey toward conscious caretaking. Once some caretakers believe there is a "behavior make-over" that will help, they tend to berate themselves if they don't have the change accomplished and in place by yesterday. Now that they know that they need to do it, they feel guilty because it's not already done! You'll continue to overstress yourself at times — and that's all right. Sometimes there simply won't be a place for you to clear for yourself or a way to reduce your stress on a particular day. But, in the long run, you can make choices that will produce fewer crises, give you consistent time off, and give you much more room to maneuver.

In the quest to establish clear boundaries, take a realistic look at how you're committing your time each week. Obviously, if you're finite, and there's only so much of you to commit, you can't have it all or do it all. That means you'll have to make choices about the use of time. You have 168 hours in a week. How are you utilizing that time now?

To answer that question, we'll borrow some ideas from Carol Osborn, who wrote the book *Enough Is Enough*.[8] (That's a very suggestive title for a caretaker, isn't it?) Carol understands women like you and me. She says that, on the simplest level, she knows that we "have trouble with such concepts as the fact that there are twenty-four hours in a day, that [we] can't be in two places at the same time, and that when [our] gas gauge is empty, the car will stop."

Getting a piece of scratch paper, start with 168 hours (24 hours a day times seven equals 168 hours a week). Subtract the amount of sleep time you need each night times seven; the time you actually spend each day (times seven) at work or volunteering; your commute time to and from work; the time you think you should or would like to spend with your kids or pets over a week's period; the time for those conversations or romantic encounters with your mate. If you're single, compute the time you need for "being in the right place at the right time."

Continuing to subtract hours, consider time with friends,

time for physical exercise, time to do chores around the house, the time it takes you to look great every day (including any trip to the hairdresser), the time you want to read, time to be in church, time to take your kids to classes, and time for holidays and birthdays (add the time you spend each year on these activities and divide by fifty-two).

Carol bets you're in the hole. If you managed to break even, she calls that "coping," and if you're in the red, at least, she says, you're in touch with reality now. What you do with that reality is your choice.

These days, time needs to be budgeted just like money. In making choices regarding your schedule, you may want to allocate time to various categories that are priorities to you and then decide how to commit your remaining time during a week. Important categories, for example, might consist of "quality time with kids," "quality time with spouse" (or "time for socializing and dating," if you're single), "personal time," and the like.

"I consider 'volunteering in the community' a vital item," says one woman. She might then assign a certain number of hours a week to that category. If she has already filled the category with an allotted time commitment, she says no to an additional request during the same time period.

Keep in mind that firming up boundaries is no small chore. Boundaries will change even from one day to the next, with such factors as how much sleep you've had, how many kids are sick, or how bad the leak in your waterbed is (you're in trouble if it requires galoshes). The best you can do is take frequent temperature readings of your stress level (many heavy sighs mean you're moving into deep water!) and give yourself permission to cut down your production level—without guilt. "When things get too stressed," says one woman, "I just make my list for the day and then draw a circle around ten things I'm absolutely not going to do that day."

Make needs—your needs and your family's needs—the basic criteria for making decisions about what you will do. One woman observes, "You may think that standing at the ironing board for ten hours is fulfilling your family's needs, but if you asked them, they'd rather you'd send the ironing out and have five minutes at the end of the day with them."

To get some perspective on what's happening out there in the world, remember: there are very few, if any, caretakers who do have their acts together. Every woman is fighting the same uphill battle and is affected by two truths: "If something can go wrong, it will" (Murphy's Law), and "Nothing ever stays the same" (Larsen's Law).

Deep down, the caretaker thinks she can keep things fixed and ordered (like everyone else) but no such luck. She can't control everything, and she feels responsible. She begins to suffer from "failed dreams."

"What bothers me is that when I was young, I had visions of what it would be like to be a mother and a wife, and it hasn't worked out like I expected," says one caretaker. "My kids don't sit down and say, 'Ummmmmm,' when I fix dinner. I always get something like, 'I don't like that!' Nobody sits down to breakfast together. Nobody goes places together. I feel so inadequate all the time because I haven't been able to make those things happen."

"I wish I hadn't grown up watching television programs like 'Leave It to Beaver' and 'Father Knows Best,'" says another caretaker. "Everybody was always happy. They never talked about bills or the mortgage or the grocery budget. They fed the children oatmeal, and nobody cried in the morning. I think we all thought, 'That's the way it's going to be.'"

The truth is that you, and I, and everyone else, are all

struggling. Underneath the surface, we're all stressed and distressed — hanging on by our nails — and it can't be otherwise in today's high-pressure, high-achievement society. The challenge is to accept the reality that we're going to continue to have lives that are "undone." Release yourself from having to be ordered in a disordered world. Remember, you will continue to have crises. And they will pass. And you will survive. You always do.

And don't sweat the small stuff. If you're convinced your life will always remain undone, you may see the wisdom in adopting a new philosophy to manage life's small stresses. Think a moment — how would you react to these situations:

• You have to wait for a person who is late.

• You find someone has taken your (pliers) (scissors) (flashlight) (make-up) and hasn't put it back.

• You realize your spouse or teen has walked off with your car keys and you need them — right now!

• The driver ahead of you is moving at a snail's pace, and it isn't possible to pass him at the moment.

• You discover that the children you just got ready for the party have been outside playing in the mud.

• The cat has mistaken your satchel for a kitty litter box.

When you encounter frustrations like these, as a juggler going a hundred miles an hour, do you typically get irritated or angry? yell at others or tell them off? do something rash? fall apart? or maybe lapse into a glum mood or sullen silence?

Everyday life is full of dozens of frustrations and disappointments. Like many others, you may react strongly to them — let them hurt you, anger you, or ruin your peace of mind. Suddenly your focus narrows to an irritating event that becomes the most important thing in the world. For that moment, you lose perspective of anything else that matters. And — zap — gone is your sense of well-being.

If you suffer when you let frustrations get to you, so do the people you love. When you become distressed, you become emotionally unavailable to others. What's worse, you can take your anger and disappointment out on them, even when they're not the cause of the problem. You need a target to discharge all the pent-up emotion you've been collecting, and you may find one in the form of the people you care about — people you wouldn't hurt for the world. Your target could be your children — the most vulnerable of those around you — who end up suffering the most.

A vital question to ask is: Does it really matter? Some things in life really do matter — your values, your honor, the safety of your family. But often it's hard to sort out the things that really don't matter from those that do. To get better at sorting out important from unimportant matters, keep asking yourself: "In five minutes (or in the long run), will this thing even matter?" Most of the time, the answer will be a resounding no. In a few minutes you'll have cleaned up the kids, passed the slow driver, found your pliers (or done without them), given away the cat, or otherwise moved through your moment of frustration. So why let the event shake you up or ruin your day? Losing your peace of mind simply isn't worth the heavy costs you and those you love must pay.

So just adopt the new philosophy: Don't sweat the small stuff. And while you're at it, add a rider: Everything is small stuff.

In addition, allow yourself to enjoy the moment. Now that you're relaxing, shaking out the tension, taking life more calmly, even releasing, think about the possibility of living more of your moments in the present. To set the discussion for this, envision yourself pulling your car into your driveway and lingering a few minutes to finish enjoying some music on the radio. What begins to happen to you?

If you're like many women, you'll begin to experience a vague, uneasy feeling. "I feel like I should be in the house doing something," says one woman.

"I begin to wonder, 'What are the neighbors going to think?' " says another. As a result, you may shut off the radio and go in the house prematurely—before you're really ready to stop listening to the music.

As jugglers, we tend to be consumed with our pasts and futures, and what others are going to think. We hurry through our todays without paying attention to our present moments. And we tend to become slaves to automatic living, denying ourselves the fullness of our moment-by-moment experiences—the only time that's ours to really enjoy.

We need to attend to our nows—to live more fully in our present experiences, says Clyde Reid, author of *Celebrate the Temporary*. To Reid, this means:

• to lie on your back on the floor in the dark and listen, really listen, to a beautiful piece of music.

• to wade in a stream barefoot and really feel the cold water running through your toes.

• to walk in the warm sand and listen to the ocean.

• to climb a tree and look down at the world below.

• to watch a bird.

• to lie in bed a few minutes when you first wake up, watching the sun coming through the window, the reflections on the ceiling, the colors in the room, and thanking God for life.

• to really take time to taste bread; to give it your full attention for just a few minutes; to smell it, touch it, to chew it slowly while it dissolves in your mouth; to think about bread and the life it brings, the strength it gives.

• to carry a child on your shoulders instead of walking sedately to the car; to roll with children in the grass and to toss them in the air; to celebrate children, who are themselves temporary.

• to celebrate yourself. You are worth celebrating. You are worth everything. You are unique. In the whole world, there is only one you, one person with your talents, your experiences, your gifts.

Essentially, Reid urges this: Live for your todays. Give yourself permission to be more free, to let things happen, and to let life bring you surprises and challenges and joy. Let go of some of the controls that bind you, and let life flow instead of limiting life by channeling it all in advance.[9] Superb advice for the juggler!

Don't Say Yes When You Want to Say No

Now let's move on to the skill of saying no, the solution to the chronic condition of "tryna"—"tryna do too much." If you're a juggler, one of the most effective ways to take charge of your schedule and your life is to learn to say no—comfortably! And, if you're a juggler, that may be hard to do. Most women raise their hands when they're asked whether they have trouble refusing a request. Consider a case in point:

"I went to the doctor for my stress," says one harried caretaker. "I was worrying about stupid little things that I don't need to worry about. The doctor said, 'You've got to say no.'

"Mostly," she continues, "the problem was my next-door neighbor. She is constantly asking me to babysit, and I am constantly saying yes. The doctor also said, 'Tell her that you can't babysit anymore.'

"So what do I do when I get home? My neighbor is sitting on my porch. 'Can you babysit Mark for me next week?' she asks. Could I say no? No! Here I had just gone to the doctor—spent fifty dollars—and I said yes again. I felt so sorry for her when she said 'I'm just so stressed out, I work three days a week, and I need a vacation,' that I caved in. But after I said yes, I realized: Here I am—the doctor tells *me* to go on a vacation and to say 'No, I can't babysit'—and now *she's* on vacation while I work my night job, take care of my three children, and have this extra child to care for all next week."

Why is it so difficult for women to say no? Here is what they report:

• "Saying no is a personal rejection. If I say no, I might hurt someone." (Caretakers don't reject people.)

• "I have a 'can do' reputation to protect. Other women are constantly amazed at what I get done, and I don't want to tarnish that reputation."

• "Someone will think I'm not doing my job if I say no."

• "It's awful when someone turns me down, so I say yes because I don't want them to go through what I go through."

• "I'm returning a favor. She didn't say no to me, so I can't say no to her."

• "If I say no, someone may not help me when I need it."

• "People ask 'Why not?' when I say no, and I don't feel comfortable with the reasons I give them."

• "If I've been asked to do something, I wonder, 'If I say no, then who will do it?' "

• "People will think I'm not wonderful. I want them to say, 'Isn't she a good person!' It would crush me if they thought badly of me."

• "If I say no, I worry that they'll wonder, 'What on earth does she *do* all day?' "

• "I don't say no because I have to be the Kool-Aid mom who does everything perfectly."

• "It embarrasses me to admit I can't do everything."

• "I'll look like I'm not very organized."

Notice that most of these reasons have a common theme.

They have to do with people—not hurting others, or warding off being rejected or evaluated by them.

A caretaker who can't please people, and keep them pleased with her, isn't doing her job, she thinks. If she hurts someone, she's worthless. If she gets rejected by someone, she's worthless, Her self-esteem is completely wrapped up in keeping her relationships in order.

If you're like the typical caretaker, saying no is an emotional event having to do with your lovability. Your very worth is at stake any time anybody wants something from you. No wonder so many women suffer at having to say no.

Now, men generally don't react that way. For most men, saying no is merely a response they use when they don't want to do something. And if someone says no to them, they just go ask someone else for what they need. Saying no is not personal—it doesn't have to do with them. It has to do with getting the job done.

"Why can't a woman be more like a man?" laments Henry Higgins in the musical *My Fair Lady*. In this case, that's exactly what women need to do—be more like a man. They need to depersonalize the no's they give and even the no's they get.

Think about it this way: *You need to give other people the right to prioritize their lives in a way that makes sense to them. Likewise, you need to reserve the right to prioritize your life in a way that makes sense to you.*

That sounds pretty reasonable, doesn't it? That means that other people have a right to say no to you and you have a right to say no to them, and it doesn't mean anything except that a request doesn't fit with someone's priorities. Remember, you do have finite time, energy, and resources. You can't give equally to everyone who wants or expects something from you. (There are literally thousands of worthy causes to which you could commit!) If you don't set limits, you'll give yourself away in big chunks and neglect people and activities that are truly important to you.

And here's something to think about: If you can't say no when you need to, that means your life is governed by other people's priorities — not your own!

So how can you say no and come out unscathed and looking good? Here are some suggestions to take to heart.

1. Don't say yes immediately. If you have any doubts, just say, "I really need to look at my schedule. I'll get back to you." That will give you time to weigh your priorities and, if you decide to decline, to figure out a gracious way to say no. One woman explains: "Just as I try to count to ten before I get mad, I try to count to ten before I say yes or no. I find people respect me when I look them in the eye and say, 'I don't know right now. I have to think about it and get back to you. When do you need an answer?' "

2. Give an explanation, not an excuse. A brief explanation can cushion a no, but you don't have to give other people your life story or plead for forgiveness. An explanation can be as short and general as "I'm sorry, I'm overcommitted right now," or "My schedule is simply too full," or "I just couldn't do my best for you, considering my current obligations." Or, as one author suggests, you can use quite vague and cosmic-sounding phrases that suggest that fate, or some giant hand, stands in your way: "I'd love to, but it won't work out," or "I'm sorry, but events have gotten away from me."[10] The point is, you have a right to say no simply because you don't want to do something. You don't have to have a good reason!

3. Use a crutch, if you need one, while you're learning to say no. "I suffered over saying 'no' my entire life," says one woman. "Finally, someone suggested I mark a red line through every day on my calendar. When I needed to say no I simply

"I won't be able to work late with you, Mr. Dunlap — my computer is down!"

said, 'I have something on that day.' That line gave me the excuse I needed until I could say no comfortably."

4. Take responsibility for your no's. Avoid saying, "I can't because my (husband) (parents) (children) (boss) (friend) (dog) won't let me." Blaming a refusal on someone else diminishes your credibility with others and suggests that you aren't your own person. Taking ownership of your no's, on the other hand, commands the respect of others. Because you're being true to you, you'll respect yourself more too.

5. Don't say yes unless you can do it without resentment. It's easy to say yes when you want to say no and then find yourself mad at the person who asked for something. You may assume she can read your mind: "Can't she tell I'm too stressed? I don't have time for this." But other people can't divine what you're thinking! They take you at your word and assume that your yes comes without any strings. So it's only fair to protect them from unfair resentment by being decisive about your yeses and no's.

6. Realize you aren't indispensable. "Several years ago I was in bed for the last five months of my pregnancy and I can remember thinking how nice it was not having anybody asking me to do anything!" says a woman. "All the things I thought would fall apart without me, didn't! The world actually went on without me!" So if you need to say no, the world will go on without you too.

7. Be empathic. Show concern for the other person when you can't grant a request: "I can see you're in a bind. I wish I could help — but I just can't baby-sit your ten children tonight."

8. Use "mixed feeling" messages to express your struggle with a request: "I feel really torn. I'd like to go to the movie with you, but I have so much to do I simply have to stay home."

9. Speak without impatience or anger. Most people don't object too much to a refusal. They do object, however, to a curt refusal — "No, I won't go to the store for you!"

10. View requests as negotiable. If you feel uncomfortable with a request or simply can't grant it, you may want to make a creative counteroffer. Say, for example, "I can't handle a whole take-in dinner, but I can chop the vegetables." "I can't go with you Saturday night, but how about lunch next Wednesday?" Negotiate until you reach a solution satisfying to both of you.

11. Share the work of this world with other people. Relates a woman: "A few years ago I was asked to be the regional chairman for a fund drive, which I accepted. I figured how many people were in the neighborhood and roughly estimated that if everybody took his or her turn, I would only have to chair the drive once every twenty or thirty years. Now, when I'm asked about the same drive, I say, 'Nope. I did that a few years ago, and it's not my turn yet.' "

12. Be firm with high-pressure salespeople. You can take half an hour trying not to hurt someone's feelings or you can

decide not to waste your time or the other person's. You may need a "broken record" skill to politely but firmly say no. For example: "Hello, Mrs. Jones. I'd like to show you this product." "I'm sorry. I'm not interested." "How can you not be interested in something you don't know anything about?" "I'm sorry. I'm not interested. I have to go now." The challenge is to state your position, a one-liner, several times (you're a "broken record") and then take your leave. It's important not to go off on tangents. Salespeople want reasons so they can deal with them.

13. Don't make it difficult for other women to say no. One woman comments: "We push each other — 'Oh, it won't take very long!' or 'I'll give you a committee.' We need to ease up on others and respect *their* needs."

Chapter 3

The Guilt Sponge

Do you feel guilty when—

—your child acts up in public, wets the bed, sucks his thumb, burps without excusing himself, gets poor grades, loathes vegetables, or punches the girl next door?

—you're staying at home and not helping with the family finances? Or you're working and not spending enough "quality time" with your children?

—you take the tag off the mattress that says "Do not remove under penalty of law"?

—you're standing in the supermarket ten-item express lane with twelve items in your basket?

—your husband is overweight or not getting enough exercise?

—your geranium dies (the one you got for Mother's Day)?

—your boss doesn't get his promotion?

—you send one of your children to school with a borderline case of flu?

—it rains the day you've planned a family picnic?

If you answer yes to the majority of these questions, you

may be a guilt sponge—a woman who soaks up blame for anything that goes wrong in her life, who always hears that little voice inside insisting, "You should have known better. You should have done better. You should *be* better."

If that description fits you, you aren't alone. Guilt is running at epidemic proportions among women today.

Though women have traditionally been beset with guilt, the woman of the '90s has increased expectations and increased responsibilities—more things to do and more things to feel guilty about not having done, or not having done perfectly. If you're a guilt sponge, why do you feel such relentless guilt? A partial answer is embedded in the traditional role women have assumed of taking care of people.

Historically, as caretakers, women have learned to be nurturers and selfless givers to others. Thus, you've probably grown up feeling responsible for other people's happiness. When someone radiates distress, gloom, or anger, you may automatically think you need to "fix" that person. But what if you can't make that person happy immediately? Then your alarm buttons go off. "You haven't done your job—or your best!" says that persistent little voice inside.

Now the guilt sets in—and flourishes—because there are so many things you can't "fix." Plus, there is no end to what you should or could be doing to make the lives of the people you're responsible for fuller or happier. Every day becomes one long, overbooked guilt festival.

Sadly, if you're like most women, you don't feel bad about just a few things that happen during a day. You tend to feel bad about almost everything. Any time anything goes wrong, you may feel there is something inherently wrong with you, that you're defective or inferior. You should have been able to control events and you didn't, so the flaw is in you.

If you have a nagging voice inside that constantly tears you down and beats you up with nonstop guilt—and you want to take charge of that voice—you'll need to understand some of the patterned ways guilt affects most women. Consider the "shoulds" and how they can tyrannize a woman's mind.

The Tyranny of "Shoulds"

Agitating a woman's guilt are often hundreds of "shoulds" that whirl around in her mind, pulling at her this way and that, confusing her, and keeping her from feeling good about herself. Here is just a sample of the "shoulds" that can tug relentlessly at her and pull her off center.

"I should—

—keep my house totally immaculate—all the time—never miss."

—look young and slim and beautiful."

—exercise every day."

—lose weight (and start my diet today)."

—be less inhibited."

—put other people's needs first."

—be there for everyone, always."

—feed my family wonderfully three times a day."

—do the dishes happily and not complain."

—provide more lessons for the kids."

—get a piano for the lessons!"

—know the answers to all the problems in the family."

—get up earlier."

—stay off the telephone."

—keep the atmosphere in my home pleasant."

—be a 'love goddess' when he wants to be a 'love god.' "

The "shoulds" that flog a woman's mind are no respecter of how much she is doing, how hard she is trying, or how much she has already accomplished. Says one woman: "I'm in constant emotional turmoil. If I take time out with the kids, I

*"Me? I tried to get 12 items through
a 10-items-or-less express check-out."*

feel guilty that I don't get the house cleaned. And if I clean the house, I feel guilty that I don't do anything with the kids. If I take care of both the house and the kids, I feel guilty because I'm not serving other people (like taking a dinner to a person who's sick). If I happen to do that, then I haven't taken care of my thank-you notes from Christmas. There's always something I haven't done."

Men differ quantitatively from women when it comes to "shoulds" relentlessly plaguing their brains, says author Barbara Holland. "Men, whether they're putting up storm windows or checking the quarterly sales figures, always seem to feel they're doing the right thing at the right time. Nothing whispers in their ear, 'Shouldn't you be painting the garage instead?' They do the job in front of them, and, when they're finished, they do something else, or turn on the football game. But women feel that whatever we're doing, short of maybe saving the children from a burning building, we ought to be doing something else."[1]

The "shoulds" that relentlessly badger a woman's mind
keep her off balance and off center. Unlike a man, she seems
to have an unruly committee in her head—each member with
a different dogmatic opinion—that confuses her and tears at
her emotions. In fact, many of a woman's "shoulds" come from
what might be termed the "theys" of this world. If you were
to make a list of all your "shoulds" (or "shouldn'ts") and
examine where they're coming from—that is, who actually said
you should do a certain thing—you may find many of your
"shoulds" unattached to any names or faces. Those "shoulds"
are coming from an anonymous "peanut gallery" floating somewhere out there in space, inhabited by the "theys" of this world
who, women report, say such opinionated things to them as
the following:

"They" say you have to be young and beautiful, clean your
own house, serve homemade bread and jam, make your own
jogging suits, and run down the street in the morning—that's
what "they" say.

"They" say you should be able to handle your home and
a job at the same time without any problem.

"They" say you should never have a single murderous
thought toward your kids or husband.

"They" say you should spend half an hour a day reading
to each child, regardless of how many children you have.

"They" say you have to can, can, can, all fall long.

"They" say you have to take hot homemade bread to the
new move-ins.

"They" say mom has to get up with the kids at night.

"They" say you learn from your mistakes, but "they" say if
you do make a mistake, that's wrong.

"They" say you should breast feed (and also love it), and
if you don't, it will stunt your children's growth.

"They" say that when you're a stay-at-home mother, your

brain turns to mush, and all you can talk about is kids, diapers, coupons, and groceries.

"They" say you have to be married before you're thirty, and if you aren't, there's something wrong with you.

"They" say you can't have just one child because he won't grow up normal.

The "theys" of this world have the power to bully a woman and thrust her into guilt without a moment's notice. Inasmuch as "they" are so opinionated and powerful, we should at least ask, "Who are 'they'?"

Are they, as author Mary Z. Gray asks, "some secret source of inside information? Some majestic tribunal judging all things, passing down edicts on matters 'they' know nothing about, acting as self-appointed final arbiter on morals, manners, grammar?" Gray, author of an article entitled "Who Are 'They' to Say," confesses she had trusted the authority of "they" for many years until her young daughter, a freethinker, questioned the omnipotence of whoever determined the rules of grammar and language. "Me and Roger . . . ," her daughter had started to say before Gray interrupted her with the correction, "Roger and I." At this point the following conversation ensued between Gray and her daughter:

"Who says I have to say 'Roger and I'? Why can't I say, 'Me and Roger'?"

"Because it's wrong. There are rules for the right way to say things."

"Who makes them up? Where are these people? I'd like to meet them."

"That's the spirit we should all cultivate," says Gray. "It would save us from being taken in by the 'theys' and their fool sayings, or their arbitrary rules for what's right or wrong, 'in' or 'out.' "[2]

Gray makes a point. What happens if you indiscriminately

absorb and accept much of what "they" say to you? In essence, you give yourself over to the vague edicts of others, robbing yourself of your own sense of self, and allowing the "theys" to have a profound influence on your behavior. For example:

You may act as if there is only one acceptable mode of dress and follow the dictates of fashion (what "they" say) so you can fit in.

You may become uncomfortable when things are out of order ("They" say, "A place for everything and everything in its place").

You may limit yourself to traditional gender roles in your primary relationships because "they" say things like: "Men take out the garbage; women do the cooking."

You may walk into a room and worry about what "they" are thinking about you.

You may follow certain traditions and rules "they" have established rather than thinking about whether they fit your life or make sense to you.

You may deny yourself the good things in life — flowers, a facial, the joy of reading a good book, time to develop talents — because "they" say if you do something for yourself you're being selfish.

You may apologize excessively for almost everything or constantly think you need to explain yourself because "they" might think you did something wrong.

Following the vague edicts of the "theys" of this world comes from not having a good sense of what you want, what you wish for, and what you need. From not believing you are complete enough to do your own thinking. And from not believing that you are entitled to make choices for yourself. You don't need hundreds of vague authorities to tell you what to do. You're in charge. You need to trust your own judgment and make your own decisions. So how do you take charge of the "theys"?

• When you think "they," try to attach names and faces to these people. Ask yourself, "Whom am I trying to please?" "Whom am I allowing to have power over me?" "Whose edict am I following without doing my own thinking?"

• Test out how you feel by replacing "they" with "I." "I (feel) (think) (want) (wish) (believe) (value) (choose) ... " If the fit is good between the judgment of others and how you really feel inside, you'll know it and you can embrace that judgment as your own. If not, you can discard the judgment and search further to define your own position.

• If you're going to use the "theys," use them to your advantage. As one woman put it, "If you can look far enough, you can always find a 'they say' that matches exactly with what *you* want to do!"

Release from Guilt

So now that you're in charge of the "theys" of this world, how can you quit being a guilt sponge? How can you stay "on center" when your ideas, opinions, views, preferences, or beliefs aren't in accord with those of someone else? Here are suggestions to help:

1. For a beginning, take a look at the extent to which guilt rules you by counting all the "should" and "ought" statements you make to yourself during a day. Write down twenty or thirty of the "shoulds" or "oughts" that relentlessly go through your mind.

2. Decide whether a "should" represents a true value of yours. Test a "should" statement by saying, "This is what I want" or "This is what I choose to do" and see how it feels. The point is to identify what behaviors, ethics, values, opinions, or preferences *you* espouse. What do *you* think is fair,

right, or virtuous? What fits with *your* life? Develop a frame of reference and a mature conscience that are filled in with attitudes, values, and styles you consciously embrace, ones that are chosen rather than imposed.

3. Distinguish between earned and unearned guilt. If you've truly been, say, irresponsible, dishonest, or unkind, then take responsibility for your earned guilt, be properly remorseful, and make amends. Then let the guilt go. But, if your guilt is unearned, unload that burden. It is the abundance of unearned guilt, which is vague, pervasive, and insidious, that makes a woman apologetic for nearly everything, even her very existence. Unearned guilt also instills a profoundly disturbing sense of shame—that she is not just *being* bad, she *is* bad.

4. Distinguish between guilt and learning from the past. Immobilizing yourself with guilt by feeling hurt, upset, and depressed about a historical event is unhealthy. The healthy position is to learn from your mistake, take corrective action, if necessary, and move on.

5. If you do insist on suffering over a mistake, at least make it time-limited. How long are you going to require yourself to suffer? An hour? a day? a year? There are no medals at the end of this life for long-term sufferers.

6. Remember that many "shouldn't haves" come from insufficient information or from not being able to predict the future. If you had known your child was going to trip on a hose and break his arm today, you would never have allowed him to go outdoors. If you had known the item you bought at full price last week would be on sale half-price this week, you would have waited. It's not fair, then, to say to yourself, "I shouldn't have done that!" You're entitled to be human and limited in your knowledge.

7. Also remember that many of the "shouldn't haves" you indict yourself with were originally sound choices. For ex-

ample, imagine you declined an invitation to a literary club
one evening because of other pressing obligations. The morning after, you run across the president of the club and she says
to you, "You should have come last night. The speaker was
wonderful!"

What do you immediately think? Most women who respond
to that question say, "I should have gone!" No matter that the
day before, they chose not to attend the meeting because of
other responsibilities. Or that they weighed the factors involved
and made an informed decision. Most women don't realize
they actually did choose. Instead, they allow themselves to be
pulled off center and to doubt themselves any time anyone
questions their judgment. And if they do happen to remember
they made a choice, they may say, as one woman put it, "I
think I made a dumb choice."

8. Finally, remember that many "shoulds" come from what
you think someone else is going to think. Fretting over others'
possible opinions of you is essentially self-imposed tyranny.
Release yourself from worrying about others' possible judgments and from caring what they think. Consider this case in
point:

"I was taking my son to preschool. We were almost late,
so I threw on my coat over my pajamas, slipped on my husband's huge, fuzzy leather slippers, popped on my glasses, and
headed out the door, thinking, 'If I get a flat, I'm dead!' At the
preschool, instead of my son getting out the van's sliding door
as he always does (which would have provided anonymity for
me), he hopped over the front seat and opened the front door.
Just then a woman pulled up in her car and saw me there,
exposed in all my 'glory' from head to toe. We looked at each
other and the *shoulds* started. 'I should have gotten dressed.'
'I should have been more organized.' 'I should have gotten up
sooner.' I wanted to kill my son for exposing me to all this.

Then, suddenly, I let myself off the hook. I realized there wasn't a thing I could do, so I smiled at the woman and said to myself, 'Oh well! I'm still a good person.' My son jumped out of the van and ran off, and I drove home in my big slippers."

Consider a "should" from another person as simply that person's view of the world. Remember the story of the little boy who came home from school with a poor report card. As his frowning father read the card, the boy observed, "Keep in mind, Dad, that's just one man's opinion." From that perspective, you are entitled to have your own opinions, your own personal preferences, and to be the designer of your own "shoulds." Your judgment about what fits for you will be different from what fits for other people — and that's okay!

"I learned a valuable lesson when I was first married," says a woman. "My neighbor came to my house while I was cooking cinnamon rolls and said, 'You're using white flour!' and 'You're putting frosting on the rolls!' She said I wasn't being a good mother because I wasn't feeding my kids nutritional things. I was just crushed.

"When she got sick, I went to her house to help her and I found that she didn't wash her baby's wet diapers — she just laid them over the radiator to dry. I realized then that we were two entirely different people with two different views of the world, and that it needed to be *my* choice whether or not I fed my kids frosting."

Release Others from Your "Shoulds"

Too often, using our internal standards of measurement, we're quick to judge others with "shoulds" that we consider are coming from The Book of Truth — not from our own idiosyncratic view of the world. Yet, our standards don't measure the truth or what is real at all. They reflect only what we know, what we have experienced, what we are comfortable with.

When others don't fit our measurements, we tend to label them with judgments like these:

- You talk too loud (or too much), or You're too quiet.
- You're disorganized (or too compulsive).
- You're too sensitive (or too insensitive).
- You're too opinionated (or never have an idea about anything).
- You're (sick) (crazy) (lazy) (crude) (rude) (dumb).

What is our message? That we know better than another how that person should be, should act, or even should think or feel. The other person's way is inadequate or defective while our own is superior.

"Shoulds" are insidious pests in relationships, causing defensiveness whenever they are directed toward others. So how do you eliminate the tendency to judge others according to your own standards? Try these strategies:

1. Release others from negative monitoring. Most of us are organized to catch others being different from ourselves. We then complain about their behavior—to them or to others—sometimes dozens of times a day.

2. Simply let others be different from you. If you can, celebrate the differences rather than seeing them as bad or as threatening. Release others from having to be like you.

3. Give up "absolute thinking." You may pigeonhole people or events by dichotomizing or dividing the world into extremes such as black/white, good/bad and right/wrong. People who think in extremes tend to use words like "proper," "correct," "precise," "right" or "wrong." Yet few things fit neatly into these categories. People, for example, are not black or white, they're gray. Thus, you'll need a "gray" frame of reference, one that aids you in considering a multitude of factors, to understand others. Pronouncing that people are, say, "disorganized" or "insensitive" or "selfish"—using a black-and-white frame of

reference—seriously interferes with your understanding of them.

4. Use opinion language. Acknowledge your awareness that you and every other person operate from different perspectives by reflecting that awareness in your language. Instead of saying "You should . . . ," use tentative wording such as: "From my (perspective) (view) (peepsight) (corner of the world), this is how I see things."

5. Remember that as you release yourself from the judgments of others, it will become easier to release other people from yours. One woman observes: "I've found that when I feel good about myself, then everyone else is okay. But when I'm down on myself, I become nitpicky about other people too. My judgments have to do with me and my self-esteem, not with them."

Release from Mother Guilt

Mothers in particular take it on the chin when it comes to taking responsibility for things they can't control, as is manifest in this mother's experience: "My neighbor and I were sitting on the porch, watching her preschooler riding my son's bike. 'Look, Mom, I have a bike just like this!' the little girl said to her mother. My neighbor said, 'Oh, no, you've never had a bike without pedals!' That crushed me. I felt just sick inside. I was allowing my child to ride around on a bike without pedals! I should have been down at the hardware store getting pedals! I was an inadequate mom!"

Mothers often won't give themselves credit for how hard they try; if something goes wrong, it's still their fault. Reports one, "I took my kids to stay at my mother's last night. I was determined to have everything they needed: underwear, pajamas, etc. I must have told my preschooler five times to bring his shoes, but he still forgot. I spent the whole weekend feeling guilty because he had to go barefoot."

Often mothers will trip their own guilt buttons just through exposure to "mother models" they see in the media. "I saw an ad in a magazine the other day that showed a little girl getting ready for school," one woman reports. "The mother was kneeling down, looking into her daughter's eyes, and saying, 'I've seen that half-full glass of milk. Aren't my children getting enough calcium?' The mother is in her perfect little Levi jeans, in a gorgeous little kitchen, with a gorgeous little girl—and I thought, 'Why can't I be like that?' "

Mothers may also increase their guilt through a habit of relentlessly comparing themselves to others, as another woman illustrates: "My husband came home from work and suggested the family go to dinner. Usually I 'redo' the kids if we go out, but I was too tired so I let them go in play clothes. While we were at the restaurant I glanced at a woman who had three little girls with her. They all had perfectly braided hair. The bows in their hair matched their socks. Their tennis shoes were sparkling white. Their clothes were perfectly pressed and they were standing there so quietly. I looked at my own little ragged threesome and thought, 'I'm a failure! Look at *her* children!' I was shattered."

One area in which mothers (especially young ones) feel acute guilt is when a child gets sick. No matter how hard they've tried to keep their child healthy, in such situations they feel implicated. They should have somehow protected him or her from the flu or a cold or a bad toothache. "I always study the doctor carefully to try to pick up how he really feels about how I'm doing," says a young mother. "I always feel he's thinking, 'She's a bad mother.' "

"I take my children to the doctor once a year before the cold and flu season hits," reports another. "We have a running joke that it's so I can prove to him I'm a good mother. I say to him, 'Look, they haven't fallen, they don't have a cold, they don't have the flu — see how wonderful and healthy these children are.' And he examines and measures them and says, 'Oh, you are a good mother.' "

Interestingly, when things go wrong, fathers typically don't take on the guilt in the health area — or any other one, for that matter. "Fathers never come in and ask, 'What did I do wrong that my kid got sick?' says a physician. It's the mother who always has the guilt."[3]

Men just seem to "keep their cool" when it comes to guilt, observes one woman, who describes a situation involving her and her husband: "There had been a mix-up. Each of us thought the other had paid the babysitter. We didn't realize we'd goofed until a day later, when she came up the street to ask me something. She just slipped in the remark, 'Oh, by the way, I haven't been paid for Wednesday.'

"I said, 'Oh my gosh! Kathy, this week has been so busy, and I am so sorry, and oh, just a second, I'll run in and get the money!' I didn't have four dollars in change, so I said, 'I'll get it right down to you!' I was fidgeting and nervous and talking eighty-five miles a minute. My husband, who was standing there, simply said, 'Kathy, we'll get you the money as soon as possible.' He just took care of the problem. I was amazed that he could stay so calm. It was horrible for me! I felt just terrible — like I've never been able to keep anything straight in my whole life. I couldn't believe I had actually let Kathy down!"

This woman felt awful that she hadn't anticipated the problem or actually prevented it from happening — a manifestation of what is sometimes referred to as "magical thinking." Women tend toward the superstitious belief that they can influence events that are totally beyond their control.

"When something goes wrong with my kids, I backtrack to the premise that if I had been a little smarter, a little faster at dealing with the problem, a little more involved with the problem to begin with, I would have been able to take care of it," says one mother. "It's as though I believe I have 'magical mother eyes,' " explains another. "If I am just there, I can keep my kids from getting harmed."

Underlying mother guilt and the sweeping responsibility mothers take for events they can't control are the "if only" guilt trips. For example, "If only I had—

—just put my children's coats on (given them their vitamins yesterday) (made them eat their carrots), they wouldn't have caught cold and we wouldn't be at the doctor's now."

—trained my children better. Then they wouldn't (fight) (have messy bedrooms) (have bad manners) (have tantrums) (leave their dirty dishes) (ignore what I tell them to do)."

—nursed my child longer. Then he wouldn't be having a problem in fourth grade math."

—paid more attention in eighth grade home economics. Then I could have made my child's Halloween costume instead of having to purchase it."

—controlled my child's sugar intake. Then he wouldn't have a cavity now."

When you think seriously about the power women sometimes inadvertently assign themselves, you know there's a hole in that kind of thinking. You know you aren't omnipotent or all-knowing—and that your ability to influence events is relatively inconsequential. And you know there isn't any way to anticipate all contingencies or to control everything around you.

Yet, you may have a habit of magnifying the importance of decisions you've made in the past. You may zip through your mind and collect all the events (relevant or remote) that might have possibly had any bearing on a problem. You may then use those events to hold yourself completely and forevermore responsible for the problem.

The next time you're having a guilt festival, pay attention to whether or not you're blowing things way out of proportion and taking responsibility for events you can't control. Remember, you have limited knowledge, wisdom, and vision. Let it be okay that you're simply a finite human being along with all the other members of the human race.

Stay Alert to Mother Bashing

Why does guilt suit mothers so well? For one reason, blaming mothers is an idea so prevalent in our culture that most of us never stop for a moment to question it, says Jean Marzollo, author of the article "Why Mothers Get a Hard Time."[4] In fact, she argues, what could be termed "mother bashing" is an accepted sport in this society, "conjuring up images of remorseful mothers pounding fists against their brows, wailing, 'Where did I go wrong?'"

When it comes to telling mother what a bad job she's doing, everybody's an expert, adds Lynn Caine, author of the book *What Did I Do Wrong?*[5] Whenever there's a disobedient or unruly child, she notes, mother is likely to get blame and/or advice (sometimes insulting) from mothers-in-law, grandparents, aunts, childless friends, cashiers, clerks, bus drivers, neighbors, and crossing guards. That's not to mention the two most likely advice-givers: husbands and other kids.

Child-care experts get into the act too. "Most child care advice assumes that if the parents administer the proper prescriptions, the child will develop as planned," says Caine. "It places exaggerated faith not only in the perfectibility of the children and their parents but in the infallibility of child-rearing techniques as well. What we read and what we are told implies that if we, the perfect ones, follow instructions, we will produce perfect children. Unfortunately, this is not quite the way it works. So when disillusionment sets in, Mom gets blamed for her child's development."

Though they may be among the least deserving of discrediting, single mothers are most likely to take the rap, observes Marzollo. "Since you do most of the child raising yourself, you get most of the blame when things go wrong."

The truth is, it's important not to put the blame on either parent when a child has a problem. There are just too many complex factors to pin blame anywhere. Besides mother and father, says Marzollo, factors that influence children include "siblings, other caretakers, place in the family, heredity, other relatives, friends, school, physical disabilities, learning disabilities, family income, health, incidents over which we have no control, and just plain luck."[6]

Be a Good-Enough Mother

So what's a mother to do if she is one who blames herself for just about anything that happens to her children and sees herself forever responsible for the way those kids turn out? Become a "good-enough" mother.

A "good-enough" mother is one who can make mistakes and still rear happy, healthy, and productive children if she but provides them with such basic commodities as love, caring, attention, and understanding. The "good-enough" mother relies on common sense and, as her own best expert, trusts her own judgment in her child-rearing. She also allows her children to develop at their own pace and respects their judgments and opinions.

If you'd like to become a "good enough" mother, consider these possibilities:

1. *Realize that you can't respond to the thousands of mes-*

*sages on how to mother that come to you by way of the culture
every year.*

Says Cathleen Collins Lee, author of the article "Mothering
My Way": "Everywhere we look there are magazine articles,
books, and even talk show guests telling us how to help our
children realize their potential in music, in sports, in reading . . . in just about everything. Although this information itself
can be helpful, it also contributes to a nagging sense that there
is an impossible number of things we absolutely have to do
as parents."[7]

Though the culture today is indulgent of children and
runaway in its messages to parents about what they "should"
do to raise a perfect child, it has not always been this way.
Taking a historical view of child-rearing, it is vital to realize
that motherhood as a full-time occupation, with its accompanying stress on doing for kids — is a fairly new development.
In an article titled "Mother vs. Mother," Karen Levine says:
"Our great-grandmothers were too burdened by their household chores to think about what . . . most of us today would
call the heart and soul of mothering. 'Baby-tending' fell historically to older siblings, children themselves, since mothers
were busy keeping the house running." Concerning real time
spent with children, stresses Levine, "the experience of fulltime
mothers two or three generations ago was more like that of
today's working mothers than like that of the many women
who think of themselves as carrying on a tradition of 'real'
mothering." However, the hardworking mother of yesteryear
had one big advantage over today's working mother: "Since
psychological concepts of mothering hadn't yet been articu-
lated in the United States, these mothers . . . weren't addition-
ally burdened with the guilt so many working mothers have
felt since the end of World War II."[8]

"Over the past few decades, many women have catered to

their children in ways that would have amazed our great-grandmothers," adds Ellen Switzer, author of the article "Are You Their Mother or Their Servant?" "What's more, they have done this with the approval of many once-fashionable psychological experts who have told them through books and magazine articles that children needed a mother's complete, full-time attention and devotion."[9]

The cultural message that kids need full-time attention, combined with bombardment of thousands of other cultural messages from the "theys" of this world on how kids "should" be raised, is enough to make any woman feel schizophrenic, especially if she's holding herself responsible for all the do's and don'ts while she's in the workplace.

There are many optional ways of raising loving, competent, self-assured men and women, emphasizes Lee. We need to choose what works best for us and for our children. We also need to trust ourselves and to be in charge of our decisions regarding how to "fill up" and "fill out" our children. Finally, we need to realize we're not pieces of elastic "that can stretch and stretch to fit the demands of any situation — even the all-important demands of child rearing."[10]

Levine sums it up with a final comment: "Life is indeed much too complicated for pat answers and universal definitions. . . . Given the wide range of mothering styles that have been endorsed at one time or another, we should all be reassured that there is no one right way to mother. If anything, women should have learned to be suspicious of anyone who attempts to tell them that one kind of parenting is right and another is wrong."[11]

2. *Realize that a "good-enough" mother has imperfect children — kids who are going to have problems — and that needs to be okay!*

"Even if you stayed home every day darning socks, baking

pies and kissing your kids' scraped knees, your life and your children's lives still would not be perfect—because no mother, no child, no life is ever perfect," observes Antonia Van der Meer, author of an article titled "Free Yourself!" And, she emphasizes, if you're in the workplace, you need to realize that most childhood problems are not caused by your working. "Kids have gotten into trouble at school, had difficulty learning to read, fought with siblings and talked back to their parents for centuries! It would be a mistake for a mother to blame these problems on the fact she is working."[12]

School is a place where mothers are particularly vulnerable to guilt, stresses psychologist Carolee Lewin-Scheidman. And when it comes to a teacher's opinion, mothers out in the workplace are particularly vulnerable. When an employed mother goes to a conference with her child's teacher, she attributes normal problems, either directly or indirectly, to the fact that she works. The difficulty comes from the pairing of two separate issues, says Lewin-Scheidman: "Johnny's teacher may tell you that he has a problem focusing on his work and, a moment later, may make some comment about the fact that you are not there for him at three o'clock every day. The parent hears the first part, feels, 'Yes, that's true,' and therefore accepts the second part as well." But, she emphasizes, "What parents, and working mothers particularly need to understand is every child in Johnny's class has some area that will require attention and work that year."[13]

3. *Take a long-term view of parenting.*

If you agonize over whether you've been an adequate parent, keep in mind the observation of marriage counselor and columnist Brent Barlow, who says: "We can never really judge how we ultimately do as parents because we are not around during the last 20 years of the child's life. The problem is that parents eventually die. So how are we to know what our children turn out to be?"[14]

In this respect, look at your own self and your own continuing development. Just as you are still in a growing mode, so will your children be for years. You may be thirty or forty years older than your children—old enough to see life from a panoramic view. Your children still have a journey to take to achieve your greater perspective of the world. You can help your kids take that journey. Barlow emphasizes: "Some of the best things parents do for children occur after they jump the nest."

So there is still time! And still hope! Your children, like you, are still growing up!

Guilt, the gift that never quits giving, lavishly bestows its favors on women in yet one final way. We turn from a wrap-up of the "good-enough" mother to a wrap-up of holiday guilt.

Give Up Holiday Guilt

You've heard of PMS, or premenstrual syndrome, that crabby mood that hits some women once a month. But have you heard of PHS, or preholiday syndrome, a syndrome caused by holidays, not hormones?

"PHS is a serious national problem afflicting many people, mostly female, every year," reports Jean Marzollo in an article titled "Making It Through the Holidays." "Symptoms of this condition may manifest as early as July, but most cases are observed in fall, reaching the highest peak in December when Christmas and Hanukkah are observed."[15]

"The first time I hear someone say there are only twenty-five or so shopping days left until Christmas, I think, 'You just ruined my whole day,' " bemoans one obvious PHS sufferer.

It's not hard to spot such a sufferer. She is an overburdened woman, staggering from the guilt she feels, emitting heavy sighs, and groaning: "Ohhhh, no! I don't have Christmas pulled together *again*."

For most PHS sufferers, holiday guilt is an annual predictable event. In November and December, a woman who is normally trucking along at a fast pace on her treadmill becomes a frenzied woman on a dead run who is wearing herself out as she tries to pull this gala season together for a Christmas just like Grandma used to have.

Although PHS is found most frequently among women, men too are affected—particularly by what Marzollo calls pocketbook panic. And any man in the space of any woman who is experiencing a symptom Marzollo calls "too much to do" has to be indirectly affected by PHS, even if he doesn't have this malady himself.

PHS exacts an untold cost on many women. At a time when other people are going ho-ho-ho and fa-la-la-la, it's the pits *not* to be of good cheer during the holidays, laments one PHS sufferer, Pamela Redmond Satran. In an article titled "I Always Flunk Christmas," she writes: "Everything about Christmas—from wrapping and exchanging gifts to decorating the tree—

is supposed to be fun." So when a woman feels anxious about the festivities, she tends to get the ultimate guilt: guilt about feeling guilty.[16]

"I know I don't have the right attitude, but especially with young children, Christmas seems so self-defeating," admits one woman. "I buy all the presents, wrap all the presents, clean up all the wrappings, put away all the presents, pick up all the presents all year, and later, often throw away the presents. Then it's Christmas again."

"I agonize over every detail, clear down to the last stocking stuffer," relates another. "The worry I have about hurting other people's feelings just ruins my whole Christmas. I worry whether there will be enough presents for each child. Will they be the right presents? Is my mother-in-law's present nice enough? Will she love it? Will I offend someone by not giving a gift? Will I send cards to everyone who's going to send one to us?"

The burning questions that plague many a PHS sufferer come from feeling absolute responsibility for Christmas and the well-being of the people who will either be pleased or not pleased by how Christmas turns out. At this time of year, admits one woman, "I'm so stressed that, in the main, I experience only two feelings during the holidays: apprehension before Christmas and relief afterwards."

Traditionally, women in this culture have had the assigned duty of managing the holidays. The relentless stress of feeling responsible for everything can take a toll on her good nature. Emphasizes one grumpy woman: "All I want for Christmas next year is *no* Christmas."

Now, if this sounds grim, and you're saying, "Wait a minute! I don't get PHS," pat yourself on the back for having your act in order and proceed to enjoy the Christmas season. Consider giving lessons — next July — to your fellow soulmates on how to have a relaxed Yule season.

But if you feel chronic stress around the holidays and want to quit feeling guilty because you don't have the Christmas spirit, here are strategies that can bring relief and the possibility of even enjoying the season:

1. Sometime around Columbus Day, sit down with your family and ask them to describe a dream Christmas season. What would help them to experience the "true meaning of Christmas"? What kinds of activities and traditions are important to them? What would they especially like to do as a family? And, most important, how would they like to help those events become possible?[17]

Relinquish your position as sole manager of the Christmas season and cheerfully make it clear that even Mrs. Claus has elves. Engage the entire family in a discussion of how to get the shopping, cooking, cleaning, wrapping, and delivering accomplished this season.

2. Agree as a family to put your family in focus this year and every year from now on as a gift to yourselves. Then make every other decision regarding your time commitments and the giving of gifts for Christmas from this priority position.

Children have much more fundamental needs than gifts at Christmas time, say Jo Robinson and Jean Staheli, authors of the article "Bring Home the Joy." They need time with you. "Parents are often away from their children more in December than in any other month of the year, as their lives become crowded with shopping and social events. And when they're at home, they are often preoccupied with holiday chores and money worries," they write. "This constant busyness can make December a lonely month for children. Even though they are showered with gifts and affection on the 24th and 25th of

December, this two-day burst of attention is rarely enough. Children need to feel loved in a steady, constant way."[18]

3. Couple a much more intense focus on family activities and traditions during December with realistic gift expectations for family members. You may find that cutting down on gifts will be easier than you imagined, especially if children's needs are being met in other ways. Discuss with extended family members also practices of gift-giving and, if needed, ways of cutting down.

4. Determine your budget and stay within it. You don't have to spend a small fortune to be a good parent or spouse. Avoid equating the size or cost of the gift with your love. A present is simply that—a present. Give practical gifts you can afford and, if you want to give more, make commitments to yourself to give throughout the year gifts of personal care to the people you love.

5. Make one grand, extravagant list of everything you have to do between now and Christmas and then cut it in half. Decide how you can take shortcuts—lots of them. You can't do everything, so concentrate on doing well what you like doing best. Remember, you don't have to be overcommitted, overscheduled, and overharrassed. It's your choice. As you consider reducing your production, keep Christmas activities that have meaning to you and that you really enjoy doing.

6. Stop taking the holidays so seriously. Things will turn out. Give up rushing and start saying "Merry Christmas" and looking in the store windows while you're out and about. Laugh and smile more and also decide to enjoy whatever you're doing, whether it's shopping, baking (even with young children), decorating the tree, stocking-stuffing, or wrapping gifts. Make each thing you do a pleasant, satisfying experience in itself (that's how kids enjoy the holidays) instead of seeing everything as part of one long Yuletide endurance test.

7. Give up the guilt festival this year. Forget all the "shoulds" and "oughts" and do the things that make sense and that make the pressure tolerable.

Remember, there is no right way to celebrate the holidays. Shape this time to conform to your own wishes and values and to the needs of your family. With just a few hours of reflection before the holidays, you can gain control of the Yuletide season and create experiences you and your family can really enjoy.

Chapter 4

The Pleaser

There is in this world a malady known as "approvalitis," which afflicts any who require the endorsement of others to feel good about themselves. More widespread than the common cold, this ailment exacts a terrible toll from its victims, who chronically refrain from taking independent action for fear someone might disapprove. Not trusting themselves, they look to others for approval of the way they think, feel, and behave. And if others refuse to dole out that approval, they crumble.

At the core of approvalitis is the excessive need to please or to accommodate. One appropriately accommodates "when one has two pieces of bubble gum and shares one with a friend, when one offers the better seat in a theatre to one's companion, or even when one says, on coming to a doorway, 'After you,'" explains George Bach in his book *Stop! You're Driving Me Crazy.*[1]

Some, however, practice a false kind of accommodation in which they yield to another not so much out of good will as out of fear of conflict, Bach says. This forced yielding causes stress for approval seekers, for the price is higher than they want to pay. But saying no is not an option, for they fear there may be even greater stress, and even open combat, if they don't accommodate.

Women fall easy prey to approvalitis because their early training typically teaches them to equate their worth to loving and being loved — and to pleasing other people. That women want to please is not the problem. Neither is the problem that they draw satisfaction from meeting the needs of others. The problem lies in two other areas. First, a woman who has been taught to take care of her husband and children, and to gain satisfaction vicariously through their achievements, may completely sacrifice herself for others, only to feel empty and cheated as her children leave and her husband does not fill the "empty place" resulting from the sense of role loss. She "may come to the bitter realization that her role was not sufficient to last an entire lifetime."[2]

Second, a woman may put all her eggs in one basket. She has to please or, in the words of one woman, she is "nothingized" — she has no worth. Her very sense of self comes from being valued by or approved of by other people, and any situation that even hints of disapproval can be devastating because it calls her very being into question. Many women, in fact, will go to great lengths to avoid disapproval, disallowing the validity of their own needs and yielding at the slightest pressure to resolve conflicts in someone else's favor.

Being other-centered and dependent on validation from the outside world leaves women extremely vulnerable to the capriciousness and whims of people and events over which they have no control. Those who operate from the organizing principle "I'm unlovable if I'm not validated" reel when they experience negative messages from their world, or when the expected approval — the approval that they won, that they earned — is not forthcoming.

The stark reality is that there is no direct relationship between being "good" and "pleasing" and gaining abundant gestures of approval. At best, these rewards are only intermittently conferred by others. The disapproval, or the dearth of approval, activates a woman's worst fears: that she is going to disappoint someone she loves, that someone will decide she is unworthy, that someone will stop loving her. For some women, there is no threat more terrifying than the loss of love or approval.

The inordinate preoccupation of many women in pleasing others exacts a heavy price. Preoccupation with anticipating what they should be and how they should act to ward off disapproval (or to gain approval) wears heavily on their sense of self.

Caretakers and a Sense of Self

One caretaker uses the story of Peter Pan to illustrate what happens to women when they lose themselves in their relationships and don't develop a firm sense of self. "In the movie *Peter Pan* is a dog that most people don't remember—the caretaker, Nana," she says. "Nana takes care of the kids, makes their beds, gives them their medicine—does everything for them. She is walked all over, but she never says a word.

"In the beginning of the story, the father gets angry because he can't find his cufflinks, and he trips over Nana because she is trying to save the medication of one of the kids that's falling over. She's trying to help and to be a good caretaker. When he trips over her, guess who he's mad at? Nana! He takes her downstairs to tie her up outside. She sits and watches him frantically hunt for the rope—which she has in her mouth.

"Then Peter Pan comes and sprinkles pixie dust on the children so they can all fly off. Little Michael, the baby, sees Nana and takes Tinkerbell, the fairy, to her. After Tinkerbell sprinkles fairy dust on her, Nana tries to fly away too—but when she gets to the end of the rope, she can't go any farther. She has allowed herself to be tied up."

The caretaker who relates this story sees Nana's position as typifying that of many women. "Like Nana," she says, "we often spend our lives doing what other people expect, trying to please everyone all the time. Our main objective in life is to be good at the expense of developing a clear self. In the end, like Nana, we may pay dearly."

Women fall along a continuum with regard to how completely they have developed a sense of self, a concept that involves a firm sense of uniqueness and separateness from others combined with a high regard for self.

On one end of the continuum stands the woman who has a clear idea of who she is, where she stands, what she wants, and what is and isn't acceptable to her. She is able to represent who she is to others without fear or apology. She can give freely and fully to others, but she reserves a part of herself for herself. Her confirmation of her worth and "goodness" comes generally from within herself, and her clear sense of self is not ravaged by the whimsical moods and opinions of those in her world.

On the other end of the continuum is the woman who sacrifices her awareness of who she is to conform to the wants and expectations of others. She, in effect, merges with others to the extent that she loses sight of herself. Too much of her is negotiable under pressure from other people. Too much of her time is spent reading others' behaviors and trying to anticipate the right responses—those that will elicit approval rather than disapproval. And too many of her emotions are tied up in a never-ending cycle of feeling hurt, anger, and then guilt, as she encounters responses that don't confirm her basic "goodness" or positive intent.

Where do you fall on the continuum with respect to having

a clear, well-developed, and firm sense of self? Read on to answer questions that may help you hone in on that issue. These questions have to do with the aspect of pleasing, inasmuch as excessive pleasing lies at the heart of an underdeveloped self.

• Do you usually feel you're wrong when you encounter someone who has an opinion different from your own?

• Do you find yourself crushed when someone disapproves of you?

• Do you need your opinions and choices validated by someone else?

• Do you apologize at the drop of a hat?

• Do you constantly make self-deprecating statements ("I'm not at all attractive, good at sports, capable, or well-informed")?

• Do you believe most people are better than you are?

• Does your adequacy and lovability depend moment-by-moment on whether you're in the "good graces" of someone else?

• Are you careful to avoid confronting other people or showing them you're angry?

• Do you assume that if you just try hard enough, you can please everyone?

Now add up your *yes* answers and interpret your score:

0–1	You are off the hook.
2	You may qualify as a pleaser.
3	You are definitely suspect.
4 or more	You are a confirmed pleaser, in need of help.

The more yes answers you have, the more likely it is that your sense of self is in need of repair or firming. One way to begin immediate "construction" on yourself is to analyze how you deal with disapproval from others—the next topic.

Managing Disapproval

Most women cringe at even the thought of disapproval and, in fact, will go to great lengths to avoid it, as one woman illustrates: "I locked myself out of my car. I hesitated calling my husband for help because he was some distance away and I knew he would be annoyed if he had to come bail me out. But since I didn't have any other viable option, I called him to the rescue. Then I discovered that a car door was unlocked. My husband had already left his office, so I did the only thing I could to avoid double disapproval—I pushed down the button and locked the car!"

A woman such as this also has fine-tuned antennae that alert her any time anyone registers disapproval or anger. Even a hint that someone thinks she is "out of order" or "not doing her job" can pitch her into anxiety or depression.

Are you, like this woman, hypersensitive to negatives from others? To get an initial impression, consider the following scenario: You pass a friend or colleague in a hall and that person doesn't acknowledge you. What do you immediately think? Most women who are asked this question report that responses such as these flash through their minds:

• He doesn't like me, (or) He's mad at me.
• What did I do to offend him?
• What's the matter with *me?*

Women tend to default automatically to the explanation that the problem lies with them, not with other people. Consider these situations reported by two women:

"My neighbor said to me, 'I have to talk to you because everyone in the neighborhood is saying you don't pay your babysitter enough.' I cried for days over that. I couldn't believe

I was such a worthless human being that I didn't realize I was supposed to pay my babysitters more."

"I catered a wedding as a favor for a friend and created this beautiful scene behind the wedding party with a wrought iron backdrop draped with flowers. In the middle of the scene I placed a mechanical bird that made a constant mechanical chirping sound — the same note — over and over again. Halfway through the wedding reception the father of the bride came up to me, stuck his face within an inch of my nose, and said, 'Where is that blankety-blank bird?' I looked over at where I had placed the bird, and it had been right behind his head the whole evening. I was just heartbroken! I had put my all into what I thought was a wonderful touch of atmosphere, and here I had caused these people more misery than joy!"

In these two situations, each woman's self-esteem plummeted as she encountered someone who called her judgment into question. In the situation involving a woman who passed a colleague in the hall, there was not even a tinge of disapproval — just the absence of an expected response. Yet even a cue as ambiguous as simply not being acknowledged by someone can trigger feelings of inadequacy. In essence, the woman mind-reads others and makes judgments about their attitudes and intent based on vague information. She then behaves as though those perceptions were true.

In their vulnerability, many women feel that they are constantly being evaluated by others. "That happens to me. I know!" says one. "When I'm in a group and people don't look at me in a certain way — if they don't look interested, or if they don't smile — I conclude that they aren't going to like me or that they don't want to get to know me. So I just avoid them."

"It happens to me, too," says another. "Like when I'm talking with someone and I'm not even thinking about what I'm saying. I'm thinking, *Am I saying the right thing to her? Am*

I making myself understood? Am I saying these things so she'll like me? Am I being over-critical? Am I being this or that? I'm running through this computer checklist in my brain, trying to make sure I'm being the right kind of person for her. That's a lot of work!

"Then, when I'm through with the conversation, it still isn't over. I walk away thinking: *Does she think I'm stupid? Does she like me? Did I do all right? Does she think I'm disorganized? Does she think I should have had all these kids?*

"And who are these people I'm talking to? They're the people who are walking away from a conversation with me, thinking, *Gee, I'm starved!* We believe these people are so focused on us, as if they cared. And they really don't."

This woman is right on target. Most of the time people aren't preoccupied with or making judgments about other people or their flaws. The little errors you think you've made really aren't even noticed. One young woman reports, for example, "I said something I wish I hadn't at a party. It was probably only a sentence or two, but I agonized over that for several days and couldn't get it out of my system until I apologized to the person I'd talked to. What shocked me was that she couldn't even remember my comment!"

Relating to the preoccupation of many in gleaning information about how other people feel about them, a woman observes, "To be quite frank, there must be a certain egocentricity in most of us to feel so watched, so criticized, and so evaluated!" Another observes, "We'd do well to remember the words of one sage, who said: 'When you're twenty, you worry about what everybody thinks. When you're forty, you decide you don't care what everybody thinks. And when you're sixty, you realize 'everybody' hasn't been thinking about you.'"

Complicating their vulnerability to disapproval is the fact that women live in a sea of mood changers — people who are constantly shifting from one mood to another. (You, in fact, are one of those mood changers!)

You cannot, then, escape disapproval. It is embedded in the human condition. It will always be there, lurking in the backdrop of your life, ready to strike when you least expect it. That is why, if you suffer from approvalitis, you may want to completely overhaul your attitude toward disapproval. Here are principles to consider:

1. *Anger and disapproval will not kill you.*

Any anxiety or feelings of being "nothingized" that you experience when someone is angry or disapproves probably come from your childhood and dealing with what Sam Keen calls the giants of your world: "Every child enters a world that is already populated by giants—Mothers, Fathers, Adults. The giants seem godlike, because they know what we want before we ask and they have unlimited power to please or punish us. They seem to be able to read our minds. If we please them, we are rewarded by their smiles and approval. If we don't, we're ignored or punished and fear we may be abandoned."[3]

Now that you're an adult (in fact, actually appearing as a giant to the children in your world), the giants are only giants in your mind. They no longer have the ability to control you (unless you let them) or to devastate you (unless you let them). However, you may still view the world through a child's lenses, feeling a child's diminished feelings, as you encounter anger and disapproval, not recognizing that the people to whom you gave so much power no longer have survival significance to you. And not recognizing that you are a giant now and that you have choices about which feelings you generate inside when you encounter these conditions.

The new awareness concerning your own empowerment that can come is delightfully expressed in the comment of a teenage football player who lifted his mother above his head and remarked, "I wish I'd known you were such a peewee when I was a little kid."

You've *always* survived anger and disapproval. You will continue to do so. But perhaps, if you adopt principles espoused here, you may survive others' negatives more gracefully—perhaps without the apprehension and diminishment that may have flooded over you unbidden in the past. You may need to remind yourself that you are a giant, on equal footing with any other adult in your world. And that anger doesn't kill. And that it passes. And that you can gain control over your own moods when someone doesn't happen to like what you're doing. It may even pay for you to get philosophical if someone chooses to disappear, as did a woman who was constantly distressed by her mother's intense and often unpredictable anger. She simply learned to make herself impervious to the anger by thinking, "Oh well, she'll either hate me forever or she'll get over it." And, incidentally, her mother always did "get over it."

2. People's anger and disapproval have to do with their choices, not yours.

Others are in charge of their own anger and, in any given instance, will make three basic choices: whether or not to get angry; whether or not to stay angry; and whether or not to express their anger destructively. The same holds true for disapproval. Take any ten people and you may not find even two who will respond in exactly the same way about something you've said or done. Each person's judgment has to do with his or her own experiences and background, not whether you're an acceptable person. An angry or disapproving response has to do with the other person's childhood programming, anger style, mood at the moment, and dozens of other factors not within your control. Consider various reasons why people may become disturbed or disagreeable that have to do with them, not you, as reported by four women:

"Once at work I took a call from a lady who was really hostile. I excused myself from the phone for a moment and asked myself, 'Why is she so angry?' When I returned to the phone, she said, 'Tell so-and-so that my husband passed away three days ago.' "

"I had an appointment with the dermatologist the other day, and by the time I got there I was so mad at the auto mechanic who hadn't fixed my car properly that I really tore into the doctor for not curing my skin problems."

"I'm a teacher, and one day a student blew up in my classroom, yelled at me, and left the room, slamming the door behind her. The next day she told me she'd gotten drunk two nights before and her mother had kept her home from school and yelled at her all day. She was just upset."

"My boss was really grumpy at work all day long. I spent the day wondering what I'd done wrong. After work she left the store, but she returned when she discovered she'd locked herself out of her car. At that time she began talking to me. I found out that she wasn't feeling well and that her grandson was seriously ill in an intensive care nursery. Finally she asked, 'Margaret, do you sometimes feel you are jinxed?' So it hadn't been my fault at all."

The point is, there are innumerable reasons that people direct stress and distress toward other people that have to do with themselves, not others. When you incur someone's anger or disapproval, it may be for no better reason than the fact that you got in the way and became a handy stress conductor. In the worst case scenario, it may be because you actually made a mistake or erred in some way. The point still holds. Others still have a choice. On one hand, they can choose to work with you in constructive ways. On the other, they can choose to spew out anger or relate in other destructive ways.

3. *Develop explanations for people's behavior that have to do with them, not you.*

Consider how this principle works. Pretend you're driving along the freeway observing the speed limit when another car zips past you and in a flash is out of sight. You and your friends humorously begin speculating about the reason for the driver's rush:[4]

• He's rushing to the hospital because someone has been in an accident (or his wife is having a baby).

• He's late for an important appointment.

• He collects speeding tickets for a hobby.

• He has a spasm in his right foot.

• He feels important when he speeds.

• He's practicing to be a race driver.

• He just got a life insurance policy he's testing out.

• He just robbed a bank.

• He has a policeman on his tail.

• He wants to see how fast his new car will go.

You and your friends played a game, but in playing it, you produced many ways of seeing the same situation. You actually used a skill of infinite value to you in real life, the skill of developing perceptual alternatives.

Now apply this skill. Let's say you take a risk—you reach out to a new person and get a cool reception. Maybe your first response is to conclude that she doesn't like you. Then, recovering from your humiliation, you pause to permit other views to emerge:

• Maybe she is shy in new situations and doesn't know what to say.

• Maybe she is preoccupied and it just doesn't register that you are making an overture.

• Maybe she is having a bad day and doesn't feel like reaching out to anyone.

• Maybe she is offended by something you've done. If so, that's *her* problem. Your intentions are sincere.

Although there are numerous ways to interpret any given situation, the meaning you choose will determine the situation's effect upon you. If, in this case, you cling to your first conclusion that the other person is rejecting you, you may feel hurt and dejected. On the other hand, if you broaden your perspective and consider other explanations, you can choose the ones that make the most sense to you. That way, you control your interpretation of the situation — and your mood.

4. *There are no people who are supreme beings in this world. There are only people who are different from you — not better.*

You can compute the meanings of relationships on either a horizontal or a vertical plane. If you view relationships on a vertical plane, you will consider others as being either above or below you with respect to value. A woman who suffers from approvalitis utilizes the vertical plane. She automatically thinks, when she incurs disapproval, "If that person thinks I'm bad — then I *am* bad" or "If that person says it is so, then it must be so." In essence, her position is this: "Your view of me is much more important than my own opinion of myself. You are the Source — the receptacle of all wisdom — and your view of me is indisputable. You are always correct, and if you disapprove of me, my worth is reduced."

In contrast, if you view relationships on a horizontal plane, you compute people as different but equal in value. From this perspective, each person has a right to his or her own position, including a simple preference. If someone challenges your position, you may simply say: "I understand we're different, and each of us is entitled to our own opinion. My opinion is ... " By the same token, if someone disapproves of your behavior or, horrors of horrors, challenges your worth, that person is entitled to his or her opinion — but that is all it is, an opinion (and a poor opinion at that!).

Computing an incident that happened on a horizontal plane, a woman relates: "I was in charge of a recognition dinner for two people who were leaving an organization. It was a touching event, with many people in attendance. The next day I was informed that a woman who had left the organization eight months before felt she should have been recognized. Previously I would have been devastated, feeling I had hurt this woman through my oversight. I would have thought it was obviously my fault — I had done something wrong — I'm worthless. However, I realized I felt empathy for her. I was thinking, 'Isn't it too bad her programming teaches her to feel that if people don't recognize her, she hasn't done a good job.' I wanted to give her some articles and a book!"

5. *View yourself as separate from others and as being in charge of your own moods.*

You exist separate and apart from others. There are no shared brains, no lifelines from you to others that connect your moods to theirs, no buttons others can push to create anger and frustration inside you. That means that you, not others, are in charge of your moods.

Columnist Sidney Harris drives this point home with an anecdote from his own life. Stopping at a newsstand with a friend who purchased a paper, he noticed that when the friend thanked the vendor politely for the paper, the vendor remained cool and silent. "A sullen fellow, isn't he?" observed Harris.

"Oh, he's that way every night," said the friend.

"Then why do you continue to be so very polite to him?" asked Harris.

*"Yes, I'm 'just a secretary.' And I understand
you're 'just a vice-president'."*

Replied the friend, "Why should I let *him* decide how *I* am going to act?"[5]

Harris's friend refused to take on the problem. He did not let the other person disturb his own equilibrium. By viewing yourself as separate from other people, you can do that too.

6. *When someone shows disapproval or is in a bad mood, view the problem as residing with the other person.*

For instance, while driving home with a friend in a blinding snowstorm, Lanette had trouble seeing through her windshield. As she inched her way through an intersection, the driver in the car behind her began honking his horn. "That driver is annoyed because you're not moving faster," Lanette's friend commented. "That's his problem," said Lanette. "My problem is getting through the intersection."

When you encounter another person's bad mood, consider this: You were probably doing okay—you were in equilibrium to this point—so try to stay that way. The other person's mood doesn't have to be your mood. Think about yourself as having a shield surrounding you, protecting you from anger coming your way. Deflect that anger. Leave it where it belongs: with the other person. That person is allowing anger to consume him or her. Don't immobilize yourself by doing the same.

If you view the problem as residing in the other person, you may find it possible to manage that person with a light touch. One woman did so when her car stalled in an intersection and the annoyed driver behind her honked impatiently. Exiting her car, she walked back to him and said, "Sir, I'll gladly honk your horn if you'll start my car." After breaking into a gale of laughter, that is precisely what he did.

7. *Recognize that others don't always have their acts together.*

To protect yourself from taking on the negative moods of others, from responding to anger with anger, you need to accept others for the imperfect people they are. Give people the room to have bad days, to be cranky, to misunderstand, to misjudge situations, to make mistakes — just as you do. Develop tolerance, if you will, for the imperfections of others and for their noise-making.

When people are noisy — when they criticize, attack, complain, condemn, have loud temper outbursts — remember that the problem lies with them, not with you. At that moment you may be dealing with a person who is hurt, maybe even scared — a person who is probably warding off bad feelings about him- or herself. All that shows is the anger. Underneath this anger, however, may be a tender and vulnerable part of the self this person is trying to protect. It is as though deep inside of the adult is still a small child — a child who is afraid of disapproval and terrified of being abandoned or rejected. It is that child, the two-year-old, who screams and makes loud noises, who shows the anger. Instead of saying, "I hurt — I am in distress — help me," the two-year-old often gives out the loud message, "There's something wrong with *you!*" At that moment, the child is communicating ineffectively — looking outward and blaming others — rather than looking inward and trying to understand the source of the frustration.

To avoid taking on the problem when the two-year-old in another person responds with anger, try thinking, "This person is hurting. I'll search for the feelings that underlie the anger."

8. *Listen.*

If you accept the position that you are separate from others — that you don't have to take on their moods, and that the choice of becoming angry or showing disapproval has everything to do with another's choices and nothing to do with your worth — then maybe you can handle a disagreeable person differently. Instead of reacting, you might just try listening — which leaves the problem with the other person. When you listen, you enter the other person's world and try to see things from the inside out. You follow what that person is saying to you without interrupting, giving advice, introducing new topics, or mixing in any of your own opinions. Instead, you focus on reflecting, in fresh words, the other person's points, step by step, as you understand them.

Consider Carolyn, who parked alongside a country road to feed her horse, which was pastured in a nearby field. After tossing her horse some hay, Carolyn turned her car around in a farmer's driveway to head back for town. Out of his house came the farmer, ranting and raving: "Get off of my property! You're trespassing! All you city people are alike. You shoot my animals, you tromp down my crops and tear down my fence, and you litter all over my land."

Carolyn resisted an impulse to take on the problem and blast the farmer back. Instead she tried to capture what the farmer was feeling: "It just burns you up that so many city people take advantage of you. They don't seem to care about you or to respect your property," she offered for a start.

"That's right!" said the farmer. "And furthermore . . . "

Carolyn listened to that response, and the next, and the next. As she turned to go ten minutes later, the farmer called to her. "Wait!" he said. "If you ever need anyone to feed your horse when you're out of town, I'll be glad to assist."

9. *Make inquiries.*

To ascertain in what way another's anger or disapproval relates to you, ask these questions:

• What specific behaviors of mine didn't you like?

• What specific behaviors would you have liked instead?

• What specifically made my behavior unpleasant (disagreeable) (wrong)?

Once you have that information (devoid of the anger or disapproval), you can decide whether you want to change or to apologize. Sometimes changing may be to your advantage. It may help you to improve relations with someone or to modify a style that generally interferes with your relationships.

10. *Set limits.*

Though you may try to aid an angry person to discover what's wrong, you have a right not to take verbal abuse. A case in point is Tracy, who worked in a billing office. In the throes of being verbally accosted by a customer, Tracy set limits by saying, "If you'd like to discuss this problem, you'll need to stop yelling at me. You have a right to yell but I have a right not to listen, so if you're going to continue, I'll need to hang up. The choice is yours. What would you like to do?" "Wait," said the customer. "Don't hang up. Just give me a minute to regroup. I do want to talk to you."

Another option for dealing with an angry person is to respond similarly to this: "I'd like to understand what you have to say, but I find myself getting angry and defensive because I feel under attack and I don't want to feel that way. Please help me by describing the problem more calmly."

If your message doesn't work the first time, play as if you're a broken record, and keep emphatically repeating your position until the other person changes his or her approach. Do not let yourself be distracted by any other topic that the other person brings up during this time.

In managing verbal abuse, keep in mind the story of a man who attacked Buddha, to which Buddha responded, "Son, if someone declined to accept a present, to whom would it belong?" The man answered, "To him who offered it." "And so," said Buddha, "I decline to accept your abuse."[6]

Strategies to Combat Approvalitis

In overcoming approvalitis, it is vital to represent yourself, to stand for what you believe, want, or need. Here are strategies that will help.

1. *Quit over-apologizing.*

Most women, operating from an "over-responsible" position, are prone to apologize excessively, often for events over which they have no control.

"I'm a great 'I'm sorry' person," admits a woman. "I'm sorry that—

—my son's shorts aren't clean."
—I have an ex-husband, because it makes my mother mad."
—I have to work weekends."
—I only fed my family pizza tonight."
—my child can't find his socks."
—dinner isn't on the table yet."
—I didn't get organized today."
—my child hurt your child's feelings."

"I even apologize for apologizing so often," she admits.

Excessively apologizing actually constitutes a form of self-abasement. Observes one woman: "Women apologize for phoning you—'I'm sorry to bother you.' They knock on your door—'I'm sorry for interrupting you.' You trip over their feet

and they say, 'I'm sorry my feet were in the way.' That's 'wom-
anitis' — women apologizing for simply existing."

Not only do women apologize excessively — many of them
apologize profusely! One woman illustrates: "This is an 'I'm
late for something' apology: 'Oh, I'm sorry I'm late! My little
boy wouldn't go to school this morning, so I had to take him,
and he cried and ran after the car when I let him out, and
when I got home I got a call from someone who saw him
running up the street, so I had to go back over and pick him
up and take him back to school, but he didn't want to stay, so
I had to sit with him for a while until he would go into his
classroom, and it took up my entire morning. That's why I'm
late. I'm sorry!' "

"It's as if you have to tell your whole life story when you
feel bad about something," offers another woman.

If you, like these women, over-apologize, you can curb this
aspect of approvalitis by listening to yourself and analyzing
situations in which you apologize. Apologizing is an admirable
habit unless it is used to excess. Then it becomes a form of
self-deprecation designed to turn away anticipated disapproval.
Over-apologizing also gives messages to others that you really
aren't comfortable with yourself. And it can turn other people
away; they may become increasingly uncomfortable and annoyed as they try to convince you that you did no harm.

2. *Stop trying to get others to agree with you.*

Avoid using statements like these: "Don't we, honey?" "Isn't
that right, Fred?" or "It's really hot today, don't you think?"

3. *Don't preface your statements with qualifying remarks
to buffer any disapproval you might encounter.*

Avoid such qualifying phrases as these: "I know you'll think
this is crazy, but . . . " "My way of thinking is probably weird,
but . . . " "This might not be right, but . . . "

Illustrating the way she disqualifies her remarks, one

woman relates: "I always say, 'I read in a book that ...' or 'I heard that ...' because I'm afraid that if I take ownership of it, people will say, 'That's a dumb idea.' And if they *do* say it's a dumb idea, I say, 'Yeah, that's what I thought, too.' "

You may figure that rushing to discount your own statements will prevent others from doing it for you. That way, you don't face disapproval. "I'm going to make sure that if someone disapproves, I've already done it for that person. Then it won't hurt so bad," admits a woman.

If you want to "firm up" your "self," you'll need to force yourself to let your statements stand by themselves and use "I" language — "I feel ... " "I think ... " "I wish ... " — to make your points. You'll probably be pleasantly surprised to find that most people will respect your opinions.

4. *Firm up your statements.*

Don't use "weasel words" to avoid taking a stand. A cartoon showing a woman sitting in a restaurant, looking at the menu, succinctly captures the propensity of some women to avoid taking responsibility for themselves. The caption reads: "Well, to be honest, maybe I'm way out of line on this one, but I'm pretty positive that I probably don't want the sole, I almost think."[7] Using such modifying phrases as "pretty positive," "probably," or "almost" give speech a tentative, uncommitted quality.

5. *Give up words that belittle or diminish the statements you make.*

Watch out for words like "only" ("This is *only* an idea, but ... ") or "small" ("May I make a *small* suggestion") or "just" ("I'm *just* a secretary"). Also, eliminate such self-deprecating responses as these:

- "I just look so terrible today."
- "I'm running late again — as usual."
- "That was a stupid remark I made. I'm such a dummy."

• "I bet I'm the most scatterbrained woman you know."

• "I'm sorry to bother you—I know I'm a pain."

Represent yourself in social situations as though you are your own best friend and advocate. That means cutting out all the slams you give yourself.

6. *Don't advertise your mistakes.*

If you feel guilty about being caught in your misdeeds, even if they are only imaginary, you may rush to point them out to others. "I came to get some soup, but I forgot it, so I had to come back to the store," a woman says to a stranger in a supermarket. By indiscriminately relating her error to anyone within hearing distance, this woman advertises to another that message that "I'm flawed. Please excuse me for *being*"—and she succeeds in calling attention to something no one would have even noticed. "You don't need to offer explanations for your choices and decisions to people who don't need or deserve them," says an author. "The hotel clerk doesn't need to know why you're checking in, and the butcher isn't interested in the fact that your daughter is allergic to beef."[8]

7. *Allow yourself to take some risks.*

Said a woman who is gaining confidence in herself, "I was about fifth in a supermarket line with my hands too full of groceries. Finally I put the gallon of milk I was carrying on the floor and kicked it along with my feet. I never would have done that before out of fear that someone might disapprove. But I was frankly pleased I had been just a little bit daring. I said to myself, 'Who's going to care in fifty thousand years?' "

8. *Trust your own judgment.*

One woman tells the story of having gone into a restroom only to encounter a man standing there. After rushing back outside, humiliated because she had gone into the wrong bathroom, she looked at the bathroom door, which read "Women."

Her judgment had been accurate but she hadn't given herself due credit.

Because she doesn't trust her own perceptions, a woman with approvalitis will often "shop" for people who will confirm her judgments. "I'm a shopper," confesses one woman. "I'm always looking for people to give me permission to have a particular feeling or opinion or to make a certain decision. The other day I admitted to a friend that I have really let down with Justin, my third child. I've enjoyed him much more than the first two — and he doesn't have to pick up every block! I wanted her to say, 'Oh, I'm easier on my younger children, too.' When she finally did, I thought, 'Whew! I can feel okay now!' "

If you would like to depend on yourself more, follow this simple rule: *Be the one to endorse your own feelings, opinions, and decisions.* When in doubt, defer to your own judgment with the same confidence as Suzanne, the child described here. Says Suzanne's mother: "When my second grader was learning how to write, she'd bring home all her work to show me. On a number of papers her teacher had circled her K's in red. When I pointed out to Suzanne that she was not making those K's correctly, she responded: 'No, Mom, that's the way I make my K's.' It didn't bother her a bit that they weren't like the teacher wanted, so I thought, 'Well, okay, so that's how you make your K's.' "

9. *Don't express your opinions through other people.*

"The other day I had a ten-minute conversation with a friend and, when I walked away, I felt I had just spent ten minutes with her husband," one woman relates. "Every thought she had was attributed to him — 'Jim said it was due to . . . ' and 'Jim says you might try this . . . ' I had actually had the conversation with him, and he wasn't even there!"

"Sometimes we can't even take credit for a great thought

that is ours," says another woman. "Instead of owning our idea, we try to give it more respect by saying, 'My doctor says this,' or 'My husband agrees with me.' We think that if we do this, we'll be taken more seriously."

A woman with approvalitis often feels uncomfortable entering the "thinking area" that has been reserved for people who are "better" or "more educated." "Our ideas will get out into the atmosphere, but they are orphaned by their insecure 'parent,' " observes a woman who is overcoming her bout with this ailment.

Coming out in the open, learning that she can depend on her own self for accurate information about herself, can be an exhilarating experience for a woman. It leads to growing self-confidence, as these comments of enlightened women illustrate:

"The world opened up when it dawned on me we didn't all have to be homogenized."

"My life changed when I realized there were as many different frames of references as there are people—and that I was entitled to my *own*."

"Previously when I encountered an opinion different from mine, I used to think, 'I don't see it the way you do, so I must be wrong.' Now I just think, 'Thirty-one flavors at Baskin Robbins! We're all different. You do it your way, and I'll do it mine.' "

Making Effective Decisions

If you're going to overcome approvalitis and have a firm self, you need to be able to make decisions without panicking or feeling paralyzed. But that's no small order for a caretaker.

"Decision making is hard when you have a whole audience of people who have their say even if they aren't there," says a woman. "You have what your mother used to say, what your dad used to say, what your husband says, what your neighbors might think, what your friends *do* think, and what the perfect mother out there is thinking."

Continuing, she observes: "The voices of these people are ever-present, so when you make a decision, the implications go far beyond, say, what color of wallpaper you're choosing, or whether or not you should wear a certain skirt. Every decision is a major event — an issue of how you're going to please everyone. If you make the 'wrong' decision, you have a whole room full of people telling you what an idiot you are and that's a big risk to take."

This is the pleaser speaking — that part of the caretaker who wants to be liked and who doesn't want to disappoint or be rejected by anybody. "The stakes are so high that sometimes I drive myself crazy wondering if I've done the right thing," says one pleaser.

Decision making can also bring out the guilt sponge — that part of the caretaker who feels responsible for fixing everything and who feels culpable any time she can't control anything. Thus, any time the guilt sponge makes a decision, she risks the possibility that factors beyond her control will affect others and she will be at fault. "I agonize so much about failing that I sometimes just stall over making a decision, hoping someone will come along and make it for me," says a guilt sponge.

And decision making can bring out the perfectionist in the caretaker — that hard-driving woman introduced in the next chapter who relentlessly considers every possible alternative. She may not want to commit until the last moment in case something better comes along. "Sometimes I end up with so many choices I feel immobilized," a perfectionist observes.

It's no wonder, with all the different, and often contradictory, pulls of a woman's cultural programming that she sometimes has a hard time making decisions — and that she sometimes gets stopped dead in her tracks!

One reason you may have difficulty, says author Andrea Williams, is that "your mind craves what is simple, clear-cut, and obvious. It tries desperately to avoid what is indefinite, unpredictable, or complicated. Your mind wants to *know*, and you're asking it to *guess*." A decision is always only a guess, she observes! For that reason, you may run into trouble making decisions when you assume that —

— you *should* know exactly how everything is going to turn out. (You don't.)

— there is a perfect, right answer. (There isn't.)

— all loss, pain, or discomfort you or others experience could somehow be avoided if only you could figure out which is the "right" choice. (You can't.)[9]

Though the circumstances surrounding decision making are usually ambiguous, and uncertainty is a life condition you'll have to live with, making decisions can be less difficult. Consider these strategies for improving your skill:

1. Adopt the philosophy that making any decision, any move, even the wrong one, is better than just sitting there.

2. Use a balance-sheet approach to write down the advantages and disadvantages of each course of action.

3. Remember that no matter how difficult the problem, you always have options. Work until you can see them.

4. Plan on making some "wrong" decisions and decide now you're not going to penalize yourself because you didn't have adequate information or couldn't foresee the future. You will have done the best you could. Besides that, you have to risk to grow.

5. Remember that you'll always run across people who won't like your decisions. But, as one woman cogently observed, "Try to be all things to all people — and *you* disappear." So please yourself — that you can do!

6. Don't get hung up going *right* just because someone

says "Go *left*." It's easy to slide into old habits of rebelling against what others want for you instead of asking yourself, "What do I want?" Do what you want, even if it happens to conform with others' choices. That way, you're in control. Says a woman who makes this point, "Sometimes I say to myself, 'I need to do what I know I need to do, even if my mother tells me to.' "

7. Remember that with a little thoughtful weighing of pros and cons, a quick decision may be as good as one that takes a day. The amount of time spent on a decision is generally not an adequate indicator of its quality.

8. Quit looking for people to tell you what to do. You may be an expert at that.

9. With heavy-duty decisions, keep in mind there's no such thing as a perfect choice — it's all relative. Each decision leads down a different path in life — not necessarily better or worse, just different.

10. Realize that many decisions can be changed, and that many aren't irrevocable. So move ahead and give yourself permission, if necessary, to change your mind or to make adjustments later.

11. If you're panicking over a deadline, check to see if you can have more time. You may find the time limit imposed by someone else is actually more elastic than you thought.

12. If you agonize over small decisions, stop it! Most decisions you make simply don't matter in the long run.

13. Develop the everyday habit of being decisive. Start with small decisions, such as what you want for breakfast or what you're going to wear. Go with your first choice and don't look back. Then go on to bigger decisions. You may be out of the habit of asking yourself, "What do *I* like?" or "What do *I* want?" and then moving definitively ahead. Developing decisiveness can help you develop self-definition.

Mary Ellen Donovan, author of an article titled "This Is DEFINITELY What I Want — I THINK!," cheers you on here. She says: "It's easy to say, 'This is what I *should* do,' or 'This is what I *ought* to do.' But the hardest thing for anyone to say is, 'This is what I *want* to do.' "

Many women are afraid of the consequences of defining themselves clearly, but not defining themselves also has consequences, she emphasizes: "If a woman hasn't cultivated the habit of acknowledging what she wants on a routine, everyday basis, then it's absurd for her to expect herself to be able to figure out what she wants when it comes to major issues like relationships, careers, and childbearing."[10]

If, on the heels of Donovan's sobering words, you want to combat indecisiveness, the first firm decision you can make is to decide more and suffer less. Now see, wasn't that easy? You just carved out a bit more self-definition.

Make Anger Work For, Not Against, You

To combat approvalitis, a woman must also learn how to represent herself effectively when she experiences anger.

Women are on a continuum when it comes to expressing anger. At one extreme, some women — culturally programmed to please and to be "good" — rarely show anger. They may, in fact, rarely recognize their anger, as these feelings may convert readily to guilt and depression. Others are in the middle of the continuum — thinking they shouldn't get angry, but they still do, sometimes frequently. They keep trying to stifle their anger and to ignore it, because being "good" means avoiding anger and conflict at all costs. But the anger keeps surfacing — overcoming them, grating on their self-images as well as their relationships. Some frank souls — women who are not shy about getting angry and stating their differences — fall toward the other end of the continuum.

Regardless of where they are on the continuum, however, many women are prone to use fighting, complaining, and blaming as indirect methods of expressing their stress and distress, which only tends to preserve the status quo of their problems and relationships.

Harriet Lerner, author of *Dance of Anger,* has written about women at the two extremes of the continuum. At one end, women who are victims of what she calls the "nice lady" syndrome direct their primary energy toward protecting others and preserving the harmony of relationships at the expense of defining a clear self. By diverting so much effort into "reading" other people's behavior and keeping relationships on an even keel, they become increasingly less expert on their own thoughts, feelings, and wants. At the other end of the continuum, a woman who spews forth venomous anger — without clarity, direction, and control — allows herself to be written off and provides others with an excuse not to take her seriously. Lerner asks: "Have you ever watched another person get cooler, calmer, and more intellectual as you become more infuriated and 'hysterical'?" If so, the nature of your fighting or angry accusations may have actually allowed the other person to get off the hook.[11]

Despite their radically different appearances, keeping anger to yourself and destructively dumping it on others are simply two sides of the same coin. The outcome is the same. In either case, you're left feeling helpless and powerless.

In venting anger, Lerner observes, it is amazing how frequently women "march off to battle without knowing what the war is all about. We may be putting our anger energy into trying to change or control a person who does not want to change, rather than putting that same energy into getting clear about our own positions and choices."

How can you become more effective in dealing with anger?

How can you decide what the war is all about before choosing whether to march off to battle? Consider these possible strategies:

1. *Decide if anger is a problem.*

Henrie Weisinger, author of *Dr. Weisinger's Anger Workout Book,* suggests five signals to make that determination. Anger gets in your way—

—when it is too frequent.

—when it is too intense.

—when it lasts too long.

—when it leads to aggression.

—when it disturbs work or relationships.[12]

2. *Face your anger.*

We all get angry—it's a natural part of the human condition. The stirrings you feel inside come from a physiological arousal, a state of readiness occurring in your body to deal with hurt, frustration, and fear. When you're angry, you're simply prepared to act. So when you feel those stirrings, don't tell yourself you shouldn't be angry or that you probably aren't angry. Give yourself permission to experience what is happening inside. Those feelings aren't wrong—they simply *are.*

3. *Use anger as a signal that you need to focus inward to determine why you're out of equilibrium.*

"Anger becomes a tool for change when it challenges us to become more of an expert on the self and less of an expert on others," Lerner emphasizes. Become introspective, she urges, by asking questions such as: "What about this situation makes me angry?" "What is the real issue here?" "What do I think and feel?" "What are the things I will and will not do?"

Don't be surprised if it takes some time to answer such questions, she continues. "It is an action of courage to acknowledge our own uncertainty and to sit with it awhile. Our anger can be a powerful vehicle for personal growth and change if it does nothing more than help us recognize that we are not yet clear about something and that it is our job to keep struggling with it."[13]

4. *Recognize that you can choose how to express anger.*

Anger as such is neither positive nor negative. However, how anger is expressed will determine whether it destroys everything or everyone in sight or is a vehicle for positive change.

5. *If you do express anger, describe all the feelings you're experiencing.*

Anger is not a primary emotion. It surfaces after you experience such emotions as hurt, disappointment, or fear. People will be more understanding if you express your pain, rather than just your anger.

6. *Use an "I" message (an upcoming topic) to express your anger.*

If it applies, tell the other person that being angry bothers you, that you prefer *not* being angry, and perhaps say: "I hurt. I'd like to change what's happening between us. I'd like to feel better about us. I'd like to work this out and get about the business of loving again." At times, after pensive thought, you may also need to tell another person where you stand, what you want, and what is and isn't acceptable to you. In essence, say, "This is my position" rather than "This is how you have to change."

7. *Learn to cut down on your anger episodes.*

If you explode frequently, use a golf counter to count your anger responses for a week, with the ultimate aim of reducing your explosions by 90 percent. Studies indicate that self-monitoring, by itself, alters behavior.

8. *Try to find out what makes you angry.*

Keep a daily anger diary and record each time you become angry. Do an "anger autopsy" to discover the situations and events that trigger your anger. Most likely, the same old things set you off time and again. After determining what they are, design new and creative ways of approaching these potentially explosive situations. If, say, you ordinarily see red when you walk into your teenager's messy bedroom, decide now to handle the situation with humor rather than grimness and raw anger.

9. *Notice physiological signals that warn when you're getting angry.*

When you get mad, the adrenaline begins to flow. Your muscles flex. Your stomach tightens. Your heart beats faster. You breathe faster. Your neck and forehead get hot. You're ready to strike and then suddenly you explode. Interestingly, though, you can't explode until your body goes through physiological arousal. Have you ever seen a relaxed person fly off the handle? One way to derail anger responses is to interrupt your body's physical preparation to act and to find alternative ways of discharging pent-up energy. Consider these possibilities:

• Talk more slowly or whisper.

• Breathe longer and more deeply and instruct yourself repeatedly to relax.

• Change your body position. If you're standing, sit down. If you're sitting down, lean back.

• Keep your hands at your sides or in your pocket.

• Get a drink of water—literally cool yourself down.

• Punch a pillow.

• Remove yourself from the pressure scene and find a cooling-off place to release the tension.

Accompany any of these strategies with this self instruction: "I refuse to take my frustration out on the people I love. I choose to calm myself."

10. *Find a code word.*

Explosive anger is like a runaway train going a hundred

miles an hour down the track, says author Neil Clark Warren. When you see that runaway train coming, you need to pull a lever to shift it to a side track, and then slow it down until it eventually stops. To do this, develop a code word like "Think!" that stops your behavior from running over you. Then, rehearse your word. Say it out loud, and make it remind you of sobering questions like these: What do I really want out of this encounter? Do I want to fly off the handle and end up embarrassed? apologetic? guilty? sick of heart because I've hurt someone else? Or do I want to find some way of bridging my differences with this person? of becoming close? of being better understood? What is the best way to accomplish these goals?[14]

11. Practice exchanging "hot" thoughts for "cool" thoughts — thoughts that cool you down rather than heat you up. For example: "I need to keep my cool, or this situation could really get out of hand. I can cope. Take deep breaths. That's right. That feels better." "I can handle this. If I lose control, I'll be the loser." "Whatever he says doesn't matter. What really matters is that I control myself."

Also concentrate on cool thoughts sympathetic to the other person's position: "She must be very hurt by something she perceives I've done to insult me like that." Listen carefully to the other person's point of view *while* you're angry at him or her (this has to be one of the toughest things in the world to do). Nothing dissolves anger more quickly than truly understanding another person's position.

Use "I" Language

The secret to representing yourself — your needs and feelings and opinions — involves using "I" language, responses that start with the pronoun "I" and put the focus on you rather than on other people. Using "I" language, you claim ownership of your perceptions and your actions: "I think . . . " "I feel . . . "

"I want . . ." "I need . . . ." Your messages describe your own experiences, and any listener knows that you, not others, are responsible for your thoughts, feelings, deeds, and needs. See how clear and up-front these messages are:

- It's important to me.
- I want to think about it.
- My view is different.
- I'm relieved you called.
- I enjoy that picture.
- This is what I like.
- This is my impression.

Does stating what you really think, or feel, or want, or need sound simple? Actually, it would be—except for one thing. As a caretaker, you've likely had lifelong training for being indirect and hiding how you feel. Afraid that you'll hurt other people's feelings, that they may perceive you as impolite, or that you're actually selfish if you declare yourself, you may have chronically shrouded your feelings and intentions. Being tactful, caring, and civilized—all caretaking positions—has meant deferring to others at the expense of having a self.

Consistently representing yourself involves identifying and overcoming ineffective habits of expressing yourself that may get in the way of that objective. These habits include:

1. *Using questions.*

Questions can hide real needs and feelings. Maybe you're riding with a friend and the thought, "I'm hungry," comes up. Instead of saying, "I'd like to stop for lunch," you may say, "Wouldn't you like to stop for lunch?" Another time you may be excited about seeing a new movie in town, but instead of simply stating that fact, you ask, "Wouldn't you like to go to a movie?"

2. *Using vague pronouns.*

You may use cover words, such as *people, some folks,*

everybody, they, we, or *it,* that hide your real feelings or intentions. For example:

• "*We* shouldn't spend so much money." (You mean, "I'm uncomfortable with the amount of money *you're* spending.")

• "*Everybody* says this is a good movie." (You mean, "I'd like to go to this movie because I've heard it's wonderful.")

• "*People* will think you're impolite if you don't go to the dinner." (You mean, "I'm worried about what people will think of *me* if you don't go to the dinner.")

• "*Nobody else* would put up with the way you're speaking to me." (You mean, "I'm annoyed at the way you're speaking to me.")

By far the most insidious pronoun to get in the way of representing yourself is the word *you.* Watch how this little pest, which is often accusatory, can interfere:

• "*You* are insensitive" (meaning "I'm hurt you didn't call when you were going to be late").

• "*You* don't love me" (meaning "I don't feel loved").

• "*You* shouldn't have gone to the spa tonight" (meaning "I'm disappointed we didn't have time to spend together" or "that you weren't home to help me" or "that you forgot our anniversary for the third year in a row").

Notice, in each instance, that the first response puts the focus on "you" and the contrasting response puts the focus on "I." Whenever your responses put the emphasis on another person rather than on yourself, your inner alarm needs to go off. "You" messages obscure your feelings and needs and they also bring out strong negative feelings in others. People don't like being told what they're thinking or feeling or what they're doing wrong. Sadly, you may think you're explaining your feelings by using "you" language, but you're not. What you're doing is utilizing blaming responses that encourage others to attack or to defend.

3. *Identifying what you'd like.*

When you talk about what you *don't* like, you're obscuring what you *do* like. Imagine being stranded on a desert island. The pilot of a helicopter overhead, who will be making only one pass, calls out to ask you what supplies you want dropped from the aircraft. For best results, you need to tell him what you want. If you give him negative responses ("I don't want perfume," "I don't want evening clothes," "I don't want enchiladas"), you may starve! The moral of the story is that people are much more likely to know what you want — and to provide it — if you give them positive and instructive information.[15]

4. *Being congruent — communicating your true feelings to others.*

Learning to express feelings means learning to face them. In effect, you say: "I realize there are certain risks involved in being real, or true to myself, but I also realize I'm responsible for that self. I'm therefore willing to face the consequences of open expression and commit myself to communicating my feelings accurately to others."

Ironically, there are far fewer risks to relationships when you are congruent than when you are not. Anger and resentment foment when problems build up, sometimes resulting in such turmoil and bitterness that people abandon relationships. When you behave in concert with your feelings, you choose to be open and accepting of yourself, confirming your own value. In effect, you choose freedom — freedom to be yourself — over the bondage of living constantly with stored and festering feelings.

5. *Being responsible for the way you communicate.*

Being open does not mean being destructive. It is vital to edit out overt hostility and abrasiveness in your responses, even if it means delaying a response to get control of yourself and your approach to another person. Unfortunately, often by the time you notice you need to express feelings, you may be angry or frustrated. Under emotional stress, it is easy to dump raw anger and devastate others or attract an equally harsh response. Pause, then, to think about what to say. Aim to build, not to destroy, relationships.

Remember that you're not expressing your feelings to an object but to another living, breathing human being who has the same vulnerability to pain as you do. You can choose to blurt out your feelings in whatever ways they come to you or you can rehearse in your mind ways of expressing yourself that are kind and sensitive and even gentle.

6. *Listening to others.*

As carefully as you try to express feelings, your messages may still cause pain. To reduce defensiveness and make your messages more palatable, rephrase what you hear. As a rule of thumb for keeping a relationship in repair, explain yourself in less than one minute and listen to others' reactions for at least five.

7. *Reserving judgment as to who, if anybody, should change.*

Don't make the error of assuming others should change simply because you've explained your feelings. It may be, in fact, that *you* should change, something you may realize as you release festering feelings and can think more objectively. You may find that you've had unrealistic expectations, or the indignities you've suffered are imagined rather than real.

Chapter 5

The Perfectionist

Maybe you are the type of person who has high standards and who takes pleasure in the healthy pursuit of excellence. That's good.

Then again, maybe you set standards that are way beyond reach and relentlessly knock yourself out trying to achieve them. That's bad.

In fact, if you frequently strain to reach impossible goals, you may be a compulsive perfectionist who drives herself for perfectionism in every aspect of her life and who measures her self-worth entirely in terms of her own achievement.

Take the case of an admitted (and now reformed) perfectionist who relates this incident: "One Thanksgiving we were invited to my mother-in-law's home, and, among other things, I'd volunteered to bring a relish tray. Now, this was not your ordinary relish tray. I took oranges and a grapefruit and stuck parsley into them until they looked like a mound. Then I prepared celery trees, turnip daisies and lilies (each with tiny little carrot centers), and radish spirals and roses, and arranged them into an integrated flower garden on the parsley hill.

"By the time I was finished with the garden, which took me most of two days to make, I was too exhausted to go to Thanksgiving dinner. Too frustrated, too. So—I put my six children (who were scrubbed and polished), the relish-tray garden, a scrumptious broccoli casserole, and eleven assorted homemade pies in the car and sent them with my husband off to grandma's.

"The comments about my relish tray were wonderful, but I wasn't there to hear them. I never did get to the dinner. I was home—just fuming—because other people expected so much of me. I didn't even take a shower and get dressed for the day until everyone had left. Now I realize that *I* was the one expecting so much of me! I made the choices. All I needed to do for that dinner was prepare a simple relish tray, buy a few pumpkin pies, and take a vegetable dish. The drive to spend two days making a relish garden, the elaborate casserole, and the exotic array of pies came from inside me, in an effort to make other people think I was wonderful. But all I did was make myself completely miserable."

This woman spent the first thirty-five years of her life pushing herself every day to the limits of her endurance. And what were the benefits in trying, as she puts it, "to always be perfect"? "I got a lot done," she says, but in further contemplating her answer, she reflects: "Many of those things I didn't really need to do. I think now of the time I missed with the kids, the time I missed taking care of myself, the resentment I had toward so many people, and I realize I paid an enormous penalty for trying to be perfect."

Perfectionism, as is true of other aspects of women's programming, falls along a continuum. On one end is the woman who has a compulsive drive to achieve a flawless product in everything she does. She sets unrealistically high standards and then berates herself mercilessly when she doesn't measure up to them. Anything less than a perfect performance is unacceptable, but she may not even be able to savor what she considers an ultimate achievement because perfection is her norm. She rarely gives herself a pat on the back, constantly focusing on what she hasn't achieved rather than what she has. She winds up "feeling haunted by her incompletes rather than heartened by her successes."[1]

On the other end of the continuum is the woman who strives to meet high standards but who acknowledges her finiteness and limitations. In completing a task, she senses when she has reached maximum returns. She can let go of the task—and find satisfaction in it—without having always done her best. She can also prioritize tasks and choose which ones deserve the most effort. She comfortably embraces the motto: "If it is worth barely doing, just barely do it." This woman's drive to achieve comes from enjoyment in and enthusiasm for achieving, not from a fear of failing, so she can stop and relax without an inner gnawing that, in momentarily not performing, she is doing something wrong.

The woman driven by perfectionism operates from a position of unconscious caretaking. Her motives for performing and doing for others are beyond her awareness; and her unrelenting push to achieve overambitious, if not impossible, goals imposes high costs on her physical and emotional well-being. She doesn't know when to say "I've done enough. This is good enough." She has no concept of herself as having boundaries—of there being only so much of her to expend on her activities.

On the other hand, the woman who has control over her drive to excel operates from a position of conscious caretaking. Her expression of self derives from a drive to create rather than a drive to impress (to "earn" self-esteem). She is aware of her limited time, energy, and resources, and respects her finite boundaries.

Moving to a position of conscious caretaking with respect to perfectionism is a quest, not an event. Where, then, are you with respect to this continuum? Can you identify aspects of your behavior that please you? Areas in which you have made progress? Areas you want to get under control? The remainder of this chapter has been designed to aid you in any quest to free yourself from perfectionism. Remember, as you read on, that the basic qualities embodied in perfectionism—being hard-working, attentive to detail, accurate, thorough—represent basic strengths that serve you. The quest is to gain control of these sterling qualities by gaining control of your perfectionism.

The Myth of Perfectionism

Is there such a thing as perfection? Not according to David Burns, author of *Feeling Good: The New Mood Therapy,* who says that perfection is the "ultimate illusion." "It simply doesn't exist in the universe," he argues. "The harder you strive for perfection, the worse your disappointment because it's only an abstraction, a concept that doesn't fit reality." And if you don't believe this, he urges, just look around. Everything can be improved, which you'll notice if you examine it closely or critically: every person, every idea, every work of art, every experience. This includes, of course, your own performance.[2]

To give up perfectionism, you have to give up the lingering notion that you really could be perfect in some area if you tried hard enough. The truth is, you can never be perfect in this life—anywhere, ever.

You will also need to give up the notion that there is some woman out there who is perfect, who does have her act completely together—someone whose performance you have to match! "I have that image," says a perfectionist. "I believe there is someone out there who looks like a million dollars, has her household together, cans forty bottles of peaches a day, conducts preschool herself, teaches her children at home, always makes bread from scratch, never sleeps, and never gains weight when she gets pregnant. I have her in my mind and, because she exists for me, whatever I accomplish is never good enough."

Finally, you need to give up the notion that you're what author Dorothy Briggs calls a "Special Case."[3] In your head you may realize that people can't be perfect, but in your heart you may feel you're different — *you* can't afford imperfection. Your "Unacceptable Me" is quantitatively worse than any other person's, so you have to strive to make up for it by looking wonderful, even if that means pushing until you drop. As a "Special Case," you may also believe that you're the only one in the world who makes mistakes and that you're the only one who can't be forgiven for them.

A penetrating question to ask yourself is this: Why are you the only one (of the five billion people on this planet) who needs to be perfect? *All* people make mistakes every day of their lives.

Perfectionism and All-or-Nothing Thinking

Women in general and perfectionists in particular tend to evaluate their personal qualities using labels — extreme, all-or-nothing categories — often dozens of times a day, as reflected in the following statements:

• "I'm so fat. I shouldn't be sitting here with all these skinny ladies."

• "I don't have anything to say to these women. I'm so practical and boring."

• "What a stupid comment I made. I'm sure I offended them. I always say dumb things."

• "I should have thought of that idea myself. I am so self-centered. I can't think of anyone else."

If you habitually use labels like these to describe yourself, you are making sweeping generalizations that totally ignore the many complex facets of your actions or character. In one fell swoop you can wipe out your uniqueness, thinking of yourself only in terms of the label you've used.

Labels divide your characteristics into black-and-white categories: they are either good or bad, beautiful or ugly, desirable or undesirable. They thrust you into an either/or category, and *you* become the label. Typing yourself in this manner is distorted and misleading, for labels are abstractions that don't exist in reality. They are also insidious, for each new situation in which you apply a label becomes one more "proof" to you that you indeed *are* inferior or inadequate in the ways the label suggests. The label itself designates you as a "finished product," destined to remain as you are all the days of your life, with no room for growth or change.

What labels do you use when referring to yourself? Consider this list:

disorganized	stubborn	insensitive
boring	overprotective	timid
lazy	weak	insecure
unmotivated	indecisive	impatient
inadequate	too serious	too tall
unlovable	too intense	too short
ugly	outspoken	too fat
unattractive	anxious	too thin
selfish	too talkative	too emotional
weird	too practical	not confident

stupid	too reserved	not musical
clumsy	temperamental	not mechanical
careless	nervous	not athletic
irresponsible	plain	dumb
forgetful	too meticulous	a poor cook
sloppy	opinionated	a poor speller
controlling	immature	a poor sport

Labels such as these discourage you from exerting the effort and taking the risk of trying to change. They are also self-perpetuating. What can you do to avoid labeling yourself and to stop destructive thinking that inhibits your growth and keeps you from any chance of attaining high self-esteem?

1. Realize that you can change. Avoid using, say, a label of "I'm dumb" and of then supporting it with conclusions such as "That's just me," "I've always been this way," "I can't help it." You have the ability to change anything you would like to change.

2. Remember that a label presumes you must achieve perfection in order to be a viable human being. Not so! You will always be in a state of imperfection—on a continuum—with respect to any dimension you utilize to measure yourself.

Speaking to this point, one woman relates: "When I was talking with friends, I labeled myself 'uninformed' because I wasn't aware of all the election issues. Later I thought, 'I don't need to know about every movie that's been out, or every book that's on the best seller list, or every election issue in order to be an adequate person.' I'll never be informed about *everything*."

3. Recognize that when you use negative labels, you wipe out any positive characteristic you have or any positive thing you've ever done in your life. Take the statement "I should have thought of that idea myself. I'm so self-centered, I can't

think of anyone else." Such a statement ignores all the generous, selfless efforts you've ever made on behalf of others.

4. For a week, keep track of the negative labels you use. Then throw them out of your repertoire. Instead, be descriptive and stay with the situation at hand: "I wished I'd thought of that idea, but I didn't, and that's all right."

5. Think gray. Instead of thinking of your characteristics or performance in absolutes, think of them in percentages, reminding yourself that things are usually somewhere between 0 and 100 percent rather than simply black or white.[4] Instead of saying, "I'm so self-centered — I never think about other people's needs," say, "Probably 95 percent of the time I *do* think about other people's needs."

6. Try thinking of your behavior or performance in neutral terms. Imagine using the label "failure" as a description of an animal's behavior, says Wayne Dyer. Consider listening to a dog barking for fifteen minutes, and then saying about the dog: "He really isn't very good at barking. I'd give him a 'C.' " That's absurd, Dyer says. "It is impossible for an animal to fail because there is no provision for evaluating natural behavior. Spiders construct webs, not successful or unsuccessful webs. Cats hunt mice; if they aren't successful in one attempt, they simply go after another. They don't lie there and whine, complaining about the one that got away, or have a nervous breakdown because they failed. Natural behavior simply is! So why not apply the same logic to your own behavior and rid yourself of the fear of failure."[5]

Even if you want to improve your behavior or performance, consider your present performance as simply natural behavior, a neutral starting point for change, instead of some awful flaw in yourself.

7. Remember that these points apply to other people as well. When you label others, you see them as totally bad or

deficient and wipe out their personality or essence. You are not giving the other person specific information about a specific behavior that occurred in a specific situation that bothered you. That makes it difficult for the other person to even consider a change!

Perfectionism and Mistakes

Perfectionists typically live in mortal fear of making mistakes. When they inevitably make a mistake, they tend to shame and scold themselves, as does this mortified woman: "When I dusted this morning I broke three things. Three! Two were keepsakes originally belonging to my husband's grandmother and the other one was a piece of glass from a picture frame. I berated myself for hours over my goof."

Although women who tend toward perfectionism are perhaps the hardest on themselves when they make mistakes, this kind of critical self-jabbing is not atypical of any woman who makes the grave error of confusing her *worth* with her *growth*. To distinguish between the two, first consider the concept of *growth* and the following principle: *You have a right, as a fallible human being in the process of becoming, to make mistakes.*

For most of us, life is a learning process. Each crisis we encounter requires that we change and grow. As fallible creatures, imperfect in our nature, we are always in the process of becoming—always accumulating wisdom and experience. We will never, if we are lucky, arrive at a point where we have completed our growth process. In that process of growing, we will make mistakes, which is to our benefit, for it is out of our errors that much of our learning takes place. In fact, making mistakes is absolutely essential to the growth process.

Now consider the concept of *worth* and this principle: *As a human being, you are intrinsically valuable simply because you are.*

A popular poster depicting a young boy who looks like a ruffian succinctly captures this concept. Beneath the boy's picture the caption reads: "I know I'm okay because God don't make no junk."

On this point, Dorothy Briggs, author of *Celebrate Your Self,* writes: "You are an unprecedented event in the universe." Most of us give lip service to our uniqueness and then lightly toss the fact aside, she observes. Yet the likelihood of another person genetically put together in our unique pattern at any time in the past, present, or future is so infinitesimally small as to be inconceivable.[6]

Briggs makes the point that our universe does not indulge in duplicates. Each of us is an unrepeatable creation—a miracle. As that miracle, we have intrinsic worth.

Consider these statements to see how women typically confuse growth and worth:

- "I lost my temper. *I'm an awful person!*"
- "I locked myself out of my house. *That was so dumb!*"
- "I spilled the milk. *How careless of me!*"
- "I'm growing new life forms in my refrigerator. *I'm a horrible housekeeper!*"

In each statement, the woman first describes her mistake, a growth issue, and then labels herself, making the mistake a worth issue. The task, then, is to simply substitute a neutral statement for the label. For example:

- "I lost my temper. I'll learn from the situation and do better next time."
- "I locked myself out of my house. I'll hide a key outside so it doesn't happen again."
- "I spilled the milk. I'll get a rag and clean it up."

• "I'm growing new life forms in my refrigerator. That's very creative."

Notice that these reactions simply focus on the problem. They do not assassinate a woman's personality nor do they diminish her worth. Of these illustrations, the first three — losing one's temper, locking oneself out of the house, or spilling milk — might be considered genuine mistakes. The fourth situation is not; it involves a woman simply noticing something she hasn't accomplished and then indicting herself for it when she says "I'm not a good housekeeper."

Herein, then, lies an important point: A mistake is often not a mistake. People often define themselves as having done something wrong under conditions in which they really haven't erred.

According to one dictionary definition, people make mistakes when they misunderstand or make a moral judgment.

You're not making a mistake when another person thinks you "ought" to do something differently. When someone remarked that a comment one woman made was "just plain stupid," the woman responded: "I reserve the right to say things *you* think are stupid and not feel bad about it." This woman knew she hadn't made a mistake. She just wasn't thinking the way her friend thought she "should."

Neither are you making a mistake when you base a decision on the best information you have and then realize later that with further information you would have made a different decision. You simply did the best you could with the information available at the time. It doesn't make sense to chastise yourself for that.

Even if you make a mistake, don't be hard on yourself. When you flub, don't scold or shame yourself. Or deny your mistake. Or apologize profusely as though you had committed an irrevocable and unpardonable sin. Simply practice the

"kindly grandmother" stance, says Dorothy Briggs. Then you're neither overly indulgent nor harsh with yourself. The biggest mistake you can make is clinging to past mistakes. So, just consciously face mistakes, learn from them, and then lay them to rest. In fact, "Put a statute of limitations on past errors and refuse to wallow in self-punishment year after year," she recommends.[7]

One woman describes the way she lets herself off the hook when she bumbles: "When I realize I've blown it, I pat myself on the back, because I've learned Step One: I've recognized, at least afterwards, that I made a mistake. Step Two is recognizing my mistake while I'm blowing it. Then Step Three — the really great step! — is recognizing the mistake before I blow it. Then I've really made progress!"

As you work to put mistakes in a neutral zone, keep in mind a comment made by one sage: "In the over-arching cosmic view of things, with death at our left shoulder, what difference does it really make?"[8]

Everyone has the right to be wrong, and the right to grow

from his or her mistakes, without others emphasizing the mistakes with finger pointing. Most people beat themselves up inside so severely when they feel they've made a mistake that they don't need help in highlighting their error. Yet, letting others make mistakes without penalty is perhaps one of the most difficult challenges a perfectionist faces. At the heart of her problem is that she assumes that other people can or should be perfect—and being perfect means doing things her way.

If this description applies, and if, in your heart of hearts, you know you need to give people more room to make mistakes, read on. Previously we talked about methods to release yourself from your mistakes. Now consider ways to release others from your judgments—and from being perfect:

1. *Releasing others from being perfect means allowing other people to be different and allowing them their separate reality.*

A poignant story of a five-year-old boy who went with his family to a restaurant illustrates this point. When the waitress asked the boy what he wanted, he responded, "I'll have a root beer, a hamburger, and french fries." His mother countered, saying, "No, bring him roast beef, peas, potatoes, and milk." When the waitress returned, she placed in front of the boy a root beer, a hamburger, and french fries. There was a very pregnant pause at the table and then the boy said, "Gee, Mom, she must think I'm a *real* person."

Writer Carl Rogers uses this analogy to capture the need to accept those we love in their imperfect condition: "When I walk on the beach to watch the sunset I do not call out, 'A little more orange over to the right, please,' or 'Would you mind giving us less purple in the back.' No. I enjoy the always different sunsets as they are. We would do well to do the same with people we love."⁹

2. *Releasing others means allowing them to be inconvenient without penalty.*

The acid test for such a release results when something of value to you is at stake—perhaps an object, or your time, attention, or schedule. Take the case of Roxie, whose test came when she was making a double batch of waffles on a Sunday morning with her eight-year-old daughter. The daughter grabbed the bowl of batter out of Roxie's hands to place it beside the waffle iron—and up in the air went the bowl and down came the batter, spattering all over the kitchen. Seeing her daughter's tears, Roxie stopped herself from the scolding that was on the tip of her tongue. Catching her breath, she said quietly, "It was just an accident." And then she said, rather gleefully in front of her husband, "Don't worry about it, honey. Daddy will clean up the mess, and you and I will make another batch of waffles." Roxie remembered something else at that point: the lemon meringue pie she had turned upside down years ago when she had tried to help her own mother. Her daughter had done nothing more than make the same kind of mistake Roxie made when she was young.

3. *Releasing others means making a commitment to protect their fragile egos.*

As you consider giving others more latitude, think about them as vulnerable human beings who have the same inner insecurities and tender feelings as you have. Protect them from the wounding you can inflict, as one woman illustrates:

"Nineteen years ago, when my husband and I were poverty-stricken newlyweds, he gave me a music box with three glass figurines on it. I treasured that music box, which played 'Let Me Call You Sweetheart.' It sat on the coffee table until my toddler picked it up and broke one of the figurines. I shouldn't have left the box there, of course, but I didn't consider that at the time. I was so furious, I spanked my son until his bottom turned red. Afterwards I felt so bad that I vowed never to do that to him again. From that day forward I resolved to build his self-confidence and protect him from my anger. I put the broken music box in the bottom drawer of my chest, where it has remained the past nineteen years. Every time I open that drawer, it reminds me of my resolve not to hurt him."

4. *Releasing means taking a no-fault view of a situation.*

Viewing negative events as accidents is difficult because we tend to see them through a "blame" framework. Says a struggling mother, "Inside I feel someone has to be at fault. If my child spills his milk, it is not an accident. I gave him too big a glass or it was too close to the edge of the table, and I should have foreseen the problem and moved the glass. Or he spilled his milk because he's a klutz, so I'm going to send him to his room."

Negative events do happen and people do have responsibility for their respective parts in those events. But there is a difference between responsibility and fault. People don't go out of their way to cause accidents or mistakes, nor do they usually behave deliberately in ways to make other people angry. If you search carefully for the cause, you will find a person who is hurt or preoccupied or perhaps uninformed, not a person who is intentionally trying to make your life miserable. Or you may find a person who is just going about the business of being himself, even if it is irritating to you.

5. *Releasing means giving others permission to make mistakes.*

Consider how several women have accomplished this with their families:

"The other day my four-year-old dropped his cookie, which left some crumbs on the floor. He was looking at me, and I just picked up the cookie, blew it off, and handed it to him while I kissed him on the forehead. It was a new experience for both of us. I didn't pounce on him simply because he made a mistake."

"Twenty years ago, when I had four young children, my husband and I took his parents and our children to a restaurant, where one of the kids promptly spilled his milk. As I reacted with frustration, my father in-law said, 'If you'll just accept the fact that milk spills at every meal, it won't bother you anymore.' I've tried to apply that philosophy over the years with my children, and it has saved us all substantial wear-and-tear."

"I try to deal with my child's mistakes as though they were committed by an adult visiting my home. If my neighbor spilled milk there, I'd say, 'Don't worry about it.' I try to treat my child the same way."

"I told my children something I had read recently—that we're all allowed to make ten mistakes a day, and that when we err, we should remind ourselves of that. Then one day my kids were carrying in the groceries and one of them dropped a bag, breaking a big bottle of spaghetti sauce. My child pointed out the obvious: 'Mom, I made a big mess!' 'That's okay,' I responded. 'We all get to make ten mistakes a day.' 'But I've already made five!' he lamented. 'Well, this just makes six,' I said. That put a big smile on his face."

"I've tried to deal with my children's mistakes with humor. Recently my son, who has four younger sisters and doesn't get along with them that well, came bombarding down the stairs, shouting, 'I'm so sick of these sisters! They're always getting into my stuff. I want a padlock on the door!' A few minutes earlier I had gone into the laundry room and found he had thrown all the clean laundry on the floor, looking for a shirt. I had been mad about it, but I didn't say anything. I just counted to ten. So when he said the same thing to me about his sisters, I looked at him and very calmly said, 'I know just how you feel. Someone pulled all the clean clothes out of the dryer. It makes me so mad, I guess I'll just have to put a padlock on the laundry-room door!' That brought him to a screeching halt, and we were both able to laugh about the situation."

"My five-year-old is perfectionistic, just like me. He also sings. While he was performing the other day, he missed a couple of words. Afterwards his teacher gave him a treat. Later he told me, 'I don't think she would have given me that treat if she'd known I messed up on those two words.' At that point I realized I needed to help him be less critical of himself. Our family already has a tradition of sharing special things at the dinner table, so we just added the *faux pas* we make every day. Now we have good hearty laughs over our mistakes and delight in simply being human. The kids have learned it's okay to mess up."

The last line about sums it up. The challenge is to let other people know that it really is okay to mess up. (And, of course, to believe that yourself!)

Perfectionism and Control

A woman with perfectionism in her makeup is a woman who is trying to control her environment. When things around her fall apart, she tends to fall apart too. Her worth depends on her keeping her world in order. That also means keeping people in order.

Says a released perfectionist: "I used to never let my children make anything in the kitchen because I assumed it was my responsibility to watch over a food project and make sure that it was done right and tasted good. I also dreaded their playing dolls or getting the trucks or puzzles out because I was afraid someone might see the clutter. If they wanted to put something on their bedroom wall and it wasn't the right color, didn't match, or looked out of place, I would rearrange it. I was afraid someone would come in and think I decorated the room. Essentially, my choices had nothing to do with my kids' choices or their expressions of creativity. I didn't allow them to be who they were. We have a funny way of thinking that's how you take care of people!"

From the perfectionist's perspective, the people in her charge are extensions of herself. Relates one woman: "I've always viewed my husband and kids as my 'representatives.' When we first married, David wouldn't wear socks, and that just devastated me. Even today, he doesn't like to have his shirttail tucked in, and he lets his hair get too long before he gets a haircut. If he walks out the door and doesn't look great, it's my fault—I'm the caretaker, and he ought to reflect me. If he doesn't look good, I don't look good. It's the same with my kids. If I send Lisa to school and her hair doesn't look wonderful, it bothers me all day. I say to myself, 'The teacher will think I'm not a good mother because I haven't done her hair well.' "

Another woman confesses, "I feel as if everything about my child needs to be perfect, including his schoolwork. That's why I hate parent-teacher conferences. I feel like *I'm* getting the report card."

When it comes to her "extensions" or "representatives," the perfectionist always feels as if she is getting the "report card." Because of this, she may find herself excusing behaviors of others that she can't control.

One woman explains, "When my two-year-old is teething or tired, I'll say, 'I never knew what it was like to have a boy!' That's my excuse for him, especially when he's punching someone in the face. Another excuse I use, when Jenni doesn't look perfect, is 'She dressed herself this morning.' "

Because she feels indictable, the perfectionist may put in-ordinate pressure on those she is "in charge of" to conform to her expectations and her view of how the world "ought" to be ordered. Responses like these are not unusual:

"I've made Sarah's life miserable because she typically wants to wear something to school that doesn't match, and I won't allow it. I always say to her, 'They'll think you're an orphan.' Then she'll cry and scream and say she isn't going to school, and we end up in an emotional battle."

"My head is filled with everything I need to do to and for my children — to the point where I often plan the fun right out of their lives. I say no too much, too automatically. I'm so busy keeping things under control that I often don't give my kids the autonomy they need."

The perfectionist is also likely to get angry — often — and to yell and scream when she doesn't get her way. It's not that she wants to do that, but her back is against the wall, the stakes are high, and people aren't cooperating. They're doing what *they* want to do, not what *she* wants them to do. And they're creating disorder at the same time that she needs order to keep her self-esteem intact.

Perfectionism and Martyrdom

In addition to her anger and resentment, a perfectionist is prone to inflict guilt trips on others. Because she has extended herself so far and stretched herself so thin, she feels overworked and underappreciated, and she lets her family know with guilt-producing statements like these:

• "Look at all I've done for you. You could at least do this for me."

• "If you loved me, you'd do what I asked."

• "I've slaved my whole married life for you, and this is all the thanks I get?"

Because perfectionists view what they do for others as givens demanded of them, rather than choices freely made, they tend toward playing martyrs. The anger they experience and the guilt they elicit in others springs from the sense of "being used." This feeling is confusing, because it is closely related to the positive feeling that one is "of use." The sense of "being used" relates to a feeling of depersonalization—that our services have been separated from ourselves and that our uniqueness has been denied. On the other hand, the sense of being "of use" relates to the utilization of ourselves, the feeling of usefulness, which provides great joy and pleasure.[10]

The motives the perfectionist assigns to others will determine whether she has the satisfying feeling of being useful or the humiliating sense of being used. Consider the way some women describe their roles: "All I was good for was to be everyone's servant." "The hard thing after you're married—and you still want to go to school—is that you're still expected to do everything else." "People give us this all-encompassing power that's supposed to make things better and make others happy. It's like we're supposed to be angels of mercy. In large part we are—I love the nurturing and loving parts of being a woman—but we're asked to perform at the highest level. We're not allowed to miss a step."

Notice that these responses infer that someone else is responsible for the perfectionist's stress. If she tacitly views herself as being driven by others who don't understand or appreciate her or care about her burdens, she will be angry because she believes she is being victimized.

Perhaps the most basic difference between the conscious caretaker and the unconscious caretaker is that the conscious caretaker views herself as being in charge of her choices regarding any overload, while the unconscious caretaker assigns the fault and the blame for her overload to other people.

Most women are taught to serve, but they can take on so much that serving becomes servitude by their own making, as one woman astutely observes. They often then become chronically resentful because they view people as expecting too much of them and giving them too little in return.

One woman explains: "I lived with the false notion that if you give and give, it will all come back to you. But it never does. No one ever notices how you are feeling or asks you if you need a break. I waited for years and years for someone to do that. I'd often get angry at them because they weren't doing the things for me I had hoped they would."

Women thus contribute substantially to their runaway burdens, as Ellen Sue Stern, the author of *The Indispensable Woman* observes: "The more you do, the more everyone expects," she says. "And the more you expect of yourself. You set the tone. At first, you second guess other people's expectations, imagining you must perform, regardless of what messages they are actually conveying. Before long, what's imagined becomes real. After a while, your employer, friends, and family tailor their expectations to match your image of yourself, happily agreeing to your persistent offers of help. Even those closest to you take your apparent lack of vulnerability at face value and stop extending their support."[11]

It is vital, then, to accept personal responsibility for your own choices. You are a significant source of your own pressures, and you play a large part in perpetuating your own burdens. Your informed choices can now release you from many of those pressures and burdens.

Perfectionism and the Independence of Others

The perfectionist gives, and gives, and then gives some more. In her giving, she sometimes takes over, assuming much too much responsibility for the people in her charge, as illustrated in the following comments made during a women's seminar:

"I know every day that if I fix everybody's breakfast, I'll be late for work," said one woman. "But every day I still do it. Every day I say to myself, 'Tomorrow, I'll just turn on the griddle and they can make their own pancakes.' But while I'm putting my makeup on in the other room, I think, 'I'll bet they're letting those pancakes burn,' and I'll run back in the kitchen. Sometimes I even cover the pancakes to keep them warm while my children are playing around. It's crazy, but I still do it — I know better!"

"I have a hard time delegating," another woman commented. "One day I got really brave and thought, 'I'm going to delegate a little job here.' I asked the kids to clean the table off and do the dishes (which I do ten times faster). As they did the work, I felt bad for them. I couldn't win either way."

"As you [the presenter] have been talking," said another, "I've been thinking that this is the first day my husband has ever been alone with his five children. Ever! So I am sitting here with tired bones because yesterday I cleaned the house. I got all the kids' clothes ready and put meals in the refrigerator. I took care of everything just so I could come here today. When I kissed him goodbye this morning I looked at him and was silently proud of myself *because he didn't have to do anything!*"

"This woman's husband probably has no idea what a normal day would have been like if she hadn't done that," observed another woman. "When she gets home, he's going to say, 'You know, it was a whiz.' "

"Plus," responded the first woman, "it will be a mess when I get home!"

"I have a good analogy for our tendency to take over," another woman commented. "We start in the morning on a hike. We are all wearing warm clothes, but as the day progresses it gets hotter, and we all start throwing off outer layers of clothing. The kind of person we're talking about is picking up everyone's castoff clothing. While those in the front are having a good time, she is carrying the load. She is not having a good time—but they are!"

And what happens to the woman who overdoes her caretaking? How does she feel when she sees all of these people out there having fun while she's staggering up the mountain with all these clothes?

"Resentful," was one woman's response. "I start feeling mad at these people, and then I feel guilty for being mad at them because I'm doing what I'm *supposed* to be doing."

The pull toward caretaking is a powerful one, causing caretakers at times to rob others of their independence, as these two authors indicate:

"It is confusing to discern between taking an interest in and taking over, between making ourselves useful and making ourselves indispensable," says one.

"By taking responsibility for others' happiness, we invite them to become dependent—an invitation that the truly healthy human spirit always vigorously refuses."[12]

Responding to the propensity of women to "take over" others' lives, the women at the seminar continued:

"Taking over our children's problems does them a disservice. They grow up with mother doing everything for them, and when she eventually stops, they think, 'Why isn't she doing this for me anymore? I must not be lovable.' "

"Taking over also handicaps them. My mother did everything for me, so I grew up with the image of being the caretaker. But I didn't have enough confidence to carry out the role because my mother always did everything for me!"

"Taking over certainly doesn't make kids self-sufficient. I'm always trying to find answers to their problems. I have to find the answers, because my kids need immediate relief from them. If I solve the problems, I think, then they'll be happy. But it only takes about ten minutes before they have another problem."

"Do you know what we've been doing? We've been programming ourselves to go into depression when the kids leave home. *Nobody wants us, nobody cares,* we think. We feel empty, and since we haven't invested in ourselves, where do we go? Clear to the bottom."

"We think we want our children to be independent so they can live without us. Then we're disappointed when they *are* independent and *do* live without us. Really, we've done a good job — we've done what we've started out to do — but we find it distressing when our children leave because we've been robbed of our role."

"We need to quit becoming so intensely involved in other people's lives. We need to help them to be free and independent."

Allowing other people to have autonomy may mean "giving up the God role," says Elizabeth Berg, author of an article by the same name as her counsel. Recognizing she has lost control of most of the forces that can affect, influence, or devastate her daughter Jenni, Berg faces her own limitations. Sometimes she can cushion a blow, but she cannot save her child from learning from her own choices and experiences. Addressing the need to let go, Berg acknowledges with some sadness that "the time has come for Jenny to deal with some problems alone, to find her own way of removing psychic splinters. It is time for the fallout from her actions to be her responsibility."[13]

Releasing from Perfectionism

In this world there is a bubbly, upbeat woman who, when asked why she always seems so happy, responds, "It's because I have low standards."

This woman's response reflects her conscious position that

she can't do it all—and that's okay. This is the position any woman must adopt if she is to come to terms with her perfectionism. She must release herself from the self-imposed tyranny that comes from straining unremittingly toward impossible goals, and then relentlessly indicting herself when she can't achieve them. As it is, the endless details she has to accomplish are like grit grating on her mind—ever with her, ever pushing her down, wearing her out.

If this sounds like you, would you like to lose five pounds of "grit" (in one month's time, with satisfying results or a money-back guarantee)? If so, consider these strategies for lightening your load and clearing your mind:

1. *First, face yourself!*

The positive side of perfectionism is that it pushes you toward your full potential. The down side is that you ignore your limitations. In stretching too thin, too far, too often, you court frustration and exhaustion, maybe even total collapse.

Several possible habits may exacerbate your exhaustion. Most women today adhere to the "add-on" principle: "I'll just add on one more teensy-weensy commitment (without giving up anything!). My datebook shows my next available opening at 2:00 A.M. a week from Thursday. Of course, I'll do it. I can handle that!"

Most also operate—too often—from the "I have to make it" principle. A woman can't, say, just purchase brownies for a child's school party and smash them with a fork so they look homemade. No. She has to make them. And they have to be fresh, no matter what time bind that puts her in.

Finally, most cleave to the "I can't ask for help" principle. When it comes to saving children from burning buildings, women will ask for help. But the situation has to be about that dire, and the woman that desperate. Even one who needs seven clones to accomplish all her self-imposed assignments says,

"Hey, no way! I don't want anyone to think that I can't handle my job all by myself."

These habits are symptomatic of the Invincible Woman syndrome. Any woman so afflicted tells herself, "I'm tough. I can do anything you ask. Anytime. Anywhere. Just give me a challenge!"

Now, if you're suffering from this syndrome, you need to realize you're *not* invincible — undaunted, perhaps, but not invincible. You need to use adjectives like *bounded, finite,* or *limited* to refer to yourself. There is an end to you. You can't do it all. You must make choices. Facing these facts (after you've had a good cry) will help you release from perfectionism.

2. *Decide, with this new perspective on your finiteness, to quit demanding of yourself that you do everthing perfectly.*

Consider how one woman became a victim of the "I have to make it" principle because she hadn't given herself clear permission to be less than perfect. This particular instance is related by an observer at the scene:

"My mother-in-law, three sisters-in-law, and I went to the craft store. We all know that to be a successful mother, you have to do crafts, right? There was a darling craft made up and all ready to buy for about ten dollars. One of my sisters-in-law decided she wanted to buy the item, but my mother-in-law and the other two sisters-in-law began applying pressure: 'Oh, you can *make* that for a lot less money! And you do such a good job!' So my sister-in-law (who really hates crafts and who normally just purchases any item she wants) bought the supplies. Afterwards I asked her, 'How much did you spend?' And she said, 'Twenty-four dollars.' She had spent more than double the money for the privilege of making the craft herself and feeling perfect as a homemaker!"

Many women, like this one, are trying to function at an illusionary 100 percent level. There isn't a place for a 95 percent or 85 percent or 50 percent performance. The woman who is an ultimate perfectionist is probably fighting for her self-esteem every minute of her life because every detail undone accuses her of not doing her job. One price of perfectionism, then, is that the perfectionist is not free. Her life is controlled by her list of unaccomplished things.

Another price is that she usually isn't enjoying what she's doing. She is a victim of finished-product thinking, focusing on the end result rather than the satisfaction of doing something. For her, the joy of doing a task well may also give way to fear of not doing it perfectly.[14]

Still another price is that perfectionism eventually erodes a woman's energy and ability to cope, including reduced immunity, chronic exhaustion, low self-esteem, impaired relationships, depression or burnout, and potential collapse.

The perpetual drive toward 100 percent can also be hard on a family. Says a mother, "I was going crazy, as usual, preparing for my son's birthday party for the entire third grade class. Suddenly it hit me, as I was blowing up the twenty-ninth balloon, that what's good for me may not be good for my child. Having a mother who knocks herself out driving to four different stores to find the crepe-paper streamers that are the right color may not be so great. The child may have the kind of birthday party you'd see in a TV commercial, but he doesn't see his mother smile all day."[15]

Releasing yourself from taking care of everything perfectly may be hard to do—but it can be done. Reports one woman: "All I had to do to feel bad about myself was to look through the kitchen window at the apricots falling off the tree in the backyard. I could hear my mother's voice saying: 'Diane, it's slothful to let those apricots go. It's the same as wasting money.' Now that I'm liberating myself, I give myself permission not to do something simply because someone else says I should.

I've been canning apricots every summer for the past fifteen years and I don't even like apricots. So I've decided that next year I'm going to tell my mother she's welcome to pick the apricots when they're ripe so we won't waste money."

3. *Cut down on the number of things you're doing.*

"When you start to center yourself, and you become clear about your limitations and your priorities, you realize you can't do a million other things," a woman comments.

In their busyness, perfectionists often don't realize how unrealistic their goals are, as one illustrates: "I was startled the other day when I asked a co-worker, 'Floyd, what goals do you set for yourself when you come to work and there are a million things to do?' And he said, 'You know, if I can accomplish *one* goal, I feel really good.' 'One goal?' I said in astonishment. 'I have twenty!' So now I'm trying to relax a little bit and give myself full credit if I only accomplish ten things. Men's views are so different—and maybe they're more relaxed because they're more realistic."

In your quest to become more realistic, consider how other women are cutting down. Says one: "When my neighbor was sick, instead of making something, I ordered a pizza, bought a liter of root beer, tied a balloon on the bottle, and took it all to the family. I reasoned that when I'm sick, the last thing I want to do is organize and serve dinner, which is what you do with everything homemade. With a dinner like this, there would be no dishes to return or wash—and what family doesn't like pizza!"

Another comments, "I had four kids, and when I was working fulltime, I sent all their clothing that needed to be ironed to a rummage store. I decided I didn't need that additional stress. Someone asked, 'How can you afford to do that?' to which I said, 'We just wear less.'"

In cutting down, you may want to apply the "Anti-Doing

Formula" from Margorie Shaevitz's book *The Superwoman Syndrome*.[16] Ask yourself these questions:

- Does this really need to be done? Why?
- Can someone else do it?
- Do I want to do it? Why?
- Is it important for me to do it? Why?
- Is this something that I can *not* do? Why?
- What is the worst thing that will happen if it doesn't get done?
- If I choose to do it, who can help?
- Can I pay someone else to do it? Who? How much?
- How much time will I save if I hire or ask someone else to do it?

Shaevitz's motto is: "When in doubt, dump it!" As you consider what to "dump," give yourself permission to make choices that coincide with your personality and preferences. Decide what is right for you and stand firm.

4. *In your quest to cut down, remember that some things are not worth doing and others are not worth doing well.*

A time-management expert asks, "Why should you spend 45 minutes meticulously mending a skirt waistband that will always be covered by your sweater when you could do an adequate mending job in just 10 minutes?"[17]

Why not dare to be average in some things? David Burns, earlier quoted as saying that perfection is an illusion, also says averageness is an illusion, but it is a useful construct: "By lowering your standards so that you can be 'average,' not only do you tend to feel better about what you do, but you also tend to do it more effectively." To experiment with this notion, choose any activity; and instead of aiming for 100 percent, aim for 80 percent, 60 percent, or 40 percent. Then see how much you enjoy the activity and how productive you become. The results may surprise you.[18]

"It's rough being a working mother—but I manage."

Says one changing perfectionist: "The concept of being average has really helped. When I need to release myself in some area, I just say to myself, for example, 'This year, I'm going to can fruits and vegetables just average.'"

"The idea of a continuum has aided me in dealing with perfectionism," observes another woman. "I've gotten away from viewing myself as either perfect or worthless. Now I give myself credit for what I do. For example, this winter I often went to aerobics twice instead of three times a week. And instead of chastising myself all week because I missed on Friday (and saying to myself, 'Aren't you a slob!'), I gave myself one hundred points for each class, and one thousand points was worth a dinner out. Over the winter I went to aerobics twenty times, and that amounted to two thousand points, or two dinners out."

"Just be thankful you're as far along as you are," one woman stresses, relating this humorous verse to make her point: "I'm not what I *should* be. I'm not what I *could* be. But I thank the Lord I'm not what I *used* to be."

5. *Try to do some things badly.*

Add a little of Lisa Strick's philosophy to your new approach to perfectionism. Strick, author of the article "What's So Bad About Being So-So?," says that she enjoys singing badly, drawing badly, and playing the piano badly. Unfortunately, she laments, "doing things badly has gone out of style. It used to be a mark of class if a lady or gentleman sang a little, painted a little, played the violin a little. You didn't have to be *good* at it." But, she continues, "in today's competitive world it seems as if we have to be experts — even in our hobbies."

Let's put a stop to all this right now, Strick urges. Let's each vow to tackle something new this week — and make sure we never master it. Sing along with grand opera. Create peculiar-looking objects out of clay. Make souffles that fail. Be like the two-year-old who has a gift for tackling the impossible with zest (and isn't discouraged by failures). Enjoy being a beginner again — and rediscover the pleasure of creative fooling around. "As for me," she says, "I'm getting a little out of shape, so I'm thinking about tennis. It doesn't look too hard. Given a couple of lessons I should be playing badly in no time at all."[19]

6. *Just let yourself be where you are without indicting yourself.*

This applies, for instance, to things undone up ahead. Because you're always on call for emergencies, your schedule is going to change often. The things you thought were going to get done, won't!

To illustrate this concept, one "derailed" woman relates: "One day when my children were young, my baby was very unhappy and I must have nursed him a hundred times. All he would take were 'bird swallows,' and I didn't get anything done. When my husband came home, I said, 'Before you ask me what I did today, I want to tell you that I spent the day taking very good care of your child.' And he said, 'That's what's most important. I feel satisfied if you're taking good care of my children.'"

Similarly, another woman says, "I had twin baby daughters, as well as a two-year-old son, and my hands were full. One day their needs consumed me all day and I didn't get a thing done. When my husband came home (and he's always liked his dinner ready when he arrives), the first thing I did was start apologizing, telling him, 'I couldn't get one thing done today because of the kids.' And he said, 'Well, you got them one day older, didn't you?'"

The concept of letting yourself be *where you are* also applies to *what you know.* Says one woman, "I remind myself that this is the first time I have been a mother of this child. This is the first time I have been a grandmother. This is my first time through life with many things—and I won't always do the perfect thing or have the perfect answer."

This concept also applies to your physical self. Systematically, take crucial stress and play breaks without accusing yourself of being slothful. Says a woman about the all-consuming caretaking role, "It's almost as if a beautiful prom dress that says 'caretaker' has been hanging in your closet your whole life. Finally you fill out enough to grow into that dress. You feel great. The only thing is, you can't wear that dress all day and all night—but women do! We're always working. We never take time to change—to allow ourselves time to play or to take time off."

How do you know you've made significant inroads in releasing yourself from perfectionism? Here are sample responses from women who are gaining conscious control over their standards:

• "I can look at a dusty shelf and say 'I'll dust it on Friday.'"

• "I'm at the point where I can invite people over to eat

and if the chicken is raw, it's raw! I just put it in the microwave. It doesn't reflect on me."

• "I used to tackle everything with the same effort and give every detail equal weight. Now I save my maximum effort for the most important tasks."

• "I'm getting good at applying the principle of selective neglect. I just say to myself, 'That will have to wait,' and I don't feel uncomfortable about it."

• "I've quit thinking I have to do everything perfectly."

• "I'm much more at ease with making errors, like the lady who was about to serve the turkey on Thanksgiving when it slid off the platter. She just picked it up and took it back to the kitchen, telling her guests, "I'll get the *other* one.""

As emphasized earlier, tempering perfectionism is a quest, not an event. Be good to yourself and treat yourself with compassion by noticing and celebrating even your most minor victories. And be like the little boy who, just before he was to give a talk, asked his teacher, "Is it okay if I do the best I can?"

That's all you can ever do in this life. Just do the best you can.

Chapter 6

The Depleted Woman

Take a Caretaker who thinks she's invincible and who has no inkling that she has physical and emotional limits, that there is any end to her, or that there is any need for personal boundaries.

Add to her programming the Juggler, who frantically juggles innumerable details (more than she can possibly handle effectively), while constantly adding to an ever-expanding "should" list more and more things she "ought" to be doing.

Combine with the Perfectionist, who thinks everything she does should be done faultlessly and who rarely believes she has done anything "good enough."

Stir in the Guilt Sponge, who soaks up blame for anything that goes wrong in her life — most of which she can't control.

Blend with the Pleaser, who tries to please all the people all the time — and can't, so she thinks the flaw is in herself and she tries even harder.

Intermix all these characteristics with the woman's gnawing feeling that she is being selfish anytime she takes time for herself, her tendency never to relax, and her tendency to give up her needs whenever they bump up against those of someone else.

And what do you get? You guessed it! A Depleted Woman!

And, because she never lets down in response to chronic, unrelieved stress, you also get a woman on her way to burnout—or already there. The road to burnout is a gradual one, with symptoms quietly eroding a woman's ability to cope. Burnout's first warning symptoms are often physical: headaches, insomnia, chest pains, stomach problems, flu, colds, and chronic exhaustion. In its more advanced stages, burnout produces irritability, crying jags, forgetfulness, temper flareups, and a sense of worthlessness. "It's like being premenstrual all the time—you eat too much, cry too much, yell too much," reports one sufferer.[1]

At the extreme end of the spectrum, burnout can become life-threatening, with a woman totally depleted of physical or emotional reserves and significantly impaired in her ability to cope with daily living.

What characteristics make a woman particularly vulnerable to burnout? The very kind alluded to consistently throughout this book. The women most prone are those who are highly conscientious, motivated, reliable, industrious, dedicated, and committed to excellence. Ironically, these sterling characteristics, unchecked, can lead women to feeling driven, irritated, angry, exhausted, overwhelmed, desperate, and alone—all burnout symptoms.

Actually, women wouldn't be such prime candidates for burnout if they weren't trying to do such a good job. Observe Herbert J. Freudenberger and Gail North, authors of *Women's Burnout*: "Potential burnouts are an enterprising group, not usually satisfied with simple security or the status quo.... To the contrary, [they're] personal strivers and achievers with high expectations of themselves and the world around them. They're not content to quit and 'pack it in.' "[2]

Potential burnouts are also women who are accustomed to burnout symptoms, say these authors. They've become so used to the stress and pressure endemic in their lives that exhaustion is considered the norm. Women toss off complaints of fatigue, lost motivation, and waning enthusiasm "as though they come with the female territory—not to be taken too seriously."[3]

Further, potential burnouts are women who see themselves in need of behavior makeovers in order to handle *more* stress. Women who are burning out are ashamed of their inability to juggle the myriad aspects of their lives. Rather than looking for a way to heal themselves, they are looking for ways "to regain energy in order to return to the same arenas with renewed vigor. They want to know how to become stronger, more resilient, better—anything to help keep their momentum going."[4]

Thus, while burnout is a *life-style* issue, having to do with chronic frenetic pace and chronic overextension in response to daily stresses and pressures, a woman is likely to view it as a *personal* issue having to do with her own incompetence and mediocrity; this, in turn, means to her that she needs to "get tougher" and "drive harder."

Because the vulnerability to burnout is inextricably linked to women's cultural programming, it is no respecter of persons. Any woman can slip into burnout—young or old, married, single, divorced or widowed, with or without children. One group most susceptible, however, is the mother in the workplace.

Referring to such women, one author remarks: "Combat soldiers, intensive-care nurses and overburdened executives have long suffered from what has only recently come to be called burnout. The new candidate for this state of depletion is the . . . working mother, who lives under constant stress, who continually caters to the needs of others and who finds herself used up even at the start of the day. It's in the nature of the double role."[5]

Another author writes: "Working requires us to make constant transitions — to move swiftly from a professional mindset to one capable of dealing with chicken pox or tantrums. Racing to get home, juggling schedules and babysitters, trying to keep our marriages happy and secure, and meeting our own frequently unanswered needs, it's no wonder so many working moms are felled by exhaustion and conflicting feelings."[6]

But whether mothers are working at home or at the workplace, the story is similar. In either arena, women press themselves to the wall and don't let themselves off the hook. Hester Mundis, author of an article entitled "So You Think You'd Like To Stay Home . . . ," humorously describes the effects of unrelenting stress on a homemaker: "As a general rule, by bedtime you already had two to five run-ins with your kids, muttered several unprintable comments about your husband and kicked, thrown, or torn to shreds one or more inanimate household objects."[7]

Change is one of the major reasons for women's burnout, especially in their mothering role, says Joseph Procaccini, author of *Parent Burnout.* Procaccini draws an analogy between mothers and another highly burnout-prone group, air traffic controllers, observing: "Most people assume air traffic controllers burn out because they shoulder the massive responsibility of guiding planeloads of people to safety. Actually, the major cause of their stress is change: It is 9 A.M. and there's a 747 coming in and two small planes going out. The winds are calm, visibility is unlimited. At 9:01 all that will be different. Air-traffic controllers constantly need to adjust to new realities.

P.C. VEY

"Don't worry, kids. Mom's just a little tired tonight."

They must stay intensely connected to those realities because the stakes are so high. Mothers are in pretty much the same spot. Kids come and go, the emotional climate in the household changes from minute to minute. Kids are constantly changing, and so is the family as a whole."[8]

Change, at a cultural level, also contributes to burnout. A woman is constantly coping with a world that is increasingly frantic and in turmoil, observe Cynthia Lynch and Maurine Ward, authors of an article entitled "Doing the Fizzle." "Women today are stressed by conditions unique in all of time," they say. "They have been thrown into what the futurist Alvin Toffler describes as a 'fire storm of change.' In the course of two decades, practically every woman in the Western world has faced a reevaluation of her own identity and social functions." Imagine, if you will, "today's woman being thrown into a huge centrifuge — a machine moving at great speed, using centrifugal force to separate materials of different densities. In such a machine, it is not surprising that many women are suffering internal as well as external fragmentation."

Adding to the stress is the fact that women now face a staggering array of choices, say Lynch and Ward. Once channeled into traditional life-styles with little possibility of nonconformity, women now experience a myriad of choices, almost all of which carry certain stigmas. And for many women, these authors emphasize, having more choices just means having more things to do.[9]

The profound societal upheaval compounds the stress of modern mothers, observes Carol Tannenhauser, author of the article "Motherhood Stress." "Many women feel caught between images of the mothers they watched on 1950s television and those they see today striding across the cover of Sunday supplements, briefcases and babies in hand," she writes. "When [they] inevitably fall short of their expectations, they feel frustrated, inadequate, resentful and guilty. And the self-destructive cycle of burnout begins."[10]

The burnout that women experience occurs gradually. Freudenberger and North,[11] for example, list twelve phases that blend into and overlap with each other:

1. The compulsion to prove—to have impact on the world.

2. Intensity—characterized by an unwillingness to delegate.

3. Subtle deprivation—waning attention to one's self.

4. Dismissal of conflict—inattention to inner fatigue, irritability, and the nagging feeling that a problem exists.

5. Distortion of values—measuring worth through approval of others, house, acquired goods, or competence on the job.

6. Heightened denial—unconscious denial of emotions, fears, frustrations.

7. Disengagement—psychically detaching from self and surroundings.

8. Observable behavior changes—behaviors reflecting withdrawal, anger, disillusionment.

9. Depersonalization—loss of contact with self, body, priorities.

10. Emptiness—feeling hollow, cleaned out, drained, useless, void, depleted.

11. Depression—not caring any more—desire for continual sleep and escape.

12. Total burnout—physical and mental exhaustion may imperil a woman's very survival.

Awareness of burnout is the first step in the cure, these authors stress. Then comes understanding where you are with respect to burnout, taking steps to recover, and learning how to prevent burnout in the future.

Given the typical cultural programming of women, you would be unusual if you didn't experience off and on (or most of the time!) the early, and even advanced, symptoms of burnout, particularly fatigue, irritability, and frequent temper flare-ups. Fatigue, that sluggish "I-can-hardly-drag-myself-around" feeling, is particularly rampant among women. In fact, in one nationwide study of six hundred women, one-third of the respondents reported chronic fatigue.[12]

To recognize how simple it is to ease into burnout, one has but to consider an observation of Procaccini's: "Burnout begins the minute energy drops in relation to demands, be they physical, mental, emotional, or spiritual."[13] Women today are always trying to somehow square excessive demands with flagging energy—walking the tightrope between energy imput and energy outgo, and not noticing they're on the tightrope and that they might fall off.

Life-style Changes to Avoid Burnout and Depression

If you recognize symptoms of burnout in yourself, consider the following life-style changes that will help interrupt the course of burnout and eventual depression.

1. *Exercise.*

The world's best remedy for keeping yourself in repair is exercise. As an antidote that can strengthen emotional as well as physical well-being, exercise is by far the top candidate. Here is only a small sample of its enormous health-promoting benefits. Exercise —

• boosts brain power, bringing an increase of blood and oxygen to the brain, thus giving you an intellectual edge.

• allows your body to utilize nutrients to their maximum efficiency.

• develops a fine-tuned body and well-toned muscles that promote flexibility and coordination.

• increases bone density and muscle strength.

• gives you a sense of empowerment and growing control over your own life and body as it increases physical health, appearance, and body image.

• reduces stress level and the chance you'll eat to relieve anxiety, anger, frustration, or down moods.

• alleviates — and often prevents periodic lows by re-leasing in your bloodstream endorphins (chemicals) that elevate your mood.

• allows you to go to sleep more quickly, to sleep more soundly, and to awake more rested.

• slows down the aging process, reducing the rate at which you lose aerobic capacity.

• keeps the skin more elastic, promoting better skin tone.

• suppresses appetite and enhances a feeling of satiety, or fullness.

• burns extra calories for up to fifteen hours after exercising. Exercising twice a day gives 24-hour calorie-burning benefits.

• increases your muscle mass—the major calorie-using tissue in the body—and decreases fat, which simply stores calories. The more muscle you have, the more energy you burn, and thus the more likely it is that you can retain a desired body weight.

• reduces the risk of osteoporosis, heart disease, and some forms of cancer, and enhances the immune system's ability to fight off colds, flu, and other bacterial and viral infections.

If you add up all the benefits, you can see that exercise is vital to a woman's well-being. Unfortunately, when women go into an overload mode, they begin to eliminate the very energy boosters they need. Says Dr. Holly Atkinson, author of *Women and Fatigue:* "Exercise is often the first thing to go . . . in an attempt to get everything done." Yet, "if a woman could do one thing to combat chronic fatigue, I'd say exercise."[14]

So are you ready to exercise your cares away? If you're a nonexerciser, do I hear an "Ugh"? But just think—how can you resist the immense benefits of exercise? Start with a few easy bends and stretches, maybe a jog around the house or block. Start easy and work up. Remember, *any* exercise helps. Then, if feasible, move eventually to any good aerobic exercise that speeds up your heart and breathing rate. Choose several kinds of exercise you enjoy—jogging, swimming, walking, cycling—and alternate during the week. Do aerobic exercise, at a minimum, for twenty minutes a day, four days a week. An optimum would be thirty minutes a day, five or six times a week. But build slowly. Caution several experts: "If you are already exercising, don't overdo. Strenuous exercise . . . can cause 'sports anemia.' The symptoms: weakness, fatigue and irritability."[15]

*"Don't think this means I'm going to give up
my aerobic dancing class!"*

2. *Nutrition.*

In addition to exercising regularly, another way to keep yourself in repair and improve your overall health is to take stock of your nutritional habits. What goes into your body does make a difference.

Many a woman, in the process of nonstop sixteen- or seventeen-hour-a-day caretaking and performing, pays little attention to her eating habits or to ingesting the types of food and nutrients that could actually support her high outlay of energy. Instead, she chronically pushes her body day after day, expecting it to serve her without consistent and adequate fueling and repair. Eventually her body, deficient in the resources needed to keep pace with her will to perform, wears down and she enters a state of what experts call nutritional burnout.

Aside from a woman's "pushing" response, nutritional burnout can also be caused by emotional stress (anxiety, grief, anger, even irrational fears), which can also deplete the body of certain nutrients, many of which are critical to healthy brain function. Relates a medical expert: "Take someone who's just a little depressed or a little stressed because of things going on in his life. That person might find himself eating poorly. And that could lead to nutritional deficiencies that push him over the brink, into true depression."[16]

In addition to depleted intake, there's also the problem of nutrient loss. Another medical expert explains: "When you're under stress, hormones are released, and they in turn increase the speed of many functions and systems of the body. With this faster rate, a large amount of nutrients are pushed into the bloodstream and excreted. The body loses nutrients all the time, of course. But when you're pressured, you lose more."[17]

Adds Emrika Padus, author of *The Complete Guide to Your Emotions and Your Health:* "If the stress drives you to drink — alcohol or coffee — or smoke, you can count on even greater losses. Alcohol, coffee, and smoking destroy B vitamins. And, to make matters worse, coffee acts as a diuretic, flushing the water soluble vitamins — the Bs and C — and essential minerals out of your system."[18]

The loss of nutrients can dramatically affect the functioning of the brain, which is a vital part of the physical self. And *real* food — with its vitamins and minerals — is just as important to the brain's functioning as it is to the functioning of other organs in the body. Says Padus: "A number of new studies have demonstrated that nearly a dozen specific nutrients can alter the biochemistry and function of the brain. A deficiency in any one of them — even slight — can result in such common emotional problems as fatigue, irritability and depression."[19]

That a well-nourished brain is a stronghold against fatigue, irritability, and depression needs to put on alert any overextended caretaker who is concerned about burnout. The bottom line is that no woman can continue to push her body and ignore her nutritional fuel needs without consequence.

So what to do? If you're a caretaker anxious to avoid burn-out and depression, bring your eating habits into line with these guidelines recommended by nutrition experts:

• Eat a variety of foods at each meal to get the nutrients you need (more than forty different substances).

• Establish consistent eating patterns, including three meals a day.

• Eat foods low in fat.

• Eat little sugar.

• Eat ample low-calorie, high-volume, high-fiber foods.

• Eat primarily lean meats, poultry, and fish.

• Cut down on red meat portions.

• Use minimal amounts of fat in preparing foods.

• Eat low-calorie snacks.

• Drink six to eight glasses of fluids daily.

• Limit sodium.

• Limit alcohol.

• Limit caffeine.

When you add exercise for efficient food consumption, this list addresses total nutritional care of both your brain and your body. If you are not following these guidelines, consider making changes that will give your body and brain the nutritional fuel they need.

3. *Preventative health care.*

A final way a woman can keep herself in repair is to systematically take care of her physical well-being throughout her lifetime, but that's not something she'll do easily. The same reluctance she has about spending time or money on herself in other areas of her life typically crops up when it comes to taking care of her body.

Says Valerie Logsdon, a gynecologist practicing at the Millcreek Women's Center in Salt Lake City: "If I told a woman her husband had one chance in ten of getting breast cancer (and that's an incredible risk!), and that she needed to make sure he was doing monthly self examinations, she'd do it. But if I told this same woman she had one chance in ten of getting breast cancer and that the best way to find this breast cancer early is with regular self exams, she typically wouldn't do it. In this culture women tend to sacrifice themselves entirely for others — and when it comes to health care, sometimes that means at the expense of their own lives.

"Every day I see women who have put themselves in jeopardy: a woman who hasn't had a Pap test for ten years, or one who spots postmenopausally and postpones doing anything about it for two years while she takes care of other people," observes Logsdon.

"I remember a sad case of a nurse I treated while in medical school that affected me deeply, a woman about forty, with a husband and five kids, who one day opened the refrigerator and hit her breast. She noticed that night that she had a sore where she hit herself. It didn't get better — it got bigger — and it started draining, but she put off going to a doctor because she was busy and had her kids to take care of. When I saw her she had a breast cancer as big as a tangerine. This was a condition that was clearly abnormal, experienced by a woman who clearly knew better, but she put off taking care of it because she had other things to do. I did a mastectomy, but the cancer had already metastasized, and she died."

If a woman is to take care of her physical well-being and to systematically track her health, what steps does she need to take?

"It all boils down to a yearly health exam," responds Logsdon. "An exam is a health-screen for major problems that affect a woman's physical and emotional health, including all of the cancers that she's particularly vulnerable to — breast, cervical, endometrial, rectal, or ovarian. It also provides a woman with a relatively tight link with a physician with whom she feels comfortable. Women need that link because many of their health problems will be in relationship to their periods, pregnancies, and sexual intercourse, and those are difficult things to talk about to just anyone.

"Add to a yearly exam the tasks of taking calcium daily to reduce chances of osteoporosis and of doing a monthly breast exam forever," Logsdon continues. "Since the incidence of breast cancer increases dramatically after age thirty, I always recommend a screening mammogram sometime between ages thirty-five and forty; between forty and fifty, every other year; from fifty on, every single year. The amount of radiation that comes with a mammogram these days is very low so women don't need to worry about inducing breast cancer."

And how do you do a breast exam? Logsdon explains: "The best time is right after your monthly period, because prior to that your breasts are more lumpy and tender.

"First, stand in front of a mirror, put your hands over your head, and push down, which spreads out your breasts and tightens the muscles. Check to make sure your breasts look normal to you — that there are no lumps, bumps, dimples, or wrinkling of the skin.

"Then take a shower and use the slipperiness of the soap to do a breast exam. Essentially, just feel your breasts in an orderly fashion — circles, squares, crosses, lines, back and forth — however you want to. The goal is to memorize what your breasts feel like, to know where all your normal lumps and bumps are.

"Then dry off and lie on the bed before you get dressed. Put one arm over your head, which again spreads out the breasts, and use your other hand to feel for lumps. If you've been doing this monthly, you'll recognize any changes that take place either abruptly or slowly. Anytime you discover an irregularity that doesn't go away with a month's cycle, bring it to the attention of a physician."

In summing up, Logsdon advises women: "You function best — for the family or others — when you're at your best physically and emotionally. If you can't take care of your physical well-being for yourself, do it for other people, because it really does make you a much happier, healthier, and more energetic person."

Depression: The Clinical or Chemical Disorder

Through life-style changes and through monitoring and controlling her stress level, a woman may be able to reverse the course of burnout and to increase the probability that she won't fall prey to true chemical depression. Sometimes, however, all the life-style changes in the world can't break the hold of hopelessness and despair. Complex forces acting upon a woman induce a major physical depression — and she is literally taken over by a profound despondency that one author has described as "a veritable howling tempest in the brain."[20]

In such a condition, the woman is often too exhausted, too overwhelmed, or too confused to even consider, say, an exercise or nutritional approach to address her depression. Neither may she be able to benefit from therapy until her physical disorder has been medically treated.

Depression-the-chemical disorder (as contrasted with depression-the-blues) is a dark cloud that sometimes comes in on a victim like a weather front: "It can steal up as insidiously as a November fog, chilling the heart, sapping the will even to get out of bed in the morning," says one author. "It is known as clinical depression — and it is not to be confused with the everyday 'blahs' that most people encounter at one time or another, like passing rain squalls in their lives. Clinical depression is something else, a full-scale tumble into the void. It can last for months and recur over years with — at its worst — devastating effects."[21]

"It was like a weather front," says Terry, a recovered victim of a fourteen-year depression. "I might have a day or two that was sunny or partly cloudy, but the front would come relentlessly back. There were no triggers for the change in mood — the sadness, the anger, the hurt that swept in. I couldn't find any way of lifting myself out of this dark mood, and in the back of my mind was always the thought there was something terribly wrong with me. I felt so hopeless."

Like a weather front, clinical or chemical depression often comes subtly and the symptoms are often mild enough to permit a sufferer to go through the motions of life at home and at work. As months go by, the sadness, the mood swings, the low tolerance for stress, the withdrawal from people, numbed feelings, and other symptoms that gradually develop seem normal to the depressed person, who often forgets what she felt like before the depression descended.

As an alternate scenario, the adult has never known what it is to feel good. Since the "weather front" — depression — has been in place most, if not all, of the victim's life, that person has no standard against which to measure his or her emotional and physical well-being. Asked by a psychiatrist how long she had been in poor spirits, one victim said, "Since the sperm hit the egg. I can tell by the way other people act that they're happy, but I don't know what that's like. I never have a happy day."[22]

The mistake most victims make in diagnosing their condition is that they view it as an emotional deficit they should be able to control through sheer willpower. One factor confusing the issue, says a *U.S. News & World Report* article, "is the colloquial use of the word depression to describe a range of unpleasant, but inevitable consequences of living. One is 'depressed' after a bad day at the office, or the breakup of a love relationship."[23] In addition, says another source, the statement "I'm depressed" is an American cliché used to describe just about any mood that isn't buoyant.[24]

To a lay person, the word *depression* suggests that the sufferer can remedy the situation by "taking charge" and "snapping out of it." The lack of evidence of doing either is often viewed by both observer and victim as a weakness or character flaw.

The second factor confusing the issue is that, until recently, depression has been viewed as a mental disorder typically remedied only through psychotherapy. Only the most severe depressions were treated with psychotrophic drugs.

These days, says a *Newsweek* article, "biology . . . looms ever larger in the study of depression. For generations the condition was thought to be purely a state of mind, but in recent years there has been significant progress in understanding its causes. Today it is seen as an illness like ulcers or high blood pressure, the result of an interplay of biological and psychological forces. Many doctors now believe that victims of depression carry an innate susceptibility to the disease; the disease itself can then be triggered by external factors or by a change in the body's own chemistry."[25] At times, in fact, depression appears to occur without any precipitating event.

Because of the biological or physical base of clinical depression, "snapping out" of such depression would be about as easy as snapping out of a broken leg, emphasizes Salt Lake psychiatrist Susan Mirow. "It's very sad to see people who struggle with depression on their own, listening to family members who say, 'Oh come on, snap out of it.' "

Mirow stresses that "people don't realize there is a difference between the mind and brain. The mind is what we think of as ourselves, and the brain is an organ. When a person suffers from a chemical depression, the brain's chemicals are imbalanced . . . [and in such instances] the brain, as an organ, needs medications just as the liver, heart, or lung needs treatment when there is a problem with them."[26]

When a person is depressed, what is it that goes wrong in the brain? "Picture this," says an author: "The ending of one nerve (A) in the brain lies close to the ending of another (B). There is a gap between them. When Nerve A fires electrically, its endings release chemicals into the gap. They travel to Nerve B, where the chemicals then trigger another electrical discharge. Billions of nerves 'talk' to each other this way. Thoughts, then, are both chemical and electrical." In the case of depression, he emphasizes, "the chemical transfer between nerves has gone awry. There may be too much of one chemical or not enough of another. Or the receiving nerve cannot absorb the right chemicals."[27]

A malfunction in the brain's regulation of the chemicals or neurotransmitters causes a short-circuiting of the electrical impulses that transfer information, resulting in numerous physical and psychological symptoms. Consider the symptomatic effects of chronic chemical depression upon Liz, who has suffered a soul-numbing melancholy for many years. She describes her experience:

"What I experienced was a terrible feeling of gloom. Everything in my world was just black. I even thought in terms of the color black. There was no appeal, no interest anywhere. It was like I walked around with a cloud hanging over me all the time. And sometimes the tears would just cascade down my face without my knowing why I cried. My mind was also fuzzy. I had difficulty making decisions and comprehending when I tried to read. And sometimes when I asked someone a question, that person would get two sentences into his answer and I would be off into a never-never land. I wouldn't even mentally stick around for the answer.

"I was tired all the time and everything became a chore — even little things were hard to do. My response time was slowed, and I had this acute sense of time passing me by and my not being able to catch up. I had no interest in anything, and I pulled back from the things that earlier had given me meaning. I would often just sit and think — but no matter how much I thought, I couldn't find the answers. I didn't have inside what I needed to feel good. I felt so helpless, so hopeless.

"Night after night I had a hard time going to sleep and staying asleep. I was up a lot just walking the floor. In the morning I would feel terribly depressed and not know why. I struggled with anger that came from nowhere. The littlest thing bothered me. Sometimes I could go from a calm to a crazed person in a matter of three seconds. Then I would feel terribly guilty for the screaming and yelling I did.

"Inside I was always saying, 'I can't believe how stupid I am.' I felt like a big giant nothing. Also, the slightest things hurt my feelings, and I was constantly apologizing, usually for not much. I would need to hear the other person say it was okay I had made a mistake. I was preoccupied with death. I kept thinking, 'The world would be better off without me.' I felt I was giving nothing — that there was no way out. I could see nowhere to turn."

At one level, Liz was experiencing the physical effects of electrical messages short-circuiting in the brain — a partial result of abnormalities in the chemicals that conduct these messages. This short-circuiting of messages causes the symptoms she described: chronic black mood, difficulty in concentrating, fatigue, uncontrolled anger, sleepless nights, disinterest in life activities, and the preoccupation with death.

At another level, after years of depressed thinking, Liz has also had accompanying psychological effects — emotional fall-out emanating from years of experiencing and interpreting the world from a black pit. That emotional fallout, in turn, has interacted with her physical depression, contributing to the blackness and gloom she has felt.

Sadly, neither you nor anyone you know is exempt from such a physical depression. In fact, about 6 percent of the adult population may be in the throes of the disorder at any given time. For adolescents, the estimated incidence is 6 to 7 percent, and there has been recognition only recently that close to 2 percent of younger children may be victims as well. And you, as a woman, stand a shocking 25 percent chance of experiencing a major depression during your lifetime.

If one or more of your parents have depression, the possibility rises that you or your children may also suffer from the disorder. The single biggest risk factor for depression is having it in the family. "Depression is a family affair," explains one expert. "If one parent is depressed, the likelihood of the children becoming depressed increases twofold to threefold. If both parents are depressed, the chances are increased four-fold to sixfold."[28] In addition, studies show that an estimated two-thirds of relatives of depressed patients have been depressed.

The susceptibility toward depression is thus often a genetic legacy inherited along with the color of a person's eyes and hair. For some, depression has always been active, expressing itself even in infancy.

In recognizing their own chemical depression, many victims go on to identify many other relatives who suffer from the disorder. And, tragically, they identify some who have taken their own lives or who have gone to their graves without knowing the terrible price depression stealthily exacted from them. Victims can also often track depression back to childhood or to their teens when, like a genetic time bomb, the disorder was activitated by stress and changes in hormones.

In long-term genetic depression, no amount of psychotherapy alone will heal the disorder. Treating such depression exclusively with psychotherapy is equivalent to treating diabetes with talk therapy. Many victims, in fact, will report that years of therapy have not alleviated their symptoms. That investment has simply resulted in their becoming better-informed, and sometimes better-adjusted, depressed people.

In contrast to genetic depression, many people who do not have a predisposition to depression suffer from situational depression — depression caused by an unrelenting overload of stress that has finally worn down a victim's ability to cope. "Sure I'm depressed," a victim might say. "I have good reason. My marriage is on the rocks, my father died recently, my teen is driving me bonkers, I just had a baby, and I'm recovering from my third surgery in two years."

In such instances, though a victim has "earned a depression," the long-range effects of stress on that person's biochemistry are the same as in a genetic depression. In such instances, mood and chemistry change together. The chemicals or neurotransmitters in the brain are still altered — the brain's ability to transmit messages via electric impulses is still impaired — though the reasons for the depression may be different.

The ravages of chemical depression on victims are all the more insidious because the disorder is usually not recognized by the lay person. Nor, according to studies, is it often detected even by physicians, who, at least half the time, treat only the physical illness masking the depression. Or they treat discrete symptoms such as fatigue, headaches, constipation, digestive complaints, chronic pain, or sleep or appetite disorders.[29] The depression then continues, unchecked and untreated, to debilitate the victim. The longer the depression goes untreated, the more likely it is to become chronic and seriously damaging.

"I wonder how much more often we would seek treatment of depression if, when we had it, our skin turned green," says a victim. "Then we could recognize the depression in ourselves and make allowance for others who have this condition, like we do for people who have colds, or hay fever, or some other obvious physical malady. We wouldn't be so hard on each other."

But since our skins don't turn green, the next best option is to become well acquainted with the symptoms of depression. If you wonder if you or someone close to you has clinical or chemical depression, look for the symptoms identified on the following checklist. As you review this list, consider these factors:

• The number of symptoms. The possibility of having depression increases with the number of symptoms identified.

• The duration of symptoms. The possibility of having depression also increases with the persistence of symptoms over months or years.

• The intensity of symptoms. The intensity of symptoms correlates with the severity of depression. In fact, the more the symptoms and the longer they've endured, the more intense they are and the more serious the depression.

• The toll the symptoms are taking, in such forms as missed days at work, wear-and-tear on relationships, or withdrawal from life activities.

Bearing in mind the number, duration, intensity, and toll of symptoms, turn now to the depression checklist:

• Sleep disturbance, which may take the form of early morning awakening or chronic oversleeping.

• Loss of interest in life activities, with little ability to experience pleasure, including pleasure in sex.

• Difficulty laughing, being cheerful, or finding humor in situations.

• Physical symptoms, complaints, or illnesses that don't respond to treatment, such as nausea or digestive disorders, headaches, backaches, or other chronic pain.

• Significant anxiety, worry, or nervousness, sometimes accompanied by panic attacks, with such symptoms as feelings of terror, hyperventilation, heart palpitations, and increased perspiration.

• Low energy level, fatigue, faintness, and dizziness.

• Restlessness, irritability, low stress tolerance, hypersensitivity to noise and small distractions.

• Rapid mood swings, sometimes with frequent explosive outbursts.

• Excessive emotionality, sometimes with unexplainable crying jags and/or a pervasive numbness that keeps one from experiencing normal feelings of empathy, caring, or grief.

• Diminished ability to think or to concentrate on such things as reading, paperwork, or small details; difficulty in organizing or making decisions; poor memory; memory lapses.

• Difficulty in completing tasks, chores, or assignments.

• Withdrawal or isolation from friends, family, and social situations. Withdrawal from a spouse is particularly common, with a victim often questioning whether he or she really still "loves" the other person.

• Constant over- or undereating or appetite fluctuations; significant weight gain or loss.

• Sad or gloomy mood with feelings of emptiness, pessimism, guilt, failure, hopelessness, helplessness.

• Redundant thoughts — preoccupation with certain issues, events, or emotional material.

• Feelings of emotional exhaustion or burnout.

• Recurring thoughts about suicide or death, or just wanting to cease to exist or to go to sleep and not wake up.

• Feelings of uselessness, inadequacy, low self-esteem, loss of self-confidence.

• Neglect of hygiene, weight, general appearance; body language may take on a drawn, sluggish expression.

Note that most of the items on this list are caused or exacerbated by the physical short-circuiting of the brain's electrical messages. With medical treatment that restores the chemical balance in the brain, any symptom listed above will often dissipate in several weeks.

Depression is now seen not as a single illness but as a range of disorders with different symptom patterns and degrees of severity. Many people have *dysthymic* or chronic depression — a sometimes lifelong malaise spiked by periods of acute depression. People who incur the profoundly low moods have what is termed *unipolar* depression, with some experiencing just one major episode in a lifetime, and others, recurring bouts. Those who experience cycles of depressive lows, alternated with dramatic highs, have a far more rare *bipolar* version (formerly called manic-depressive illness). About 20 percent of major depressions are of this type.

Because it is vital to recognize bipolar depression, which may require specific medication to even out highs and lows, symptoms in the high phase are described here. These include: marked and extended elation; increased energy and decreased need for sleep; more rapid speech; disconnected and racing thoughts; increased physical, social, and sexual activity; unrealistic belief in abilities; increased irritability; and increased aggressive responses to frustration. During a period of elation, a person often experiences increased impulsiveness and reduced judgment, which may lead to buying sprees, poor investments or business decisions, sexual indiscretions, and even violent behavior.

Note that the elation phase of bipolar depression can be distinct and easily recognized, or, in some cases, it may be masked, with bipolar depression presenting as unipolar depression.

Chemical Depression and Treatment

If your depression is fairly mild, is recent, and is clearly related to a life crisis, or seems to be the result of too much stress, you may want to consider some combination of lifestyle changes, reading self-help books such as those listed below, and perhaps even therapy. With these efforts, however, it is important to assess whether your depression lessens significantly within a short period of time; for without proper treatment, depression can become a lifetime affliction. Further, with today's advances in medically treating depression, neither you nor your family need to suffer for months with the ravages of this disorder.

If you have long-standing, serious depression, it is wise to solicit both medical treatment and therapy. Experts generally agree, in fact, that both are needed to combat severe depression. Through medical treatment, your moods should stabilize, and your concentration and ability to think through problems should return. This, in turn, will put you in an advantageous position to benefit from therapy, and therapy itself can more likely be brief.

In selecting a physician, you might first contact a gynecologist, internist, or general practitioner. In selecting a therapist, choose one who is eclectic in approach and who is willing, if necessary, to coordinate medical treatment of your depression with a physician.

For medical treatment of a unipolar depression, new-generation medications are available that are not habit-forming, typically work more swiftly than those of the past, and have many fewer side effects than traditional antidepressants.

The presence of bipolar depression, or serious depression that does not respond to several trials of medication, signals the need for a psychiatrist, who is a physician expert in the use of psychotropic drugs.

If a long-term depression is exacerbated by such problems as a dysfunctional life-style, addiction, unresolved grief, a distressed marriage, or a pattern of failed relationships, it is worth investing in a regimen of therapy to address these issues. If others are substantially involved in your problems, it will also expedite problem resolution to include those persons at times in therapy sessions.

As a rule of thumb, if you persistently think about suicide or death, and especially if you have a plan, it is imperative to seek medical help and therapy immediately.

It is important to realize that chemical depression is sometimes caused or exacerbated by such factors as hormone or thyroid imbalances, undiagnosed cancer, Epstein-Barr virus, or even certain medications. Depression can also be a symptom of other illnesses as well as a disease in itself. These factors need to be ruled out by a physician. If you are depressed and have not had a physical for some time, get one!

Turning to the psychological side of depression, since chronic depression is invariably interactive with negative self-talk, it is worth investing in cognitive therapy, which will address your style of thinking about yourself, others, and the world in general. This form of therapy aids you in identifying negative thinking patterns, including typical errors in thinking. The objective is to replace these dysfunctional patterns with ones that are more productive. Changing such destructive chronic thoughts as "I'll never have another friend," "I'm

worthless," or "I'm a failure for life," for example, will consistently reduce stress; that, in turn, may help you contain future
depressive episodes. If you want to engage in self-study in this
area, you'll find helpful two books written by David Burns:
Feeling Good: The New Mood Therapy (New York: William
Morrow and Company, Inc., 1980) and *The Feeling Good Work-
book: Using New Mood Therapy in Everyday Life* (New York:
Plume, 1989). *Love Is Never Enough* by Aaron T. Beck (New
York: Harper & Row, 1988) also applies the same cognitive
frame of reference to a couple's relationships.

Indirectly, the book you're reading addresses self-talk
within a framework of women's cultural programming. Each
chapter provides alternative ways of viewing the self and relationships with others, thus giving you multiple ways of developing new, healthy ways of talking to yourself.

Chapter 7

The Woman and Her House

Y ou're exhausted. You've been working all day long but the dishes are still stacked in the sink, the front room is in shambles, and punch is spilled all over the kitchen floor.

Now imagine that the doorbell rings. What's your reaction? If you're a woman who panics — who gives a strained "just a minute" and makes a wild scramble to fix anything that is fixable within a few short moments — you probably need this chapter. Your feelings about yourself are inextricably linked to the condition of your house. Whenever your house is in order, you feel all right, but when your house is chaotic, you feel chaotic too. Your worst fears are that someone will see your messy house and know you're a slouch.

Now the ultimate humiliation — answering the door. What will you say? If your self-esteem is tied to your house, you'll likely make an excuse — maybe even plead for forgiveness. Read on for excuses women make:

• Please don't mind the mess.
• Come in if you dare.
• Just walk over the big pieces.

• I just got home from work. (It might be ten at night, but I just got home from work!)

• It's not usually like this. (You caught me at a bad time.) (I'm getting ready to clean the house.) (A tornado just came through.)

• I'm sorry. (I've had a busy day.) (I've been up all night with the kids.) (I haven't been feeling well.) (The phone's been ringing all morning.)

• You don't know what I've been through today. Let me tell you before you come in.

• Have you had your shots lately? You'll need them to come in my front room.

• I'll let you in only if you don't look. Please close your eyes. I'll guide you.

• I'm sorry but it's the maid's day off.

• The mess is my husband's fault. He's been home today.

• It's the dog's fault. (Reported by a single woman, who said, "I've got to have some excuse. He really does drag in the leaves.")

Varying in Reactions to Houses

If you don't make excuses, count yourself lucky that you have somehow escaped the cultural programming that can tyrannize a woman when her house is in disarray. Or that you have accomplished significant "emotional housekeeping" that has enabled you to make personal choices about the "shoulds" in your life. In that case, you're into conscious rather than unconscious caretaking.

Many women are not that fortunate or that well informed. At the very least, fear of others' judgments will leave them with nagging doubts about their adequacy as homemakers. At the very most, trying to hide their flaws as homemakers will consume and obsess them.

*"Please excuse the mess. We're having our home
redecorated — by our two-year-old."*

Many women will, in fact, go to great lengths to hide their
shame. Some won't answer the door. Others stand on the porch
(doors shut behind them) talking to people rather than letting
them in. Several use their vacuums creatively. This is what
some have reported:

"I park my vacuum in the middle of the front room so if
someone comes, I can just say I'm in the middle of housecleaning."

"I sometimes keep my vacuum by the bed so I can sleep
in. If someone calls, I just turn on the vacuum and say I'm
doing my morning work."

"If things get too bad, I put out my old get-well cards on
the mantel."

One woman has even trained her kids to rush around
picking up things when someone comes to the house: "Anytime
the doorbell rings, the kids and I act as a team. We all have
assigned territories."

The lengths to which women go to protect their houses
(and their self-esteem) can reach comical proportions. One
woman humorously reports: "The other morning a man was
coming late in the day to put a new top on our stove, but you

should have seen my old burners. I got up at six o'clock to make sure I'd have enough time to clean them. Later in the day I thought, 'This man can't see a dirty oven,' so at six o'clock that night I turned on the cleaning mechanism — and the oven was red hot when he came. He couldn't even put on the stove top. I ran out the door to a meeting and left my husband and the man just standing there."

Looking back, another woman can see the humor now in a situation that, at the time, devastated her. "It was Christmas and my children were small. They had made a terrible mess as we were trimming the tree, and while I was screaming at them and rearranging the ornaments, the doorbell rang — and the tree fell over! It hit the floor just as I opened the door to one of my neighbors. I said, 'You can't come in. Goodbye!' And I slammed the door shut."

Like this person, some women are traumatized when someone sees their house in disarray. Their flaws have been exposed, their nagging self-doubts confirmed. There is, indeed, something wrong with them. Relates one: "My house is what people use to determine whether I'm a good person or a bad one. A talented person or a good homemaker. It's my gallery to all the world. People can walk in and make all these determinations about me. They will know that I'm disorganized. Or sloppy. Or lazy. It all boils down to the feeling that I'm a bad person and that I'm not measuring up."

The extreme discomfort many experience when they let people in their homes and are discovered is reflected in the observations of a woman who describes her experience with a carpet cleaner: "I was so mortified. I started apologizing for everything — the mess, my appearance, the furniture that was in the way (I even tried to help him move it). I kept saying, 'I'm so sorry, I'm so sorry!' 'I'm sorry for the dog who's getting in your way.' 'I'm sorry for my messy bathroom — for the toothpaste being out (without the lid on it!) and for the spilled orange juice and my half-eaten bagel (which I was trying to eat while putting on my makeup).' "

Many women worry excessively that someone will come into their house when they're gone and thus unprepared. One explains, "I drive myself crazy if we're going on an extended trip. Before I leave, everything has to be in order because if I die on the way I don't want anyone to come in and see a dirty house." Says another, "If I were ever hospitalized or incapacitated, my biggest fear is that someone might go into my house to help. Lying in that hospital bed, I think I would be dying more of humiliation than of any physical problem." Yet another woman, whose house *was* entered by a would-be helper while she was hospitalized, recalls: "I was absolutely mortified. Here I had portrayed myself as being so organized, and now this person knew what the insides of my closets looked like."

To avoid discovery, some women go so far as to make pacts with each other. "Katie and I have a bargain that if one of us gets sick, she or I will stand at the front door to block the neighbors from entering and cleaning our houses," says one woman. "Your house is like your personhood and you are not that personally intimate with everybody—so why should you let just anybody in your house?"

Linking Self-Esteem to Houses

If your self-esteem takes a nose dive whenever anyone sees your imperfect house, it's probably because you feel guilty on several counts.

Indictment number one: You know that taking care of the house is your job. Somehow, your mother passed down to you an inner sense of what needs to be done in a house—and how. Without particularly knowing it, you have in your head thousands of details regarding your role, the traditional woman's role that you "need" to play out. Missing a beat — ignoring a detail — means you haven't done your job.

Indictment number two: You know your mother's standards — she probably tried to keep a spotless house. Can you hear her reprimands? (You don't even need her there.) Deep inside, you experience a sense of shame when something's not in order. You've failed again. You keep trying to be the perfect housekeeper but you never make the grade.

Indictment number three: If your mother's voice doesn't haunt you enough, you also have the media role model of today's woman to live up to — the woman who *can* do everything. Says Jean Fitzpatrick, author of the article "The Dirty Truth About Housework": Today's woman "has a brief case in her hand, not a toilet brush. She doesn't chase dustballs in the hallway; she goes to exercise class. But she also doesn't leave tasks undone. In her perfectly managed life, everything is under control. So it goes without saying that her house is as immaculate as her perfectly tailored suit. Why can't you measure up?"

Traditionally, a clean home was a measure of a woman's character, and her moral goodness was tied to the whiteness of the grout in her tile, says Fitzpatrick, who observes: "The home economics movement of the late 19th century . . . elevated the American housewife to the role of family health engineer in charge of domestic germ warfare. And after World War II, women's magazines preached to the brides of returned GIs that family togetherness depended on their own immaculate housekeeping."[1]

That's the legacy you have inherited. Your moral goodness, too, depends on the whiteness of the grout in your tile, and the cleanliness of your cupboards, and the organization of your drawers, and the tidiness of every other aspect of your house.

Though times have changed, the tacit message that women

are as good as their houses are orderly has not changed. Every sock on the floor, every fingerprint on the wall, is still a personal indictment—a sign of a flaw—to most women. If that description fits you, you keep cleaning up, putting away, and organizing, in constant quest of that moment when you can relax and finally feel good about yourself, when your house (and any children and husband) are in order. But it never seems to happen.

The bald truth is that never in recorded history has anyone ever finished housework. Think about it. There is always something left to be done—a closet to be straightened, cobwebs to clear away, spills to clean up. And your house and the people in it are in constant motion. You spend your life pushing back things that come floating out. Over and over and over. Nothing stays in order very long.

And so your feelings of being okay are fleeting. You keep pushing, but you never do arrive. You never reach that point where you can feel good about you because you're always encountering disorder and can never complete your job.

One woman captures the devastating effect this "house in motion" has on her self-esteem: "I can't relax when I'm in the house," she says. "Whatever is not fixed, running, or perfect means there's something wrong with me. It's personal."

Many women feel incessant guilt over their houses, especially when outsiders are around. Admitting to this feeling, a woman observes: "They may never know that the wallpaper is peeling, that there's dust in the corners, or that the light switch cover is off—but *I* know. I know I haven't done my job."

The threat of having her flaws discovered can actually consume a woman. Says one: "I'd often stay up until two or three in the morning cleaning and putting things away. I couldn't sleep until everything was in order." Another confesses, "I used to be so shackled to my house that I would rake the carpets in the morning and then send my children outside. I didn't want them in the house because they would make footprints on the carpet. I was terrified someone would see things out of order."

Being susceptible to the possible judgment of anyone dropping by can keep a woman's self-esteem in constant jeopardy. "What's so odd is that I can be sitting in all that squalor and then the doorbell rings," says one woman. "Suddenly I look at my house through someone else's eyes and go from being comfortable to being a total emotional wreck."

Interestingly, some women will let even children become a reference group whose opinions can determine their worth. A woman relates: "When my children bring in playmates and I know they come from a clean house, I have to grit my teeth and just let them in to see the mess. When they start playing and having fun, I begin to relax, but I still wonder what they'll say to their mothers."

Homemakers are particularly vulnerable to plummeting self-esteem. "When you work outside the home, you have other standards and measurements by which to evaluate yourself," says one. "But if you're at home all the time with preschoolers and your whole world consists of walking kids to and from kindergarten and running 'mother' errands, you become MOTHER with capital letters and exclamation points, and that is all you are. Then a house out of order weighs on you much more heavily—you have nothing else by which to measure your success."

Housework and Myths

Most women suffer from the myth that somewhere there really is a woman who keeps a perfect house. One woman who previously believed this observed, "Because the idea was so deeply embedded in my subconscious mind, I didn't examine its absurdity and tell myself it wasn't true. The perfect housekeeper just doesn't exist."

"The problem with comparing yourself to other women when it comes to housework is that you don't have the real story on how other women struggle with their houses," emphasizes another woman. "It's only been lately that I've realized I'm not alone. Lots of other women are beating themselves up inside every day because their houses, like mine, won't stay together."

The tendency for women to compare themselves to other women can have devastating effects on their relationships. "I have friends who won't invite me to their houses because they're intimidated by my housekeeping," says one. "My house is so orderly that they feel uncomfortable if I see their houses. What's ironic is that they don't realize I go around frantically cleaning my house before they come."

One woman whose neighbor felt chronically intimidated by her housekeeping finally took matters into her own hands. "I took her on a tour of my house and said, 'See my junky closets, and look at these messy drawers, and here is this disorganized room. Please see me as the imperfect housekeeper that I am.'"

Another myth women suffer from is that other people, particularly other women, are constantly judging them. "We need to quit making other women into the bad guys," declares a woman. "Actually, we're the ones who intimidate ourselves. We walk into someone's house in which everything is in place and think, 'There must be something wrong with me because I can't do that.' We set ourselves apart from that other person because *we* feel judged."

Women actually cause some of their own problems by pointing out the flaws in their houses, as one woman explains:

"A neighbor walked into my kitchen last night and I said, 'Oh, I'm so far behind. This day has just flown by — and I haven't even finished my dishes!' And that's when she noticed the dishes! I don't think she had even looked over that way. When she turned back, I thought, 'Oops! That wasn't very wise of me to say that.' "

Though women often assume others are going to judge them as not being "good" homemakers if their houses are not clean, this may happen much less frequently than they think. Others may actually be relieved seeing the mess, as one woman observes: "We've all had the experience of going into a friend's house and seeing that it wasn't spick and span and in order and thinking, 'Oh, thank goodness she's human.' "

Strategies for Releasing from Houses

Any tendency to link your moral goodness to the condition of your house is simply a cultural program — something you absorbed from your mother (and she, from her mother), not a universal principle. There is no "Book of Truth," with absolute standards of measurement, that correlates your goodness or worth with an ordered house.

Giving a cultural perspective to housework, one woman says: "I think of my grandmother living in a circus tent for a year in Canada with five other families. She had her children and animals, but nothing to clean or to keep in order. Sometimes I think it would be nice if we didn't have our houses for a year — only the people around us. It would help us focus on what's really important in our lives."

Another woman reports becoming acutely aware of her cultural conditioning when she spent several years in Bolivia and had a maid: "Someone else was doing the things I'd done in the States. It was Maria's house to clean, and I saw for the first time what it was like to be relaxed, to enjoy life. I also found out I was okay. I stood on my own, without my worth being dependent on my house. I promised myself that when I returned home I wouldn't let my house tyrannize me again."

As you reflect on your own attitude toward your house and the role an orderly house plays in your assessment of your worth, you may be shocked that anyone would let a house so completely rule her well-being, as some of the women quoted have indicated. On the other hand, you may also feel intensely relieved to know there are many women, like yourself, who are struggling mightily over their houses and their feelings about themselves. Whether you're at one extreme or other, or in the middle, is not important. What is important is to recognize ways your self-esteem is emotionally ensnared in your house and to consider corrective action. If you got off scot-free in this chapter—that is, you're certain your feelings about yourself aren't caught up in your house—consider using what you've learned to better understand and to find compassion for other women you deal with every day. If, when it comes to your house, you're into unconscious caretaking, and want to free yourself from programming that relentlessly wears on you (and your family), consider these strategies:

1. *Don't excuse yourself.*

An initial step in releasing is to quit defending yourself, no matter how you feel. In this spirit, one woman declares: "I'm still uncomfortable when other people come to my house and can see two weeks' worth of newspapers stacked someplace, but I don't demean myself explaining. I don't think I owe them anything, and they don't owe me."

2. *Separate yourself from your house.*

On her way to releasing herself and refusing to allow her self-esteem to rest in the hands of others, one woman says: "A long time ago, I decided that if I knew people were coming and my house was dirty, it was *my* fault. If I didn't know the people were coming—and they came—it was *their* fault." Now go a step further. It isn't anyone's fault. It isn't a fault issue. There should be no blame attached to how you choose to put the pieces of your house back in place or attack the dirt and grime that relentlessly accumulate. You have a job to do, but that's all it is—a job. And you are where you are in the performance of that job. And that's fair.

To get away from fault and worth issues, view the tasks involved in housework as simply that: tasks, not emotional events. Relates one woman: "I used to become very disturbed if something prevented me from getting my washing done on Monday. I'd look at my laundry and think, 'I'm not doing my job.' Now if the washing doesn't get done, I say, 'Oh, well.' I know I'll get it done tomorrow or next week."

3. *Change your self-talk.*

Deep inside, your beliefs about other people's reactions may trigger negative voices confirming your self-doubts that go something like this: "Oh, no! My kitchen is in shambles. My life is a disaster. Someone will see my flaws. They'll see this is all an act—that I'm really *not* adequate. This proves what I've suspected all along—I'm the disaster. I'm (disorganized) (a poor housekeeper) (a terrible person). There's no hope for me forevermore. I am truly worthless."

Counter—very firmly!—those negative voices in your head. Say things like:

• My house *isn't* me.

• What difference does it really make that an ice cream bar has melted in the garbage and leaked out all over the floor, and my neighbor sees it before I get it cleaned up?

• What difference does it make if my neighbor sees the skateboard in my front room or the trail of Rice Krispies through the hall?

• I can't anticipate or control the way other people make messes or move the pieces of my house. Nor is there always enough of me to go around. Nor can I always fix things or people the way I'd like. Nor should a clean house be entirely my responsibility—it should be *our* responsibility. Therefore I give myself the right not to have an ordered house in a disordered world. And the right to have other priorities besides my house.

4. *Quit mind reading.*

Much of your emotional wear-and-tear comes from anticipating what other people might be thinking about you and your house. One woman's candid comment aptly illustrates the mind reading women do: "Once a new person comes to my house and sees the mess and how we really live, I relax. But the anticipation of her walking in and getting that first shock is just horrible."

Notice that this woman divines what other people will think when they come to her house and then develops actual feelings of dread based on events that haven't even occurred. In actuality, she most likely is wrong in her assumptions. As one author so cogently observed: "The degree to which we believe that we are correct in divining another person's motives and attitudes is not related to the actual accuracy of our belief."[2]

If you're traumatized or uncomfortable when someone sees your imperfect house, it is most likely because you, like this woman, are making assumptions, based on little or no information, about what someone else is thinking. You don't really know, so give the other person the benefit of the doubt. If it's a man, he probably won't notice. If it's a woman, she is probably more worried about what she is saying and how you feel about her than she is about your house.

5. *Stop letting people have power over you.*

That means facing your worst fear: disapproval. Take, for a moment, the most awful case scenario. Someone actually *does* see something out of order and *does* make a judgment call, label you "lazy," "disorganized," "inadequate," or worse. So what? Who does that have to do with, you or the other person? The right answer, of course, is the other person—and that person's lack of sensitivity, compassion, or understanding. Despite the worst knots in your stomach, it does not have to do with your worth. You are still okay. Keep saying that to yourself and in time you will release yourself. And remember what one released woman said: "If there's a mess in my house that really bothers someone, that person can grab the broom and clean it up."

6. *Set your own standards.*

One released perfectionist says, "I decided that as long as no one will catch a disease at our house and I can still find the kids' socks, I can relax. I do the best I can, but I give myself permission to live comfortably just that way—doing the best I can."

Setting your own standards may include releasing yourself from your mother—from what she thinks you "should" do with your house (or from what you *think* she thinks!). One woman reports how she let her mother's high standards tyrannize her: "My mother was an immaculate housekeeper and all my life I couldn't have even one thing out of order. Then I got married, and I loved it because I could just toss a shirt in my drawer if I wanted, and it felt so good. But every time I knew my mom was coming, my house would be 'mother clean' by the time she arrived. Then one time she popped in when I didn't expect her and I was just overwhelmed. I kept making excuses: 'Mother, there just wasn't time for me to get this or that finished.' "

Another woman talks about having to deal with an overbearing mother who makes active judgments about her housekeeping: "My mother lives with us periodically, and whenever she's in my home, my towels aren't folded right, my silverware isn't organized right, my beds aren't made right—simply because I don't do things her way. I absorb her comments for so long and then I get upset. We always have one incident while she's here. Sometimes I purposely don't do things her way."

Ask yourself if, like these women, your self-esteem is still entangled in your mother's housekeeping standards. Maybe those standards worked for her, but nowhere is it carved in stone that they are valid for all eternity. The stresses and demands on women today are different from the stresses and demands in your mother's era, and you need to take the path that fits for you.

What may be ironic is that as you're unconsciously imitating standards you acquired from your mother, she may be having second thoughts about the virtues of constant cleaning. One grandmother reports on her changes over the years: "When my kids were little, I was a meticulous housekeeper and I kept tight reign on them so they couldn't make messes. Now when my four year-old grandson puts his hands on the coffee table, the prints may stay there three or four days. I've decided that handprints, or even a little dust on the coffee table, simply aren't worth getting stressed out about."

A grown daughter describes a similar releasing process in her own mother: "Saturday has always been 'cleaning day' on the old homestead, and my mother still adhered to the ritual after all her children had left the nest. When I stopped by to visit her one Saturday, I was surprised to find her relaxing in a favorite chair. 'Aren't you feeling well?' I asked."

"I feel fine."

"But you're not cleaning."

At that her mother responded, "After all these years I've finally figured out how to get it done in half the time. I simply take off my glasses."[3]

The challenge in releasing yourself from your house is to be your own judge of what fits for you. There is no true way to fold towels, to put the silver away, or to fold the sheets. There are only preferences, so make your own decisions. What do *you* want?

One woman describes how she literally had to wrench herself from engrained childhood training to do what she wanted: "I was raised by my grandmother, who taught me that everything had its place and everything was to be folded and put away in a certain way. When I was raising my children I always felt so guilty my cupboards didn't meet her specifications. I tormented myself for years until one day I said, 'It's not going to be the way it was at Grandma's. I just can't do it.' I remember just grabbing the towels, folding them quickly, and getting them out of sight. I struggled, but I walked away from the cupboard a new woman."

A woman's detractors aren't limited to well-intended but overzealous mothers. Mothers-in-law who are perfectionists and husbands who bought their mothers' programs cause considerable consternation to the woman who is trying to do things her own way. "What do I do about my mother-in-law?" asks one woman. "She's the type who catches the dust before it hits the floor, and she expects me to be a dust-catcher too."

If you're feeling pressure from *anyone* over your housekeeping, the answer is the same. Say kindly and firmly, "I realize you have different ideas about what I should do but it's important to me to do things in ways that make sense to me."

7. *Determine your priorities.*

The English word *housewife* literally originally meant "bonded to the house." Decide *not* to be bonded — or captive — to your house. Rather, regard yourself as a free agent who needs to make conscious choices about how you expend your time, energy, and resources. These choices need to reflect investments in a number of areas.

"The longer I work, the more I have a 'male' attitude toward my house," says a woman. "My work is a priority absorbing my energy. I would like to have a clean linen closet or all the drawers organized, but my priority has become one of having the house looking acceptable rather than focusing on details."

Another woman relates: "I have the attitude that if my beds are made and my dishes are done, then my house is acceptable. That takes care of my mental state and I can relax. I feel in control."

One woman says that she has decided to make her kids her priority: "If it comes to reading to them or doing the laundry, I'll do the reading—without guilt."

These women are formulating their priorities, trusting in their own good judgment, looking inward—not outward—for answers. You can do that too. Release yourself. You are in charge. You can't do everything, so do what makes sense to you.

As you set priorities, delineate the amount of housework you'll do each day. As you know, there's never an end to housework—and for many women it's always there, intimidating, pushing, prodding, and indicting them. Because of this, you need to take charge of your time. Observes one homemaker: "When you work outside your home, you leave your office, you leave your work, and you go *home*. When you work in your *home*, you don't ever leave it, and there's no boss to say 'Workday's over. You can finish up tomorrow.' You have to say that to yourself."

"I learned something from my husband recently," observes another. "After we arrived home from a vacation, he took the day off and did projects around the house all day. At five o'clock he went upstairs, took a shower, came down and ate, and was done for the day. I thought, I can learn from that. My work is never done, and there are days I've thought I needed to stop at five o'clock, but it never occurred to me I could give myself permission to do just that."

8. *Give up guilt.*

Linda Essig, author of the article "I'm a Lousy Housekeeper So Sue Me," asks sweeping questions regarding housekeeper guilt: "Are cobwebs fatal? Are children raised in homes that are spring-cleaned really more emotionally secure? Are dessertless meals a factor in the increasing number of runaway teenagers? Do sheets that are laundered every other week tend to cause learning disabilities in the kids who sleep on them?"[4]

The answer, of course, is a resounding *no!* People will survive, life will go on, crises will pass even if you miss a step. Refuse, then, to be undone, frazzled, or upset simply because your house isn't ordered. It can't be. There will always be things up ahead that need doing and things behind that you missed and that's just the way it is.

9. *Take a relaxed attitude toward your house.*

Says one woman: "I had to learn that the only way to have other people feel comfortable in my house was to be comfortable in it myself. If people come to visit when my home is a total mess, I just plop down and enjoy them. When I ignore my house, I find they ignore it, too. They enjoy the good conversation and the visit and they don't leave thinking, 'What a messy person.' They think, 'What a nice person.'"

Looking around, you can probably find a few women who are relaxed in their homes. "I have a good friend who doesn't like doing housework," reports a woman. "She would rather play the piano, read, study, do anything with her kids, than clean her house. And so when I go to visit, I never look at the house because it's always a mess anyway. I just go to visit her. As far as she's concerned, I came to see her, not her house."

"When I was growing up I thought my best friend's house was always a mess," says another. "Now I realize her family was always having fun (and they still do). Essentially, her mother said, 'Life is too short to be preoccupied with a clean house. We need to have time together.' She didn't care about the mess. Her self-esteem wasn't rooted in her house. She knew where her values were and what really was important to her."

You are unique, not like any other woman. So what you decide to do to have a relaxed attitude toward your house needs to be in your court. The common theme in the previous examples is that these women had other priorities besides their houses. You — and your own interests — need to be a priority to yourself. You can lose your sense of self if you're consumed with your house.

Sometimes, to invest in yourself, you'll need to set your house aside — without guilt. One woman reports her intrigue as she watched another woman do exactly that: "I have a friend, originally from another country, who decided she had earned the right to take a three-week trip to visit her mother abroad. She has six children, the oldest of whom is fourteen. She left, and her husband, who is self-employed, and her fourteen-year-old daughter took care of the house.

"On the 4th of July, my husband and I picked up the family for an outing while the mother was gone. When I went in the house to get the three-year-old a drink of water, I decided I had never seen such an awful mess in my life. The house was piled high with dirty clothes and there were dirty dishes everywhere. At first I thought, 'I'm a better homemaker than she is.' But then I realized she was spending three weeks abroad, enriching herself, and would come back feeling refreshed, and all that time I was still cleaning my house. She wasn't devastated

"All right, who slammed
the refrigerator door?"

by the mess. When she got back, the family simply went through the house in a couple of days and put it back in order."

10. *Give yourself credit for what you DO do.*

"If I get back to where I was yesterday, I will have made remarkable progress," says one woman who gives herself credit. Another woman says: "Instead of making lists of what I need to do, I make lists of what I've accomplished." Still another, who works outside the home, sometimes rewards herself for doing her own housework. "Last year, with the money I saved, I bought an elegant dinner ring," she says.

Putting a monetary value on the housework you do may help you to comprehend your worth, thus giving you the credit you deserve. A homemaker would be worth $48,000 a year if she were paid for even a portion of her homemaking, says management consultant Dorothy Leeds, after analyzing U.S. Bureau of Labor statistics.[5]

11. *Make people your priority.*

When you become preoccupied or obsessed with a house,

other things can become more important than people. Says a struggling young mother: "I don't even like my kids to play with toys because of the clutter. I bought one of those awful Barbie houses, and I've packed half of it up because of all the mess. I think, 'Why can't I just let them be children and play?' " This frank statement captures a frequent dilemma for women: What is more important — the house or the people in it? "My house," admits one. "I know the right answer, yet I find myself railing at the people in my house because they don't keep it clean. It seems like something I just can't control."

If you have a bad case of the tacit programming identified throughout this chapter, having a clean house may be the only way you can find even temporary feelings of well-being. In desperate attempts to patch your shredded self-esteem, you may try to keep people in rigid routines and schedules. There may be little room for smiles and laughter, for living in the moment, and for just being yourself. As one preschooler said when she surveyed her mother's freshly sparkling, uncluttered house, "You sure can't have much fun in a clean house."

The bottom line is: it *is* people who matter, not things. People need to matter more than spilled milk, a mess in a kid's bedroom, or even a broken window. One woman reports an incident underscoring the need to put people first: "A number of years ago my mother gave me a bottle of expensive apple-pectin shampoo for my birthday. I told my five-year-old daughter several times — '*don't* touch that shampoo!' Then one day I walked into the bathroom and found gleaming shower walls and an empty shampoo bottle. I lost control and started yelling and screaming at my daughter. Finally, when I recovered, I looked at her devastated expression and thought, 'What am I doing to this child I love so much?' I was bruising her fragile ego for the price of a bottle of shampoo."

12. *Hang tough (but cheerfully) to your new program.*

As you make changes to release your stress and tension, you may encounter opposition. If you've done everything for everyone all the time, you've trained your family well to expect service. "Mothers are the ones who are most aware and always jumping up," observes a woman. "Someone says, 'Where's the ketchup?' and Mom gets the ketchup. 'Where's the salt?' and Mom gets the salt. We cause a lot of our own stress by doing what other people could be doing for themselves."

As you begin to release yourself, your family will need to go through a concomitant process of releasing you too. That may mean you'll have to withstand pressure from people who are uncomfortable with your changes.

One woman, a reformed perfectionist who went from a 100 percent production level down to a mere 93 percent, created slight gaps in her performance at home. At the same time she rescued herself from depression and migraine headaches and her husband from her anger. This is her story.

"For years I was consumed with my house and angry at my husband for not helping enough. Sometimes, under the stress, I would get migraine headaches two or three times a week. When I realized the extreme pressure I was putting on myself to be perfect, I began releasing myself from my house. As I did, my husband began pointing out little things that weren't done. He would say, 'Honey, there are dishes in the sink,' and I'd say (in my cheerful voice), 'I know, dear, this is the new me!' Then he'd say, 'But honey, where's my shirt? I don't have my shirt today,' and I'd say, 'I know, but you can wear the one that's in the closet. This is the new me!' He continued pointing out little things until one day he realized I wasn't under so much pressure. I was actually happy. After that, he said to me, 'I don't know if this new program is good for the house, but it's sure good for you.' "

Note that this woman did not become slovenly—she simply

released herself from doing the impossible. (It would have taken her a hundred years of hard work to become slovenly.) As she released her stress and tension, she benefited—and so did her family.

13. *If you're pressed and can possibly afford it, hire some help!*

One employed woman's attitude is typical of the problems some women have in bringing in outsiders to clean. This woman, who is mega-stressed most of the time, says: "I could hire someone to clean my house but I won't. I want my house to look as good as if I had hired someone to do it. I can't release myself from that. I want people to know that I do the housecleaning and to hear people say, 'Boy, her house looks great, and she doesn't even pay anyone to do it!' "

This is a woman to whom "having it all" means "doing it all." But while she's trying to look good, she may be crashing. Her house is a place she *could* reduce her workload.

Whether you're a work-at-home or a work-at-work/work-at-home woman, your role in today's high stress world is unconventional. Just as your role today is unconventional, so your approach to fulfilling that role needs to be unconventional. The core issue in today's fast-moving world is "What essential household work needs to be done and who is available to do it?" Household work is simply a cluster of jobs that need to be done by the people who benefit from those services, not a test of a woman's worth. The challenge, then, is to organize your personal and family resources—time, energy, money—in ways that "de-stress" you and your family. Approached from this vantage point, hiring help simply becomes an alternative in organizing your life to achieve this objective.

As you leave this chapter, consider making it your goal not only to release yourself from your house, but to release other women from theirs as well. Despite the fact that women don't judge each other's housekeeping nearly as much as you may think, the truth is that women do sometimes judge each other. Now that you understand the emotional connection between women and their houses and how extremely vulnerable they are to the opinions of others, be good to your fellow soulmates and give them the room and empathy they deserve.

Chapter 8

Women, Husbands, Kids, and Houses

It is probably no surprise that you and the man in your life see housework differently. It may be that the issue of who does the housework is even a sore spot in your relationship. You may even argue over housework. If so, you're not alone. These days housework is an increasingly explosive topic for many couples. In fact, no other area causes more polarization and more fights among the sexes than who does the chores. Let's look at what is happening to typical couples and why.

Couples in the '90s have disputes unknown to earlier generations. Your grandparents were raised in an era when a clear division of labor between marital pairs was not only desirable but also a necessity. Today, however, sweeping sex-role changes are confusing both sexes, calling into question what were once cut-and-dried traditional role definitions.

As a result, couples are having to take chores to the negotiating table. Nearly 60 percent of American women now work outside the home, often leaving and coming home at the same time as their spouses. At the same time that women have added up to eight or nine hours a day to their already full work schedule, they have kept most of their traditional chores, a point confirmed by Arlie Hochschild, who recently published a study of two-career couples. After observing couples in their homes, she reports that most women continue to carry a far greater portion of the responsibility associated with running a home and raising children. And, she stresses, many men — even those who talk equally — do not really do much child rearing, cooking, cleaning, food shopping, or enough other chores to count. As a result, women drive home from the office while plotting domestic schedules, meals, and housecleaning — and do a "second shift" upon arriving.

What is the effect on women of their "second shift"? Says Hochschild, they spend fifteen fewer hours of leisure than their husbands, and in a year they work an extra month of twenty-four-hour days. The women in her study, she reports, tended to talk more intently than men about being overtired, sick, and "emotionally drained": "Many women I could not tear away from the topic of sleep. . . . [They] talked about sleep the way a hungry person talks about food."[1]

As a result of their overload and exhaustion, women are angry. "Why won't he help?" or "Why won't he help *more?*" the woman thinks. Her anger puzzles and upsets the man, because he can't see what all the fuss is about. He can't see her plight. "What's wrong with this woman anyway, making all that noise and vibrating like that?" he thinks. "There's no need to scream. It's just housework!"

Bearing on the puzzled look in men's eyes is a quantitative difference between the sexes. Men and women were socialized to pay attention to different details: he, to details related to work, finances, cars, yards, and the outside of houses; she, to details having to do with household- and people-maintenance.

So crumbs on the counter, little handmarks on the wall — details so vital to most women — are just not within the frame of reference of most men. To them, dustballs and dirt are invisible to the naked eye. Women go in the front room and see the socks on the floor, the cups on the coffee table, and yesterday's newspaper. Men see the couch and the TV.

Not knowing this, the woman holds the man accountable. He should know what to do. But he doesn't. For many men, there are simply no cogs. He will help, but he has other, "important" things to do. Besides that, deep inside he doesn't feel responsible. Therein lies another quantitative difference: Even though men will help, women typically are responsible for remembering details and for prompting others to do their jobs. Women, in essence, are the managers of the home.

Though the fact that they are in charge and that they have to appeal to men to help may annoy some women no end, socially and culturally men as a group have not reached a point of sharing responsibility for the management of the household. And that is what women would really like, writes columnist Ellen Goodman — not just a man who is helpful, but a man who takes over. A wife "would like to take just half the details that clog her mind like grit in a pore, and hand them over to another manager."[2]

A further quantitative difference between the sexes is that most men don't feel adept at housework, and it isn't easy for them to change. "Men's discomfort is understandable," observes a woman. "Quite frankly, I'm uncomfortable with doing things they take for granted. My husband says, 'Would you like to learn how to change a flat tire?' and I say no. 'Would you like to learn how to run the lawn mower?' I say no again. Some things I don't want to learn. Men are the same way."

To get a true picture of how things look for men today, step back twenty-five years, says Morton Shaevitz, author of

Sexual Static: How Men Are Confusing the Women They Love.
Then a man's reason for being was to make it as a man, and
men knew what was required to do that. They were expected
to work, advance in their careers, work without interruption
until age sixty or seventy, and then retire. They were not expected to clean house, wash clothes, diaper babies, or cook
meals. And not only were they *not* expected to do these
things — they wouldn't have been making it as men if they did.

Today, the traditional male prescription has been turned
upside down, says Shaevitz. Not by men. By women — wives,
girlfriends, and even mothers — who are putting it to men to
respond differently, sooner not later! Meanwhile, Shaevitz emphasizes, "men still feel the urgency to work, to be successful,
to marry, to be the bottom-line provider 'should something
happen' and to be strong." Caught between worlds, men are
feeling nothing less than overwhelmed as they are being asked
(while many of the old rules still apply) to adapt to a world
quite different from the one in which they grew up.[3]

A final quantitative difference between men and women
is that a man associates a house with being nurtured, not with
doing housework. What's more, he comes home to relax. Her
home is her office, so she can never relax. "His haven is her
workplace," Shaevitz observes. So, while she is busy doing
housework, inevitably he asks for some time, please, right
now — and she sees this, again, as very insensitive. She is not
available right now. "There's work to be done — clutter to clear
away, dishes to do, clothes to fold, children to bathe and put
to bed, and then I'll relax," she responds.

He feels hurt. Housework is more important than he is.
Housework, of course, is a nuisance, but it is not the life-and-
death issue she makes it out to be. And it certainly is not more
important than his relationship with her. He's taking time out.
Why won't she?

"Our computer confirms your own diagnosis, Mrs. Poopnagle.
You are 'too pooped to pucker'!"

He gets angry — and shows it. Now she is hurt. She expects him to understand the world the way she does. You *don't* leave dishes!

He is simply playing out his programming. "This woman is *supposed* to be available," he tells himself. Traditionally, men (especially those over thirty) were taught that women were there to take care of their needs — to support and nurture them at home. Home was a sanctuary, a place to come to for a warm meal and the devotion of an attentive wife.

Now, particularly for the dual-career couple, women aren't as available as they were, and a central issue for men is loneliness and a sense of loss or desertion. "Imagine Adam alone in the Garden of Eden and you will have an idea about the way many men feel today," says Shaevitz.[4]

While women form networks of nurturing ties with friends and family, most men do not. They tend to have buddies in whom they don't confide because of traditional programming requiring them always to have their guard up, to save face, and to appear invincible. Thus, cut off from his own sex, "a man is overly dependent on the woman as the all-purpose emotional provider," says Erica Abeel, author of an article entitled "The Hurting Husband." A man's reliance on a woman for emotional sustenance also comes from traditional sex-role definitions in child-rearing, she says. "Boys are close to mothers—not fathers—and this rapport with the opposite sex carries into adulthood."[5]

The sense of abandonment or rejection often extends to the sexual relationship, which is a primary area where men feel validated. Overwhelmed by the competing pressures of home, work, and mothering, a wife may be tired and distracted and unappreciative of her husband's sexual needs. Unfortunately, many men clam up or show anger rather than reveal their true emotions when they're feeling cut off from their wives. And women tend not to sense the real feelings of men: "I need you. I want you. I miss you. I'd like you to be more available. I'd like to feel closer to you."

All of this is going on beneath the surface of the relationship. Above, men and women are fighting about chores. Underneath, they're fighting over the ambiguity of what were once very well-defined sex-roles. And neither one knows what the fighting is really about.

The "Right" Attitude about Men and Chores

"Some men make wonderful wives," observes a woman, which leads to this point: There are in this world some perfect "househusbands"—men who, with equanimity and zest, do their share of household work and execute chores equally as well as—or even better than—their wives. And there are even some men who are perfectionists when it comes to performing work around the house.

If you are living with such an exceptional man, you may

want to rent him out. In today's world, there is high demand for a man who will ease a woman's work load, especially if he comes complete with a happy disposition. And, if you have such a man, you may want to skip the following section, which deals with eliciting men's willing, if not cheerful, help around the house.

But if you are a woman who feels overburdened, unappreciated, and exhausted — and one who frequently goes from a low burn to a high boil because your husband doesn't help or doesn't help enough — forge ahead!

If, as underscored earlier, men are slow to take on new roles, so are women slow to give up old roles. When a man does housework, he feels he is helping his wife with *her* work. He will do it, but it's hers. Deep down, women feel this way too. And, unknowingly, they make make it tough for a man to help. Too long, in fact, women have shooed men away from the areas that were enslaving them, says one author.[6]

A core issue, then, is: Do you discourage a man's giving you the help you want? To get a reading, consider these questions:

1. *Do you buy into what Patricia Volk calls "the helpless-husband syndrome"?*

Volk, the author of an article by that same name, reports that she is the one who hails the cabs, shops for presents, plans vacations, takes coats to the cleaners, and calls his dad on Father's Day. She is also expected to open the window at night. Even though the window is on his side of the bed, he asks her, "Honey, could you open the window?" Both she and her husband are reading, both are tired, and both have functional arms and legs. So Volk responds: "Wait a minute. I don't get it. Is opening the window a sex-linked characteristic? You're closer to the window but you want *me* to open it?" "You can do it better," he says.[7]

One expression of the "helpless-husband syndrome" is the husband who is cleaning-impaired. "Women are very good at letting men train them not to ask for help," says a woman. "I ask my husband to clean the toilet and it takes him three hours. He's very cooperative and he will do it, but all the time he's saying, 'But you are so good at this!' One day, I simply said, 'I've been doing this for thirty years. Anyone would be good at this if they'd had that much practice. Practice simply makes perfect . . . or permanent!' Despite my comment, he's got my number," she confesses. "He knows eventually I'll just take over rather than suffer through the ordeal of watching him take forever to do the job."

2. Do you "re-do" a chore?

What happens if you assign out a job and it doesn't get done the "very best way"? If you're like many women, you do it over. Unfortunately, you've then trapped yourself into "owning" that chore. Letting others do chores their way means loosening your grip and letting them have input. If you have definite ideas about how the dishes ought to be stacked, the cupboards organized, or the laundry folded — and a high need to tell others what to do and how to do it — it's going to be hard to keep others interested in helping.

One woman who is loosening her grip says this: "When my husband vacuums the carpet, he just goes right through the middle and that's all. It used to burn me up because he didn't get the edges and I'd have to do them. However, I don't get angry anymore. I let him do his part and then I do what's left. I'm freeing myself from being tyrannized by details and letting chores get in the way of my relationships."

3. Do you complain when your husband doesn't perform to your standards?

One woman emphatically complains, "When my husband fixes breakfast, he never sets the table. He'll have breakfast all ready and I have to set the table. I can't stand that! He should do the whole job!''

What does a husband do under these circumstances? A frustrated man speaks frankly: "I'd volunteer to fold the laundry and my wife would say, 'Not like that.' When I'd clean up the kitchen she'd criticize the way I loaded the dishwasher. And when I'd go to the store, she'd complain about the choices I made. I finally realized she'd be on my case one way or another—so I just gave up."

4. *Do you consider it a criticism when your husband helps?*

One woman who personalizes chores says: "If my husband *does* pick up, I think, 'I should have done that myself.' It's like a slap in the face."

A woman who is now beyond personalizing comments, "When I first married I thought I had to iron my husband's shirts because that's what my mother always did for my dad. But my husband objected, even though I did a really good job. He wanted his shirts sent to the cleaners. I remember crying about that, I was so upset. I don't cry anymore, though. I just accept all the help I can get."

5. *Are you put off easily by any expression of irritation or annoyance?*

One woman says, "If my husband hems and haws, I step back almost faster than you can shut your mouth." At that point, there is a danger that a woman can become a martyr. Says this same woman: "Sometimes I'll also give in and say, 'Oh, all right, I'll do it!' That's the martyr part. But then comes the penalty: 'I'll remember forever that you didn't help.' When we had our first baby, for example, I asked my husband once to watch her and he said no. I didn't do that again. I didn't want to inconvenience him. He had let me know once that he was busy. But I never let him forget that he hadn't come through when I really needed him — and that this was just another example of his undependability."

6. *Do you feel guilty when you ask for help?*

Guilt can come flooding in simply because you think you're letting someone else do your job. "I asked my husband to start dinner the other night," says a woman. "It was six o'clock. I usually have dinner on at five thirty, but I was out working in our yard and didn't want to quit. But I felt so guilty I could hardly concentrate on what I was doing. I thought, 'You should be in there. That's *your* job.'"

You can gain emotional freedom by considering a task separately from a designation of who has to do it. The issue is: How can we get the task done? Who has the time, energy, or interest right now to do it?

7. *Do you release yourself when it's someone else's job?*

"When I was first married, my husband and I prepared a Thanksgiving dinner," relates a woman who is still torn by this issue. "The problem was, I was responsible for the food and he was responsible for cleaning the house. Well, an hour before dinner, my husband sat down to read a magazine, and one of the couples came early. So the vacuuming didn't get done. I thought, 'Why didn't you tell me you weren't going to do this? I would have done it myself.' Everyone must have seen that the floors were dirty. I wanted to put up a sign: *It was my husband's job to vacuum, and he didn't get it done!*'"

In addition to a sense of responsibility, women also have a "sense of indispensability" that interferes with their handing chores to someone else. One woman explains: "I kept complaining that my husband was not doing enough in the house — 'Why do I always have to be the one to scrub the bathroom or take the kids to the doctor?'" So, she continues, "I drew up contracts dividing all the chores in half. But when he was the one who bought the kids new socks, I fell apart. It's hard to give up being the real parent, the one responsible for the children, the important one."

8. *Do you take "time out" occasionally so your husband understands what you do?*

It's worth the effort, reports a woman who knows: "My husband was unempathic about what I was going through with four children. Then I went to Europe for four weeks with my mother and sisters and left him home, running the house, caring for the kids—everything! When I got back, he said, 'Do you know what it's like to talk to little kids all day long? You can't get anything done.' And I said, 'Yes.' And he said, 'You don't feel sorry for me.' And I said, 'No.' And then he said, 'I understand now.' "

9. *Do you ask directly for what you want?*

Traditionally, women have been taught to wait and hope and hint for what they want. The trouble with being indirect is that men typically don't catch on to what women want. She thinks: "Can't he see that the baby needs to be changed? Can't he see that the dishes need to be done? Can't he see I'm having trouble getting all these children to bed? If he really cared, he'd pitch in and help." Most of the time, however, it isn't an issue of whether he really *cares;* it's an issue of whether he really *knows!*

Give Up Mind-Reading

With respect to whether a man knows, consider the difference in a woman's style when she is taking care of others and when she is expecting to be taken care of. In the first instance, that of taking care of others, a woman readily takes action. However, in the second instance, that of taking care of herself and making things happen in her own life, too often she waits. She anticipates and hopes—and then gets angry because others don't take care of her needs in the same exquisite manner she takes care of theirs. This is particularly true in relationships with men.

Laments one man: "My wife told me three times not to get her anything for her birthday, and I still forgot!" This man knows he flunked a test.

Admits a woman who gives such "tests": "Instead of asking my husband for something I want, I give him a test and he always fails. If he comes home and does a particular something, that means he loves me. If he does something else, that means he doesn't care. I have this 'thing' going on that he is absolutely oblivious to. There's no way he's going to pass my tests."

Admits another: "I wait for my husband to notice what I need. We've been married long enough that he should know. After all, I know what he needs. I just put a button on the shirt he'll want tomorrow. I served his favorite apple pie last night. I bought tickets last week so he could see his favorite basketball team play. So I think: 'Now, he *knows* I'm tired tonight, so why doesn't he ask me out to dinner?' "

Still another says: "I've been caught in the 'If I Have to Say It, It Doesn't Count' syndrome. I want my husband to do certain things by himself. So if I have to tell him, say, that I want a particular piece of jewelry for Christmas and he buys it, then I'm disappointed he didn't think of it himself. I need to quit penalizing him for not knowing and simply plan on taking responsibility by saying directly to him, 'This is what I want or need.' "

The theme in these responses, of course, is that women are waiting for the men in their lives to take care of them or to "fill them up." And men aren't noticing.

An erroneous assumption women make is that men, like women, know all about caretaking but just simply don't care enough to do it. Says an enlightened woman: "I finally realized it wasn't in my husband's genes to think about my needs the way I think about his."

The upshot is that, like it or not, you'll often have to initiate if you want something from a man—or anyone else (other people can't mind-read either). One woman describes the emotional evolution she went through when her husband forgot her birthday: "All day I didn't say anything. I just got more angry. By evening I was exhausted from all the fuming I had done. I finally thought, 'You can continue being a martyr, but it's not fun and it doesn't even work, because *he* doesn't even realize what's going on. Or you can initiate.' So I took action and asked my husband to take me out for my birthday to a perfectly marvelous restaurant—which, given his indictable lapse in memory, he was grateful to do. Then I felt better."

The most viable method of getting what you want is to simply ask for it rather than pouting, getting angry, or withdrawing. One woman explains: "We use anger to pressure other people to deliver what we want, and then we feel empty inside when we get what we want. And sometimes when we get angry, we don't even get what we want. We get what we *deserve*—the anger of someone else."

Initiating means operating from a position of quiet strength and moving decisively in a direction you want to take. It also means not waiting for others to deliver. If you're waiting for someone else and nothing is happening, simply find another way to take care of the situation. Finally—and this is vital—initiating means taking charge without playing martyr or in some way penalizing the other person. Illustrating these concepts, a woman says: "I waited six months for my husband to put up an antenna on the house. One day, when he came home, there was a TV man on the roof putting up the antenna. I simply said to him, 'Honey, I knew you were busy, so I decided I would help you by taking care of the antenna myself.'"

Asking for Help

One facet of initiating involves asking for help, which many women have difficulty doing. Consider this scenario:

Liz makes four trips up three flights of stairs to haul groceries to her apartment while her husband, Rick, watches TV on a Saturday morning. Each time she lugs more sacks up the stairs and catches a glimpse of Rick immersed in football, she becomes more angry. By the last trip, she is seething and talking to herself a mile a minute: "Why doesn't he move? He knows I need help. I can't believe he'd just sit there and let me bring up all these groceries myself. The insensitivity of this man is just intolerable."

Finally attracted by the loud banging of cans at half-time, our hapless husband makes an appearance in the pantry, remarking, "I wondered where you were." After watching for a minute, he innocently inquires, "Why do you put the soup cans on the bottom shelf instead of higher up where it's easier to read the label?"

The ensuing explosion rocks the apartment walls, setting off a kitchen-sink argument that covers every "crime" Liz and Rick have ever perpetrated against each other. In the heated verbal exchange, neither spouse recognizes the triggering event: Liz's not asking openly and directly for Rick's help.

Liz's behavior isn't unusual. Most women have difficulty asking for help for reasons they relate here:

"I can't ask for help unless it's down to a major trauma, and I'm going to die. I'm afraid the other person won't think I'm capable. It's like admitting I can't do the job."

"No one else can do it as well as I can."

"I might get turned down. I hate being rejected."

"If I ask a child to clean the bathroom and she does a sloppy job, it might be mistaken for *my* work, and I'll look bad."

"I might as well do it right the first time and get it over with."

"My kids and my husband come up with such better-sounding excuses for not doing work than I have, like homework or scouts! The only excuse I have is that I'd like to sit down for a minute."

"I have a balance system in my head. I can't possibly ask someone to do something for me unless I'm way ahead on my scorekeeping in helping that person."

"I get pangs of guilt whenever I ask for help. I anticipate that other people will think I'm pushing my work off on them."

Note that these reasons for not asking for help have to do with a woman's cultural programming, including these dimensions:

• a fear of rejection or disapproval
• a fear of bothering someone
• a fear that a request isn't legitimate
• a need to have things "just so"
• a feeling of guilt if she doesn't take care of every detail herself
• a fear of being viewed as incapable if she doesn't do her "job"

For many women, then, asking for help is an emotional event to be approached with trepidation, one beset with the possibility of rejection and lowered self-worth. However, just as the act of saying no needs to be value neutral, so does the act of asking for help. Asking for help needs to relate exclusively to the task at hand, the availability of a woman's energy, time, and resources to achieve the task, and the advisability of delegating that task to someone else. It's that simple.

Happily, depersonalizing the act of asking for help will take stress out of relating to others. Says one woman: "It's much easier to deal with others when you're not grasping for proof that you're okay."

Since most women aren't *asking*, the question is: What are they doing? In some instances, they're nagging: "Henry, don't forget to take out the garbage. How come you aren't taking out the garbage? When are you going to take out the garbage? Why didn't you take out the garbage? I can't depend on you for anything. I took out the garbage."

In other instances they're complaining: "You're always glued to that TV." "Why don't you try helping for a change?" "How come you're so lazy?"

Sometimes, we find them even getting angry. Take the wife who walks into the bathroom after her husband has just totalled it—wet towels and dirty clothes on the floor, open cupboards, soap all over the basin—the works. What does this woman want? A man who cleans up after himself. So what does she do? If she's like some women, she comes steaming out of the bathroom, giving off loud noises that sound something like this: "I just can't believe you! You're such a slob. You're just like your father. Neither one of you has ever picked up after yourself a day in your life. You act like I'm your maid, and if you think I'm just going to keep cleaning up after you, you've got another think coming."

The response of our understandably perturbed wife just about ensures she won't get what she wants. No self-respecting husband is about to accommodate to a noisy woman—he'll just shut out the din. And it's almost a sure bet he'll leave the bathroom a mess again.

The response that the wife used is personality-centered— it challenges the character of the errant husband who made this thoughtless (and maybe perpetual) error. This response can be contrasted to a request, which is task-centered in that

"You want to talk about it?"

it informs one person about what another person needs: "This is what I would like." "This is what would help."

Personality-centered statements often focus on things that have happened after the fact: "You've messed up the bathroom, which totally offended me. You're an awful person because you were thoughtless and didn't pay attention to what I needed." There is little an offending person can do to redeem him- or herself from such a past crime.

On the flip side of any complaint is a request. While a complaint focuses on the past, a request informs about what would help in the future. Trading her complaint for a request, then, our wife might ask her husband: "Would you be willing to go clean up after yourself in the bathroom right now? And would you further be willing to clean up after yourself any time you use the bathroom? That would help a lot!"

With this response, she has now invited, rather than demanded, change. Her chances of getting compliance are considerably higher with a request than with a complaint.

If you'd like to make more requests and fewer complaints, consider these guidelines:

1. Make your request brief and to the point. Avoid negative riders that poison the request: "I know you probably won't want to do this but . . . " And avoid qualifiers: "If it isn't too much trouble" or "When you have time."

2. Agree that each person in the relationship has a right to make any request he or she would like. And each person has the right to turn down a request. If each person had to fulfill a request anytime the other asked for something, the relationship would be based on tyranny rather than democracy.

3. Agree that neither person in the relationship will say yes to a request unless he or she can grant the request without resentment.

4. Also agree that because you are on the same team, you won't just emphatically say no to each other. Instead, if you're the person who made a request that doesn't quite appeal to the other person, ask for a counteroffer: "If it would be hard to grant my request, will you make me a counteroffer? What would feel comfortable to you?" Or if you're the recipient of a request with which you're not quite comfortable, make a counteroffer: "I can't fill your request quite the way you'd like, but what if I do this for you? Would that help?" In a few minutes of counterproposing, most people can come up with solutions acceptable to both parties.

Striking a Bargain Regarding Chores

If you'd like to settle the issue of who does what around the house fairly — and to move in concert to get chores done without concern or resentment — here are suggestions to help.

1. Decide to be task-centered about working out the issue of chores. This means focusing on solving the problem and using the same kinds of problem-solving behaviors at home

as you would at the workplace. As with requests, there is a difference between task-centered behaviors ("How do we solve the problem?") and personality-centered behaviors ("*You* are the problem!").

In part, being task-centered involves giving up the regurgitation of past "crimes." It also involves giving up blaming. Remember, both of you have been caught in the dictates of unconscious cultural programming. You've brought into your relationship highly specific but unarticulated expectations of how chores ought to be done and by whom—and then you've had emotional collisions as you've butted up against these tacit expectations.

2. Develop a mutual philosophy about housework. Laura Lein, the author of *Families Without Villains,* observes that families generally break down into one of four patterns when it comes to housework arrangements. Consider your own relationship as you read her description of patterns:

• Add-to. Paid work is simply added to the woman's other responsibilities for home and family.

• Helping out. Housework remains the woman's responsibility, but her husband helps as much as possible.

• Specialist. Husband and wife share responsibility both for homemaking and generating income, but tasks are allocated on a rather sex-segregated fashion according to ability, skills, training, and upbringing.

• Partners. Both husband and wife share work responsibilities inside and outside the home, with tasks determined not by traditional sex roles, but by an arrangement that pleases both.[8]

Which pattern do you have in your relationship? Which would you each like? Keep in mind that earlier arrangements may not work now, given ever-changing pressures and stresses on you and your family.

Now articulate your assumptions about housework. Should tasks be split equally? On some type of prorated basis? Opt for flexibility and for a "fair" arrangement. Look at the amount of time each person is spending in the workplace and on chores and other responsibilities, and make an effort to equalize the situation so you both have time to relax and pursue personal interests.

3. Together make a list of the household chores—inside and out. Independently mark on a copy of the list who you think completes each chore, using these symbols: H, W, Hw, Wh, and HW (H = husband does chores; W = wife does chores; Hw = husband has major responsibility, wife assists; Wh = wife has major responsibility, husband assists; HW = husband and wife share chore equally).

Using the same symbols, now mark down how you would prefer each chore to be carried out. Then share your perceptions with your partner and negotiate for any different arrangements you'd like. Take into consideration the attractiveness of each chore. Every chore, says Lein, has a "drudgery quotient" composed of its flexibility, visibility, and sociability potential. Washing floors may appear more attractive than washing dishes because that job can be accomplished anytime.

4. Exercise the quality of mercy. Times are hard, the pace of life changes, and we rarely live on an even balance, says Charlotte Whitney, author of *Win-Win Negotiations for Couples.* If your relationship is to survive, you'll need to weather such heavy demands as starting a family, changing jobs, or going back to school or work. "With that in mind, it makes sense to relax the rules now and then," says Whitney. Ignore an un-mopped floor or unmade dinner or help out by doing some of your partner's chores during stressful times. In the end, she says, "If you want a warm, sharing, loving relationship, it is necessary to be warm, sharing, and loving."[9]

Surviving with Kids

Turning now from a focus on husbands, we move to the topic of surviving with children—while keeping your cool—under stress. Consider first the subject of children and chores. A "Gumdrop" cartoon features Gumdrop, a small boy, sitting on his father's lap and saying to him: "My problem is that I'm a 'take it easy' kind of guy with a 'clean your room' kind of mom." Gumdrop sums up a key issue between moms and kids: In most homes, moms want kids to work, and kids aren't particularly interested in complying. So how do you get a "take it easy" kind of kid to help around the house? Here are strategies to try.

1. View housework as "our" work. Do you find yourself pleading with children to do *your* job, saying, "Won't you please help *me* with the dishes?" or "Thanks for doing the laundry for *me*."

"I used to do that," relates a woman, "but I've realized that housework isn't woman's work in today's world—it's *family* work! So, to give children that message, I emphasize these are chores *we* need to get done today."

Relates another woman: "When the house is spotless and the counters shiny, I say to my kids, 'The kitchen looks so nice. We did a nice job!' 'What do you mean WE?' one of the kids will ask, to which I respond, 'Well, we all helped. You helped by watching Josh. Sarah helped by cleaning up her bedroom. That gave me time to do the kitchen.' I always find some way to share the glory and the credit. When we've done well, I emphasize that the team did a good job. And when there's a goof, I say that the team had a problem."

2. Avoid stress. "Someone once said that stress is created by doing things for other people they could do themselves," says a woman. "I'm for avoiding stress," says another. "My teen

said to me, 'I don't know another fifteen-year-old who has do his own wash,' and I said, 'Look, you can have a perfect mother or you can have a mom who's there for you emotionally when you need her. I can't take on the entire burden and still be available.' "

Even if you're a woman who has chosen to work exclusively at home, it is still not advisable to, say, make your children's beds and match their socks. "I have a friend who's very fortunate and has never had to work outside her home," one woman reports. "Yet, she still makes her children's beds and waits on them hand and foot. I see these children suffering because they aren't learning self-sufficiency."

3. Give children choices. "When I asked my child to take out the garbage not long ago, he said 'no,' " one woman said. "The next time I approached him, I said, 'Honey, would you rather go in and clean the front room and do the dishes—or take out the garbage?' And he said, 'I would love to take out the garbage!' "

4. Trade your resources. You provide a multitude of services to your children. Trade those services for services you want. For example:

"Mother, may I have five dollars?" "I'll be glad to exchange the money for cleaning out the pantry."

"Mother, may I borrow the car?" "After you've finished cleaning the bathroom, I'd be delighted to loan you the car."

"Mother, will you take me to the store?" "Of course, dear. As soon as your homework is done."

5. Popularize the phrase "I'd love to!" as a family saying, and teach members that being agreeable is a sign of caring. And respond enthusiastically with "I'd love to!" or "No problem" when someone asks *you* to do something.[10]

5. Teach physical independence. What being physically independent really means is taking care of your own dirty work,

cleaning up your own messes, and doing the little personal chores you hate to do (the ones that you could probably get someone else to do by acting helpless). Countless times a day, members of your family make choices about whether they're going to clean up after themselves. And you make choices, too — about whether you're going to assume the small jobs left by other people.

Just to see how you all stand, ask those you live with to answer these questions taken from the "Physical Dependency Checklist" developed by Gary Emery, the author of *Own Your Own Life*. Then ask yourself whether you inadvertently take over areas that rightly need to be assumed by those who have created the work. Sort out just who is taking care of whom and who needs to do what to become physically independent.

- Who refills the ice tray after I use the ice?
- Who picks up my clothes from the floor?
- Who sweeps up the pile of trash I notice?
- Who puts the lid back on the catsup after I use it?
- Who refills the water jug I've just emptied?
- Who puts away the tools I use?
- Who replaces the toilet paper roll if I use the last of it?
- Who cleans up the bathtub after I use it?
- Who makes my bed?
- Who puts away my clean underwear?
- Who closes the bread wrapper after I make a sandwich?
- Who changes my light bulbs when they burn out?
- Who fills the gas tank of the car after I drive it?
- Who cleans up when I make a mess?
- Who turns off the lights or TV after I leave a room?
- Who takes care of my food wrappers?
- Who dials my calls?
- Who takes care of my needs when I visit family or friends?
- Whose work and time are most important in my family?

In the interest of your family becoming more physically independent, teach them the ACT formula recommended by Emery. *Accept* that you're responsible for yourself (for example, that you have to wash your own clothes in order to become more independent); *Choose* to do the task, no matter how you feel about it ("So what if I don't feel like learning to run the washer right now"); and *Take action* (grab those clothes, go to the washing machine, and ask someone how to run it!)[11]

A Philosophy of Child Rearing

So far in this chapter we have considered husbands, kids, and chores. Now we turn to more general topics having to do with decreasing stress on the family, the first of which has to do with strategies for managing kids. A greeting card featuring a frazzled mom is relevant. Reads the card: "Motherhood is full of frustrations and challenges . . . but eventually they move out."

Until they do, here are suggestions concerning a philosophy of child-rearing that might help.

1. *View children as little people — not short adults.*

Children see the world differently from adults and go through progressive stages of moral reasoning, which involves the development of values, of empathy and respect for others, and of a sense of responsibility, says Thomas Lickona. In his book *Raising Good Children from Birth Through the Teen Years,* Lickona observes: "These stages of reasoning are like a natural staircase, which kids go up one step at a time. The higher the stage, the broader the child's respect for others. Kids, just like adults, often slip down the staircase and use lower stages. Some kids move faster through the stages. But moral development isn't a race; it's a process. The important thing is to keep the process going."[12]

2. *From this perspective, accept children as they are.*

"Don't think of me as a difficult child—think of me
as your personal exercise coach!"

Children see the world through their own unique lenses, as one mother's story illustrates:

"On a recent camping trip, I found myself losing patience with my seven-year-old son, Danny. Whatever I tried to do, Danny was underfoot. He followed me into the tent, sat where I was going to lay his sleeping bag, and then jumped on the air mattress while I was inflating it. 'Look, Danny,' I snapped, exasperated, 'if you're in here to help me, fine. But if you're here to get in the way, get out!' Danny looked at me and, with utmost sincerity, quietly said, 'Mom, I'm in here because I love you.' "[13]

Kids are like that—often out of sync with adults, into their own world, exasperating—but if you can get past your own microscopic view, mostly just plain lovable. For that reason, try to keep a child's endearing characteristics in focus, even under the worst of circumstances.

3. *Recognize that kids' behavior has everything to do with them and very little to do with you.*

Children are a unique breed—little people who are well-intended but short-sighted. When they don't follow through perfectly (or even nearly perfectly), their behavior has to do with their age and stage of development, not with a lack of sensitivity or caring toward you.

4. Plan on children not complying — and then be pleasantly surprised when they do.

This is not an attitude to show toward kids; it is simply one to keep you from becoming angry so quickly when you're disappointed that a child hasn't followed through. Remember, kids often *won't* follow through. That is the nature of children, and getting angry won't change that. However, telling them when they *do* follow through *will* help them to change.

5. Become an ex-nagger.

Many parents repeatedly find fault, scold, and assault their children with petty complaints but view themselves as reminding, not nagging. But whether you call it nagging or not, these small complaints can erode relationships, causing emotional lesions that don't — and won't — heal until the aggravation's gone. An anonymous mother's recording of her responses during a Saturday with her teenage daughter vividly portrays the proneness of parents to repeatedly overdo criticism:

"Are you going to sleep all day? . . . Who said you could use my hair spray? . . . Clean the dishes off the table. . . . Turn down the radio. . . . Have you made your bed? . . . That shirt is too short. . . . Your closet is a mess. . . . Stand up straight. . . . Quit chewing your gum like that. . . . Your hair is too bushy. . . . Turn down the radio. . . . Have you done your homework? . . . Don't slouch. . . . You didn't make your bed. . . . Quit banging on the piano. . . . Why don't you iron it yourself? . . . Your fingernails are too long. . . . Sit up straight. . . . Get off that phone. . . . Why did you ever buy that record? . . . Take the dog out. . . . You forgot to dust that table. . . . You've been in the bathroom long enough. . . . Turn off that radio and go to sleep."

If this sounds familiar and you want to go through nagging withdrawal, adopt these approaches:

• Make a mental note of your children's behaviors that trigger your nagging, then cut down your negative monitoring by at least 75 percent. Ninety percent would be better!

• Change your language. Avoid harsh, demanding words that have "n't" endings, like *don't, can't, shouldn't, couldn't, haven't,* or *won't.*

• Give up the words *always* and *never:* "You're always late" or "You're never considerate." Used in complaints, either word sparks defensiveness or arguments.

• Put the sound of music in your voice. If your responses are saturated with resentment, sarcasm, or criticism, you'll get a cool reception and that's all. For best results, trade in discordant notes for pleasant ones and lace your requests with "pleases" and "thank-yous." Remember that relationships degenerate when "pleases" and "thank-yous" become, "Why in the heck haven't you?"

6. *Recognize that children's behavior needs to be "shaped" through positives—not forced through negatives.*

"Why is it, Mom, that when I do something bad, we talk so much about it?" says a child. "But when I try to do something good, I'm the only one who seems to remember for very long?"

This child's comment is right on target. The number of negatives children get from the time they're born until they hit twenty years of age is shocking. If, collecting from parents, teachers, siblings, and peers, children receive ten negatives a day in the first twenty years of their lives (probably a gross underestimate), they receive a sum total of 73,000 negative messages about themselves. A truer estimate is anywhere between 100,000 and 200,000.

These negative messages are rarely balanced by positive messages. If children are extremely lucky, the ratio probably runs about ten negatives to one positive — certainly not enough to offset the negatives or to build positive self-esteem, but enough to will a child a lifetime legacy of self-doubt.

7. *Focus on positives.*

Think about it: by the time a child reaches adulthood, you want him or her to be trustworthy, reliant, honest, cooperative, generous, caring, industrious, responsible — and the list goes on and on. How do you get a child with these qualities? Acknowledge them whenever you see even small fleeting evidence of their development by using descriptive feedback. For example: "I noticed you tied your little brother's shoes when he asked. That was a very caring thing to do." "You've been sticking with your homework all evening (or for the past fifteen minutes). That's what I call perseverance!"

If you'll continue to focus on positives, you may have the same experience as one set of shocked parents who struggled with a belligerent daughter. After giving her heavy doses of positives, the mother said: "I can't believe her new responsiveness. I thought we were giving her positives but she must have just been starved."

8. *Affirm and encourage your child.*

Sherry Ferguson and Lawrence Mazin, in their book *Parent Power: A Program to Help Your Child Succeed in School,* illustrate the myriad ways parents can affirm and encourage their children. Drawn from their list of "Two Hundred and Five Ways to Praise a Child" are sample responses that can reflect your child's abilities and performance:

- Where have you been hiding all that talent?
- You really outdid yourself today.
- This shows you've been thinking.
- You're becoming an expert at this.
- This gets a five-star rating.
- The results were worth all your hard work.

- I like how you've tackled this.
- A powerful argument!
- You've shown a lot of patience with this.
- This really has a flair.
- Nothing can stop you now.
- I wish I could have seen you do that.
- You've surpassed yourself.
- You really knock me out.
- Masterful!
- You're in a class by yourself.
- I can see you've taken great pains with that.
- Touchdown!
- Take a bow.[14]

In your affirming, be like the mother who made a deliberate effort to tell her child from the time he was young that he was brilliant, responsible, charming, and good-looking. This child would say to her again and again, "Tell me, Mom, what I am." One day, the mother relates, "my son came home from school with a 'pink note' indicating all his work wasn't completed. As he gave me the note, he said, 'I know I'm smart and I can do this and I'm not the kind of a kid that puts things off. And I know what you're going to say: I'm just not a pink-note kind of kid.'"

9. *Use a positive approach to deal with misbehavior.*

These steps constitute a behavioral "shaping" process that will help you when your child misbehaves:

- Describe the misbehavior. Say, for example, "When I ask you to do something, you often argue and say things like, 'You don't ever ask David to do anything' or 'I'm always the one who has to do the dishes.'"

- Tell your child why you're upset by the misbehavior: "I get frustrated when you challenge my reasons for asking you to do things. I don't have time for that. And I don't like having problems with you. I want us to have good feelings toward each other."

• Describe the behavior you want: "When I tell you to do something, I want you to say, 'Okay,' and then do it."

• You might conclude by simply adding, "So next time, would you please just say yes." Using the "next time" approach gives a child instructions regarding how you want him to change in the immediate future and doesn't make an issue of "this time."

If the negative behavior is fleeting and can be managed with a short intervention, stop here. However, if the behavior, is entrenched and warrants a fuller discussion, continue with these steps:

• Stay on the subject. If necessary, gently but firmly repeat several times what you need. Get agreement from your child that he or she will try out the new behavior.

• Encourage the positive behavior. The next time the behavior you want occurs, comment on it. Be a cheerleader for the changes your child is making. If the child is old enough, ask him or her to point out the desired behavior next time it occurs so you don't miss it.

• With younger children, temporarily use rewards to increase desirable behavior. Carry M & M candies in your pocket for a week, for example, and give your child one every time he or she says yes instead of arguing. (With teens, up the ante!)

• Give a bonus for consistent performance. For example, give your child a bonus point each day he or she says yes five times without arguing. When the child has earned five bonus points, go to lunch together.

• Cheer signs of progress. Good behavior that gets no attention may not be repeated. So let the child know several times a day that you're pleased with improved performance.

Occasionally give extra praise by telling another adult in your child's presence how pleased you are with his or her progress.

Eliminating Temper Tantrums of Kids — and Parents

Maybe your child doesn't get the dessert or toy he wants. Or maybe he doesn't want to make his bed. Or to get ready for school. Or to do his homework. And suddenly he's angry.

Or maybe you're the one who gets angry first. Even loving parents blow their top.

Either way, it may trigger a collision: two people yelling, hitting, verbally jerking each other around, and two people, when the conflict is over, reduced to emotional rubble. Managing anger — your child's anger and your own — could be one of your biggest challenges as a parent, so here is help if you need it:

1. First make a commitment to control your anger (and then work on your child's anger). Opting for control is a good choice because children imitate the way they see people near them expressing their anger. Your anger patterns will most likely become your children's anger patterns.

2. Pay attention to how often, when you're tired, irritated, or in a bad mood, you are grouchy with your children. You may consistently respond to children with impatience, a short temper, or a sharp voice, and still expect them to move meekly in the direction you'd like. If so, take charge of your responses so you don't encourage the anger and resistance you're trying to eliminate in your children.

3. Let your children know when you've momentarily succeeded in containing your temper. Point out, for example, that you usually get mad when you see muddy tracks going across your kitchen floor, but this time you are not yelling and/or mangling kids (and you probably won't if they hurry up and clean up the mud).

4. Ask the children to tell you when they see you managing your frustrations more effectively than in the past. If you are really working on containing your anger, you'll get feedback that will reinforce your growing self-control.

5. Apologize when you lose your temper or are heavy-handed. Or, even better, apologize when you make that first caustic, critical response (which will help keep a situation from escalating). It is vital that children learn to say "I'm sorry" when they've wounded others — but they probably won't learn this unless they see you or other significant people in their lives apologizing.

6. Talk to your child privately about typical situations in which one or both of you become angry. Do this when things are calm and there are good feelings between you. Describe the child's usual responses and your own. If you contribute to the problem, talk about ways you're going to change your behavior. Ask your child to think of things he or she can do to control anger and help the situation.

7. Possibly create an incentive program for eliminating anger. For example, offer to give your child a small attractive reward this next week every time you notice (or he reports to you) he has controlled his temper (or didn't lose it as badly as he usually does).

8. Together, decide on a code word like "truce" or "time out" that you can use any time things get heated. This will give you both a chance to bring yourselves back into control to deal with the problem. Don't let situations escalate in their usual manner; it won't serve any purpose.

9. Frequently point out to your child instances in which he or she has managed anger and coped with frustration in effective ways. Say, for example, "Sometimes I've seen you get really angry — even slam down your books — when you couldn't do a math problem. Tonight I know you're frustrated, but you're

staying in control. And you haven't given up trying to solve the problem. I'm impressed."

10. When you begin to see progress, point out the child's growth and prophesy that he or she is on the way to becoming a person who can control his or her temper and manage even angry feelings in a positive manner.

11. When you see younger children in the throes of a temper tantrum, regard them as being "stuck" rather than "bad." Children often shift to "automatic pilot" when they're angry and may have difficulty getting out of that mode. Instead of losing your own temper, think how you can help children become "unstuck." This may mean calmly and with dispatch putting the child into his or her room for a short time-out. Or doing something unexpected to distract the child. Or even reaching out and holding the child close to you until the mood passes.

12. When you need to express anger, select in advance words that don't wound but that let your child know you're angry. And, instead of dripping raw anger, state a rule, assert your values, give choices, or describe a problem.

13. When your children get angry, hear them out. Help them to get to the feelings that underlie the anger: frustration, disappointment, resentment, fear, jealousy, hurt, embarrassment. Try to restore good feelings between you instead of simply punishing them because you don't like their behavior. Remember, you may have inadvertently contributed to any problems they're having with you.

14. Make an agreement with your child that each of you needs to continue to treat the other with respect even when you're angry. Also talk about positive rules for expressing anger and then make sure you both follow the rules.

Strategies to Avoid Family Conflict

It happens much too often in families behind closed doors, members pitted against each other: screaming, yelling, hitting, verbally wounding the people they care about most. If this happens in your house, here are approaches that may help:

1. Agree with your family that absolutely no issues, conflicts, or negative comments are allowed at the dinner table. You may decide that any member who violates the rule gets a five-minute time out.

2. Avoid handling problems with individual children in front of anyone else whenever possible. If you have to discipline in front of other children, don't let them side with you against a sibling.

3. Stay out of corners. When you find yourself at loggerheads with your child ("You will do what I say, no matter what!"), *stop action!* Leave the situation until you have regrouped and can speak calmly. Then come back, express your frustration that things have gone so badly, and suggest that you both start over. Apologize for your part in the flare-up and give your child a chance to do the same. Allow the child to save face.

4. To help prevent quarreling, develop decision-rules specifying what happens when children encounter particular situations. For example:

• When fighting occurs in the car, the driver stops the car until the fighting stops.

• One child (sits in the front car seat) (picks the TV show) (does the dishes) on even-numbered days; another child, on odd-numbered days. (With more children, be creative.)

• Put away any object kids fight over for a day or until they have peacefully settled the issue.

5. Identify any "stress children" — children who, because

they have characteristics or behaviors that set them apart, attract constant anger and hostility from family members. Use whatever means necessary to take this child out of the role of stress conductor.

6. Don't criticize one child in front of another. And don't talk to one child about concerns, worries, or complaints you have with another child. Each child is entitled to the courtesy of your dealing privately and confidentially with his or her problems and issues.

7. Cut back on your complaints about your children to anyone, including your spouse. Complaining is a way of rehearsing anger.

8. Make a habit of talking about what is going right instead of what is going wrong, in any facet of your relating.

9. When you want your child to make a behavior change, use a "thirty-second request" as one mother does: "If I see something going wrong," she explains, "I ask, 'May I have your attention — eyeball to eyeball — for thirty seconds?' (Any kid will give you thirty seconds!) Then I make a request: 'This is what I need. Please have it done in the next half-hour.' If my kids are fighting, I just say, 'Please cut out the fighting *now*. Remove yourself from the room if necessary — but this is the end!' I go in, ask for what I want, and then I am out," she concludes. "I try to focus specifically on what I want done. The kids are glad there aren't any more lectures. They used to say to me, 'Mom, we get through listening before you get through talking.'"

10. Let little things go without comment, and give your children plenty of room to make mistakes without incurring any penalties. Remember, there are no perfect "tens" in this world.

11. Create positive relationship time to repair and maintain the bond between you and your children.

12. Agree with your partner that if one of you starts getting

heavy or noisy with a child, the other can step in and offer to take over.

13. If you're the one concerned about a child's problem, handle it by yourself—privately, if at all possible; let your spouse do the same. Also, don't sluff a problem off onto your spouse and then expect him to deal with the problem your way. And don't be a commentator when he is dealing with a child in your presence.

14. Spare your children the pain of watching you argue with your spouse. If you have to argue, do it privately!

15. Avoid playing "two against one" with anyone in the family. Don't join with a spouse against your child or form an alliance with a child against a spouse.

16. Make a rule that you will do the parenting. Don't let one child chime in and help you when you're dealing with another. Just say, "Thank you, but I'm the mother, so please stay out of this."

17. Control your voice level. Parents too often don't take responsibility for the yelling and screaming they do—which, of course, kids do model. Yelling also wounds children's fragile egos. Said one preschooler to her mother, "Please don't yell, Mom. It hurts my heart."

18. Take responsibility for your tone of voice and for every word that comes out of your mouth. Use mature language and avoid any responses that are condemning, threatening, attacking, hostile, belittling, haughty, and the like.

19. Point out instances in which children respond respectfully, treat others in caring ways, or communicate responsibly.

20. Set up rules with children that eliminate their using name calling, swearing, other abrasive language (such as "shut up"), or physical violence. Don't wait even thirty seconds to intervene if your children violate these rules.

21. Consistently model "emotional courtesies" for your children, such as "please," "thank you," and "excuse me."

22. Don't let children just "fight it out." Nothing is gained by letting kids tear each other apart. When they are allowed to physically or verbally attack others, they learn it's permissible to hurt others when they become angry.

23. Separate children when they're having serious scraps (unless you decide to referee). When you interrupt quarrels, don't take sides ("There you go again, picking on your sister"). By avoiding taking sides, you'll avoid the alienation that occurs between kids when they consistently see parents side with a sibling.

24. Don't handle aggression with aggression. If you handle children's quarreling on their level—with screaming, hitting, name-calling, and anger—you simply become one of the quarrelers and lose your ability to influence your children. If you find yourself becoming irrational as you attempt to stop a fight, leave the scene and try again when you're calm.

25. Try to handle your problems with a light touch. Use humor, smiles, and soft voice tones. Instead of demanding change, invite it through requests and negotiation. And increase the touching, holding, hugging, and "I love yous" to help create a positive family atmosphere. For a big plus in positive family relating, incorporate as part of the family philosophy (and say it often): "Everybody needs eight hugs a day." Remember, you can work out almost anything with a child you can hug!

26. Work to eliminate any grim mode of dealing with problems that may now characterize your family interactions. This includes eliminating a punishment atmosphere and approach for dealing with children's problems, including spankings as a mode of controlling them. Spankings are rarely administered while parents are in control of their anger or their hands.

Rather, they often occur in the midst of parental anger explosions, providing a vehicle for releasing pent-up frustrations.

Christie Hyde, in an article entitled "Confessions of a Non-spanker," sums up reasons for not spanking. Describing her struggle to control her hands and lungs in disciplining her four-year-old son, she says: "I no longer pass [spanking] off as something I do FOR him. . . . I have faced the fact that handling my own anger by screaming myself hoarse and slapping the smallest person in reach does not teach my child self-control or discipline. All it teaches is fear, submission, and the idea that if you eat all your greens, you'll grow up to be big enough to slug your own kid someday."[15]

"I'm reevaluating my habit of spanking," reports another mother. "People quote 'Spare the rod and spoil the child.' But the rod wasn't used for punishment or abuse. It was a staff that the shepherds used to guide the sheep. A rod was an example of influence, deliberate intervention, and kindness, not harshness and punishment."

A father who has learned that a soft touch works better than a hard one says: "I used to treat my teen like he was a Mack truck and I would stand in front of him with my arms up to stop him. Now I just run alongside him, sort of shooing him here and there to keep him in the main lane."

Accentuate the Positives, Eliminate the Negatives

Think what it would be like if your entire family usually focused on positives rather than negatives. What would be the benefits? For one thing, you would gain children who have high self-esteem. As two children, interviewed in a classic "Candid Camera" scene, demonstrate:

"I understand you're the teacher's pet," says Allen Funt. "Why do you imagine that's so?"

"I'm very bright. I'm a brilliant child," says one child.

Another comments, "I'm only six years old and everybody thinks I'm beautiful. I have jewelry—but I don't need jewelry because everyone says I look beautiful, even without anything on."

These two children, given just a minute to tell what they have going for them, respond confidently and decisively, mirroring the positive and affirming images they have seen reflected in adult eyes. With ample positives, your children will do the same.

What is another benefit? Your children will *be* positive. "My husband and I often notice what goes right, and the kids have picked it up," relates a mother. "The other day my sixteen-year-old son said to me, 'Are you ready for your unusual compliment of the day?' 'I'm game,' I acknowledged. 'Mom,' he responded in all seriousness, 'you separate the egg yolks from the egg whites unseasonably well.' "

And a final benefit? You'll have children who will tell you what you're doing right! "I took my sixteen-year-old to get his driver's license the other day and, with great trepidation, let him drive home," a mother reports. "When we pulled in the driveway, there I was, paralyzed, hands clutching the front seat for dear life. Much to my amazement, my son leaned over and said, 'I'm impressed, Mom. You did marvelously!' 'What do you mean?' I asked, puzzled. With an impish grin on his face, he responded: 'You only screamed twice.' "

So, with that sales pitch on the benefits of being positive, consider these forty signs to help you—and your spouse—to focus on what is going right in the family, and to set the stage for your kids to do so too:

• You catch your teenager actually being pleasant to one of your younger children.

• Your husband looks at the dent in the fender and inquires, "Honey, are you sure you're all right?"

• Your eight-year-old tells you the truth about breaking the antique vase your grandmother gave you — even though he knows you're seething.

• The family all piles into the car and there isn't a fight over who gets the front seat.

• Your children are playing quietly together — sharing, co-operating, and having fun.

• You're late picking up your husband and he doesn't even comment.

• Your twelve-year-old son hasn't teased his younger sister for the past two hours.

• You make it through the grocery shopping without being embarrassed by your young children (or at least as embarrassed as you usually are).

• You ask your ten-year-old daughter to do something and she says, "I'll do it." Then she does.

• Your telephone conversation isn't interrupted by a blood-curdling scream or by a "But mommy, I have to talk to you *now!*"

• Your ten-year-old spills her milk and says, "Don't worry about it, Mom. I'll clean it up."

• Your son comes home from college without his laundry.

• You change your hair color and your husband says you look super (or at least doesn't ask you how much it cost).

• You say you're taking the family out to a special restaurant and no one starts crying because you're not going to McDonald's.

• Two of your children decide to share the prize in the cereal box (a situation that usually ends in a duel to the death).

• Your four-year-old plays with the cat gently instead of carrying her around by the tail.

• Your twelve-year-old actually returns the (tape) (scissors) (pliers) (hammer) he borrowed.

• Your teenager comes home early.

• Your six-year-old doesn't have to go to the bathroom (which is at least a half a block away) while you're shopping in the mall.

• You snap at your husband and he says, "You must have had a bad day."

• Your spouse calls during the day to tell you something pleasant.

• Your teenager cracks a joke that lightens your spirits.

• Your eight-year-old decides to read a book instead of watching TV.

• Your son wipes his muddy feet before he comes into the house.

• Your teenager asks you which music station you'd like to listen to.

• You're trying to move a heavy object and your husband says, "Here, let me do that for you."

• You get in the car and there are no (Twinkie wrappers) (popcorn kernels) (pop cans) (straws) (dirty socks) (wet bathing suits) on the floor.

• You walk into your teenager's room and can actually see the carpet.

• Your husband greets you with a hug and a smile when you walk in the door.

• You open your magic chest-of-drawers and there, as usual, are clean socks and underwear.

• Your teenager listens to you (and seems to comprehend) when you give him some sage advice.

• The mess you thought wasn't going to get cleaned up (unless you took care of it) did.

• Someone says "I love you."

Chapter 9

Filling in the Woman

There are many ways you can invest in your development and achieve more self-definition. This chapter and the next are devoted to strategies that can enable you to firm up and expand your "self," the first of which is to refrain from comparing yourself to other women. To gather information about yourself in this area, answer this question: What crosses your mind when you enter a room filled with women you know? Most women who respond admit: "I compare myself with other women." And they report that thoughts like these cross their minds:

- She has a *great* wardrobe (better than mine).
- She's more organized.
- She has acrylic nails (my nails look just awful today).
- She has composure (I cry when I have trouble with my boss; she doesn't).
- She's the same height as I am but I'm twenty pounds heavier! She can eat anything and it never sticks!

Many women suffer from "comparitis." They constantly scan the women in their space to assure themselves, in their comparisons, that they're at least as "good" as others and therefore at least adequate. And, as luck would have it, they always encounter some woman who is thinner, brighter, taller, shorter, younger, richer, wittier, more organized, a better cook, a more adept seamstress, a more accomplished artist, or the like — someone who appears more proficient on any dimension they rate themselves.

As a woman, your other-oriented cultural conditioning dictates that you look outward for your behavioral cues and for evidence you're doing okay across a variety of dimensions. So how do you know if you're attractive? smart? successful? wonderful? By comparing yourself to other women and deciding where you fit on the hierarchy — something you may do, to your disadvantage, numerous times a day.

Looking outward for your validation leaves you extraordinarily vulnerable because the comparison criteria aren't within your control. You can't regulate the characteristics of other women. Nor can you keep yourself performing at a stunning level in relation to dozens of random (and enviable) characteristics of other women you happen upon daily. Thus, you can never achieve internal security, because your well-being is at risk and your worth potentially diminished anytime you encounter another woman.

One woman astutely describes the dilemma of women who constantly compare themselves with others: "It doesn't matter how much I've accomplished, I always look at someone out there who's doing what I've done so much better. My husband can list all of the things I'm doing right but I'll say, 'Yes, but So-And-So does it all — plus!' "

But presume now that a woman does find someone whom she outclasses on a certain dimension. What then? She may experience a flash of superiority for a brief moment and then feel bad about having such a dreadful thought. Say Linda San-

ford and Mary Ellen Donovan, authors of *Women's Self-Esteem:*
"If she meets someone and thinks, 'I'm (better) (prettier)
(more successful),' her next private thought may well be, 'Wait
a minute—who do you think you are? How dare you think you
are better than someone else! That's a terrible thing to think!'
One momentary feeling of superiority is instantly squelched
by guilt and moral condemnation."[1]

Comparing yourself with other women—and coming out
either on the bottom or the top—just doesn't make sense. As
a self, you are similar to the stunning and one-of-a-kind picture
created by a turn of the crystals in a kaleidoscope. There are
no carbon copies of you. Neither can you ever be a carbon
copy of another person. You are different from others, and
there is nothing good or bad about that. It is simply a statement
of fact. And if you accept this fact, then you may want to take
a hard look at why you would ever compare yourself with
anyone else.

There will always be someone who can do something
better than you can. What difference does that make? You've
arranged your time and priorities in ways that make sense to
you. You have a unique genetic heritage, a unique family background and upbringing, and unique life experiences that have
shaped the course of your life and your choices in unique
ways. It is not logical to pick out one criterion, one way another
woman is performing in a "superior" manner, and then conclude you are a deficient human being.

Chronically comparing oneself to other women is a habit
that wears on women's relationships with each other. "Women
often don't appreciate other women's talents," observes one.
"They're envious. They have an image in their minds of qualities
they would like to have, so instead of being happy for another
woman because she has a particular quality, they want that
quality. It's not uncommon to hear a woman say something

like: 'You're very articulate. I just admire that so much. I wish I could be like you.' " Observes another: "Sometimes we alienate someone who seems to be doing a wonderful job because we perceive her as doing so much better than we are. And maybe she happens to be the loneliest person in the whole group!"

Another problem inherent in comparing is that women compare their *insides* to other people's *outsides.* Reports a woman: "Two Christmases ago, I took my four young children shopping with me to exchange gifts. The lines were long and, needless to say, by the time we came out of the fourth store, my patience was shot! As we pulled into the parking lot of the last store, I yelled at my kids, 'If one of you even says one word, or runs off, or does anything when we go inside, there will be bloodshed!' On the other hand, I promised them I'd buy them some popcorn if they'd just sit quietly while I stood in the next line.

"So my children sat on the floor eating popcorn, absolutely quiet for the next fifteen minutes, while I waited to exchange a present in the last store. Noticing their docile behavior, a woman approached me and said, 'I wish the newspaper could take your picture and designate you "The Mother of the Year." ' I felt guilty because I had been so obnoxious to my children and had threatened them. It was a good example of what my insides were doing and what my outsides looked like."

Rather than comparing yourself with others, the solution is to compare yourself with yourself across a limited number of criteria. Choose several personal qualities you'd like to develop further, and set realistic goals for yourself. Then periodically focus inward and measure your own growth — the distance you've come since you last gauged your progress. And pay attention to your own satisfaction with your achievements.

Then you're on your way to being in charge of your self-worth and firming yourself.

Raise Your Compliment Quotient

Women aren't prone to absorbing compliments, savoring them, putting them to good use to increase their self-esteem. To the contrary, they're notorious for deflecting compliments — just letting them ricochet off themselves to disappear somewhere out in the far reaches of oblivion, as these responses illustrate:

• "You look gorgeous in that dress." *I wish I were a size smaller.*

• "I love you." *How can you love anybody who looks like me?*

• "That furniture is elegant." *But it's the wrong color (It needs to be cleaned) (The chairs need to be recovered).*

• "I like you in that beige outfit." *You do? But it has a lipstick stain (The hem is coming out) (I picked it up at a thrift shop) (It doesn't quite fit).*

• "You've lost so much weight!" *Are you kidding? You ought to see me without my clothes on!*

• "You look like my favorite aunt." *Oh, that poor thing!*

• "Congratulations on getting that new job." *I only got it because the manager knows my dad (They just felt sorry for me) (They were pretty hard up!).*

• "I love your taste in dinnerware." *I got it on sale (Thanks, my mom picked it out).*

• "You have such a wonderful family." *Oh, I'm just lucky.*

• "I loved your class presentation." *The copies I handed out weren't very clear (I could have done better if I'd had more time).*

• "I like the way you wear your hair." *It really needs to be cut (I really need a perm).*

• "You look great in those pants." *I would look a lot greater if I lost ten pounds (I feel so fat!) (Don't try to be funny) (You lie very well).*

• "You did a great job!" *It's a living (It's nothing) (Anyone could have done it) (Samantha did most of the work).*

• "Doesn't this house look nice!" *I haven't had time to mop yet (You should have seen it yesterday).*

With her entrenched cultural conditioning, a woman is a bit like a baseball player, poised over home base with her mighty bat, ready to return any ball (any compliment coming her way) from the players on the other team. Unfortunately, often the players (the people offering the compliments) get tired of throwing the ball and having it knocked out of the ball field, so they quit playing the game! And then what does the woman conclude when there's a dearth of compliments? "It's probably because I'm undeserving."

What is it about the way the typical woman is constructed that inflicts upon her an almost irresistible impulse to deflect compliments? Probably a major reason is that most women suffer from the "I Don't Deserve It" syndrome. Here is what various women say about deserving compliments.

• "If I *do* have a success, I think it was just a fluke, an accident. I just got lucky."

• "There's nothing special about being perfect. That's just what's expected of me, so how can I deserve a compliment?"

• "I always remember a flaw in myself or something I *didn't* get done. If I accepted the compliment, I'd feel like a fraud."

• "I feel guilty if I'm succeeding and someone else isn't."

• "I know I didn't do my best. If other people knew that, they wouldn't give me the compliment."

• "I'm afraid I won't be able to live up to someone's expectations of me in the future."

• "People see me as more competent than I really am."

Still another reason why women have trouble accepting compliments is that they feel guilty at not producing enough. As one author has observed, from their perspective women go through life working (not well enough), spending moments with their children (not long enough), cooking hasty meals (not delicious enough), and putting away T-shirts (not white enough).[2] A second reason why women have difficulty is that they systematically cancel their strengths or positive actions with a negative. "I'm good at my job," one might think, "but it's not that hard. Anybody could do the job." "Yes, I know I look nice, but it took plastic surgery to pull myself together." Ironically, in cancelling an incoming compliment, a woman often turns it around to insult herself.

In this respect, women have difficulty because their self-concepts lack structural balance, emphasize Sanford and Donovan. Women can usually accurately perceive that they have both flaws and positive qualities, but they can't put these in proper perspective, viewing the flaws as relatively minor parts of themselves. Instead, they "shove their positive attributes off to the side of their self-concepts and focus on their flaws, no matter how small, as if their flaws were the most significant thing about them."[3]

A further reason women have difficulty is that they suffer from what author Caryl Rivers calls "the luck illusion." They are prone to cancel out their achievements, believing they are lucky rather than deserving of successes because of hard work or native abilities. "They believe they did well only because they had help—or were in the right place at the right time," she writes. "When you think a good performance is due to luck—or anything other than your own ability—you can't build on your accomplishments. After all, skill and talent won't disappear—but luck can. So one of the results of falling for The Luck Illusion is that you underrate your ability." Believing you were "just lucky" makes it impossible for you to live up to your potential. Or to take risks. Or to feel in control of your life. Your self-esteem is also bound to suffer because you can't take pride in simply being lucky.

Fortunately, Rivers says, The Luck Illusion isn't terminal. You can cure it. "Once you are aware of the trap that snares so many women — underrating personal abilities — you should be able to steer clear of it. The Luck Illusion might finally go the way of whooping cough and bubonic plague. Then, when someone congratulates you for a job well done, you can say, 'Thank you. I guess I was just — good!' "[4]

A final reason women have trouble with compliments is that they often feel they're *imposters*. Speaking to this point, Jeannie Ralston, author of an article entitled "I'm a Fake!," describes feelings she experienced working at her second newspaper job: "I'd been there long enough to know the reporting ropes, but every time I turned in an article the same thing happened. I would sit at my desk as my editor read it over, trying to act busy — while my stomach was busy doing Mary Lou Retton rolls. It wasn't that I hadn't done my research or my best job, it was just that at any moment I expected men in trench coats to rush into the newsroom and my editor to point toward me and shout, 'That's her! That's the one pretending to be a reporter!' "

That never happened, of course, reports Ralston, but for years she was plagued by the feeling that someone would come along and discover that she — the writer — was a phony. It was comforting, however, to finally realize she wasn't alone! She learned that most people (70 percent, according to recent studies) experience at some point what is known as the "Imposter Phenomenon" — a belief (despite ample evidence to the contrary) that they aren't bright, capable, or creative. Everyone gropes and struggles at times, she emphasizes, and there is no magical transformation for any of us into an all-knowing, all-confident creature just because we gain some new title or new role.[5]

Learning to accept compliments means setting aside old encrusted beliefs that you're unworthy, and replacing them with thoughts that you are that intrinsically valuable person featured previously—a person with boundlesss possibilities—who deserves credit for your strengths and achievements.

As you think about beginning to absorb compliments, imagine how you would go about actually painting your own self-portrait. First, you would make a sketch and then, with your brush, you would begin filling in the details with any color and shade you wished. Now think about doing the same thing with your psychological self-portrait. With each compliment you are filling in that portrait, making it more distinct, giving it more definition, more *self*-definition. You need the detail, the color, and the shading to make your picture more complete. If you don't fill in your portrait, you'll have nothing but an empty sketch.

How, then, can you respond to compliments?

The answer? Do it graciously, with a simple thank you, a smile, and, if possible, a sincere response. Let in that compliment. Feel it. Savor it. Experience the warmth of it. Invite it into your very core with responses like these: "I appreciate hearing that. You've made my day" or "How nice of you to say that. A compliment from you means a lot."

If you agree with the compliment, comment briefly on it: "I'm glad you like this dress. It's my favorite" or "I'm pleased with the way the dinner turned out."

If you *disagree,* after a brief "Thank you," keep your mouth shut and your mind open. Say firmly to yourself: "Think about this, Self. You're about to deflect this compliment. How are you ever going to fill in this self-portrait of yours if you don't change your ways? Is there any validity to this compliment, anything you can possibly salvage and put in your self-portrait? It will be an austere old life if you just end up with an empty sketch."

Remember, there are three reasons to accept compliments graciously—even if you don't entirely agree with them.

First, to reject a compliment is to suggest that the person giving the compliment has poor judgment, is uninformed, has ulterior motives, just isn't honest, or is disturbed. View a compliment for what it is: the subjective opinion of another person. Leave the other person to his or her opinion and don't argue with it, but do try to see that person's point of view!

Second, if you're like most women, you use a double standard. You let any negative lurking-about go clear to your core (which makes you feel bad), and yet you systematically reject any positive trying to find a warm home (while accepting the positive could make you feel good). Fair play demands that you start absorbing compliments and give yourself a chance to raise your self-esteem. Fair play also demands that you quit absorbing most of the negatives that come your way. If you constantly take in the negatives and shun the positives, it's a sure bet you have shaky self-esteem and that it's bound to stay that way until you become more open to good hearty doses of outside approval. Besides that, the negatives have monopolized your thinking your whole life—and now it's time for the positives to have their day in the sun! So just say to yourself: "Move over, negatives. Come in, positives!"

Third, you *need* compliments, so start giving yourself the credit you deserve and accepting those positive aspects of yourself you've denied. You need information about yourself that will help you fill in a positive self-portrait. And you need the good feeling that springs from being validated by others who recognize your strengths and possibilities.

As you learn to absorb the positives and to deflect the negatives, keep in mind the story of one woman who reported that she was now released—that she had finally learned to accept compliments. "The turning point was the day I served my husband's favorite lasagna and he said, as usual, 'This is good!' This time I just said, 'Yes, I know.' Startled, he asked, 'What is the matter with you? Ordinarily you respond by saying that the lasagna is too dry, or that it is too spicy, or that it needs more cheese.' 'Yes, I know that, too,' I said. 'But I've decided that I'm no longer going to cheat myself out of compliments. Besides that, I've got a positive self-portrait to fill in.'"

Create a Positive Body Image

You probably know a woman like Marney. Tall, slender, with a fine-featured face, by any standards she's an attractive woman. But she doesn't think so. "I hate my body. I can't get rid of the image of lumps, and bumps, and disproportionate body parts. I feel disgust for myself every time I look in a mirror," she laments. "I even have a name for that nagging loathing I have for my body. I call it the 'uglies.' There isn't much about myself I feel good about."

Put a group of women together and what do they have in common? Most tend to feel their bodies are not good enough, pretty enough, firm enough, or young enough. And, says one author, most have "body hatred":

• They're obsessed with their bodies.

• They're dissatisfied with their bodies.

• They're willing to do painful, punishing things to their bodies (from crash dieting and overeating to vomiting or surgery) in an attempt to change them.

• When they look in the mirror, they don't see their bodies as they really are.[6]

Research by psychologist Marcia Hutchinson confirms the negative way most women see their bodies. In a report on body image, she reports that only one of the hundred women studied was not "actively waging war against fat." Though none of the women studied was seriously overweight or emotionally disturbed, each was dieting, self-rejecting, and suffering from poor body image. In view of her negative findings, Hutchinson concludes that among women "flesh-loathing exists in epidemic proportions."[7]

Now, notice that the tone of our discussion has changed. We are talking about a *serious* matter: women who hate their bodies, who are waiting to live until they lose weight, who are making a career of trimming their never-firm-enough tummies and thighs. "It's a tragic waste of human potential," Hutchinson says. "If you could harness one-tenth of the energy you spend being obsessed with your body and use it toward something that really furthered your personal development and goals, just think where you could be!"[8]

If you have a negative body image, it is probably because you see yourself inaccurately, emphasize Sanford and Donovan. These authors, who interviewed several hundred women, reported that many distorted reality about their bodies in two ways: either they viewed themselves fatter, larger, or rounder than they really were, or they saw a certain part of their body as grossly abnormal.

The women studied consistently described themselves with exaggerated adjectives, such as "oafish," "sausagelike," "built like a house," and "grossly enormous." They also saw their "distorted" bodies as being dominated by such specific features as big feet, bushy eyebrows, wide hips, thin hair, acne, pointy knees, sagging breasts, and flabby stomachs. Moreover, they generalized from one particular feature to their whole appearance, ignoring any positive attributes.[9]

Why do so many women suffer from such negative body images? The answer lies in a culture that defines the meaning

*"I used to be short, fat, and ugly. Now I'm petite, full-bodied,
and don't give a hoot what they think of my looks!"*

of women's appearances and assigns the female the decorative role. Says Rita Freedman, the author of *Beauty Bound:* "Beauty is not a gender-natural trait. There are no televised pageants in which men parade in bikinis to be crowned Mr. America on the basis of their shapely legs and congenial smiles; no fairy-tale prince so handsome that the sun is astonished when it shines on his face."[10]

Because beauty is linked with femininity, the self-concept of a woman is often shaped by her perception of her body image. Studies show, in fact, that men tend to judge themselves in terms of what they can do, whereas women tend to equate self-worth with good looks. While cultural norms are gradually changing, most of today's women have learned that their appearance is their primary asset. The emphasis on looks puts such women in jeopardy because their worth rests in the eyes of the observer who, as aptly stated by Freedman, "can bring her to life by recognizing her or snuff her out by ignoring her."[11]

A multitude of messages generated by the beautification

industries tell women that no matter how hard they try to attain acceptability, they still remain unfinished or imperfect. Capturing the impact of such messages in an essay entitled "The Mask of Beauty," Una Stannard writes: "Every day in every way, the billion-dollar beauty business tells women they are monsters in disguise. Every ad for bras tells women that their breasts need lifting, . . . every ad for high heels that her legs need propping, every ad for cosmetics that her skin is too dry, too pale, or too ruddy, or her lips are not bright enough. . . . In this culture women are told they are the fair sex, but at the same time that their 'beauty' needs lifting, shaping, dyeing, painting, curling, padding. Women are really being told that 'the beauty' is a beast."[12]

The messages concerning how a woman "should" look also vary greatly with the prevailing norm of what is attractive — and that fluctuates with the changing fashion industry and what is in vogue. "Remember Marilyn Monroe?" says one author. "She was gorgeous. She took our breath away. She'd be sent straight to a fat farm if she were alive today."[13]

A woman never has just one clear-cut image of perfection to model. Say Sanford and Donovan: "There are usually many equally ridiculous and often diametrically opposed ideals operating simultaneously. For instance, today we have the voluptuous sex goddesses Loni Anderson and Bo Derek contrasted with top fashion models Kristine Oulman and Brooke Shields, whose adolescent bodies more resemble the bodies of pre-adolescent boys than the bodies of grown women. No woman can live up to — or even strive for — both these heavily promoted ideals at the same time."[14]

Women must deal with still other discrepant messages. Author Carol Travis reports on research indicating men and women associate the curvy, big-breasted body with femininity, which in turn is associated with "nurturance, dependence, passivity, domesticity and, alas, *professional incompetence.* Therefore, researchers concluded, women who want to be thought of as intelligent, professional and competent, must look more 'male-ish.' "[15]

Adding to the confusion is still another message. Women are told that they should be reed-thin — but with a very ample bust, please! Says one researcher regarding current beauty standards: "The ideal female body is slowly becoming more and more unnatural: big-breasted woman with boyish hips and thighs." And how do many women try to conform to this absurd image? "What you get is the skeletal woman going for a breast augmentation. . . . It's not natural."[16]

The trouble is, it isn't structurally possible for most women to conform to the fashion world's emaciated look on the bottom and the playboy look on the top. One author comments: "Today's fashion designers have made an architectural sculpting of women's form. The design has nothing to do with what a woman needs to look like — what is soft or comfortable or natural."[17] Another writes: "It is a fact of genetics that most women are built wider below the waist than above. The full-scale battle of diet and exercise that developed against hips and thighs has caused more frustration and tears of self-hatred than loss of real inches. The fact that bottom-heavy has been out of style for 40 years is a poignant illustration of the feminine aesthetic at odds with femaleness in its natural state."[18]

Tragically, many women tend to view their inability to conform to all these confusing messages as evidence of their own flaws rather than as evidence of a schizophrenic culture that is presenting contradictory and impossible standards for women to achieve. For most, the only control they have over these messages is to try to trim down their bodies, so they become obsessed with their weight. Sadly, a diet often works for only a short time, and after many unsuccessful attempts, some women turn to more desperate measures, such as diuretics, laxatives, and pills. These measures, in turn, may culminate in eating disorders—a direct result, say most experts, of the culture's emphasis on thinness.

Come to Terms with Your Weight

So what is a woman to do in this culture, especially a woman whose body just wasn't meant to be thin? If you are one who is tyrannized by the scale, consider adopting these approaches:

1. Decide what is a realistic weight for you, and keep in mind these facts stressed by Carol Travis:

• The healthiest weight seems to rise with age. According to one expert, a woman of moderate height does best if she weighs 120 at age twenty and 150 at age sixty.

• Being considerably overweight is unhealthy, but being thin is just as unhealthy. Research indicates that the thinnest people have the highest death rate.

• The location of your pounds may matter more than the number of pounds. Women are biologically programmed to have fat reserves in the thighs, buttocks, and hips, and reasonable weight in these areas isn't a health hazard.[19]

2. Give up the intense focus on weight. It's surprising how many women weigh themselves three, four, even five times a day, their goal being not to fluctuate even an ounce, says Janice Kaplin, author of an article entitled "Slaves to the Scale."

Kaplin urges a woman to disengage from "moment-by-moment" scrutiny of her weight and to use the scales sparingly. Give up being a constant "scale checker," she advises, and find a weight range (allowing for a fluctuation of three to five pounds) at which you feel comfortable. Then get on the scale no more than once a week! Ultimately, she says, you shouldn't need a scale at all. Be the judge of whether you're in the shape you want to be in, and use fitness, rather than weight, to measure progress.[20]

3. Don't put your life on hold just because you think (or know) you're overweight. Other important things can become contingent upon thinness. A woman may say, "As soon as I lose weight, *then* I'll (buy new clothes) (start exercising) (plan a vacation) (have the family portraits taken) (etc.)." On the other hand, don't put off losing weight just because you're getting on with your life! Admits a woman: "I was always saying to myself I'd lose weight as soon as—

—The basement is finished."

—The yardwork is all done and the cupboards and closets are all organized."

—My baby is in first grade."

—I go to work. (I'll be a career woman then—career women always look good!)"

—My husband starts being nice to me (I'd still be skinny if I had married Dean!)."

—I save the money to pay for a weight-loss program."

If losing that ten-plus pounds means enough to you, mobilize a major offensive, get them off, and keep them off. If, on the other hand, you're not going to give priority to making your weight a goal, decide to let yourself off the hook and be content. Why go through all the pain and tears over pounds you aren't really going to take off? Or why tyrannize yourself any longer with the thought "I should lose ten pounds!"

4. Take charge by incorporating these four guidelines in any weight-loss effort:

• Decide you're worth an intensive investment of your time and resources to lose weight.

• Dedicate as much time to yourself as you would to any other significant person you take care of.

• Consider weight loss not as a temporary adjustment but as a permanent life-style issue.

• Focus first on your health; second, on weight loss.

To illustrate, consider a woman who took charge of her life, her body, and her self-esteem. Her story didn't begin with weight loss; rather, it began many months before any attempt to lose weight, with a decision to take care of herself. "Ultimately, each person faces the issue of taking responsibility for his or her behavior and actions," she says. "It was my turn to put away the child — to stand accountable and be in control of my life; to be responsible — not to any other person, but to myself.

"I realized that, as an adult, I had given away to other people everything that I was. During my marriage I had devoted 100 percent of my time caring for my children and husband. I had put my husband through school, borne his children, kept his home — made it possible for him to literally be or do anything he wanted. I had focused on developing him and so had he. And for ten years I was either pregnant or nursing. My obstetrician finally said, 'You need a rest. You've been either growing a baby or feeding a baby since I've known you.'

"It was in those years that the pounds gradually crept up on me until I was fifty pounds overweight. Partly I put on the weight because I never stopped to take care of me — I just wasn't in the caretaking equation. I also realized that my 'self' was out of focus. I had lost my personhood. I knew I needed a sense of direction. If I didn't know what I wanted, how did I know how to get there? So I made my overriding personal goal this: I would take care of myself. I would begin a lifetime self-investment program. I wouldn't quit taking care of other people; I would just add *me* to the equation. And that meant that others would need to make some adjustments so I could devote a fair share of attention to myself.

"As a first step, I began taking better care of my personal appearance. I decided not to wait until I lost twenty pounds. I would look good *now*. I would buy some clothes. I had waited ten years until I was 'the right size' and I was still wearing my sweats, my dark pants, and all my other 'fat uniforms.' I threw out all my torn nightgowns — the ones you wear because no one sees you — and bought some lingerie that made me feel attractive and feminine. I began realizing that the choices I was making in favor of myself were accumulating, like money in a bank. I was now beginning to take care of me just as I had been taking care of everyone else.

"Then I turned to my next step. I decided that, as master of myself, I was going to get my health back. I would return my body to a state in which I could enjoy myself and experience once again a love and a zest for life. I began reading everything I could about diet, nutrition, and exercise, so I could make educated choices about how to invest in myself. And — having been born a pear, not a banana — I wanted to choose a program I could stay on the rest of my life. In regaining my health, I would lose weight, I decided. The weight I had packed around for too many years had affected the quality of my life. I was brutally honest with myself because I knew I had to find weight-loss approaches I would follow. I wouldn't go to a spa because I was overconscious of my weight, so I found an aerobic exercise I could do every day at home. I also made new food choices, based on sound nutritional advice and information, that I could feed my family and myself the rest of my life. I gave up caffeine and refined sugar and flour. Then out went the fat. I added whole grains, fruits and vegetables, and lots of water to my diet.

"I took one step at a time. It had taken time to put on the weight, and it would now take time to take it off. I couldn't instantly have what I wanted. I would put 'nickels' and 'dimes'

"I tried the high-protein diet, the high-fiber diet,
the high-starch diet, and nothing worked.
Then I created the high self-esteem diet . . . "

into my 'personal savings account' — I would keep exercising and eat right *every day* — and I would accumulate slowly the returns of my investment. And the returns have come. So far I have lost thirty-four pounds and thirty-four inches. For a long time, as I saw inches melting away, I couldn't believe this was happening to me. The significant strides I had made finally hit home when I ran into a male friend I hadn't seen for several months and heard a 'Wow!' and 'You look great!' I am also experiencing better health. I was crying the other day, and when I looked into a mirror to view the damage, to my shock, instead of seeing the white puffy cheeks and a person with bags under her eyes, I saw a woman who looked good. I had made a transformation. I was different. I wiped away my tears. I was okay."

Learn to Love Your Physical Body

In addition to addressing and coming to terms with your health and weight, there are general issues related to achieving a more positive body image. How can you treat your body with compassion? Even love that body? Consider these options:

1. In enhancing your appearance, don't try to achieve an ideal set by someone else — or all the anonymous "theys" of the world. You have a right to present yourself the way you'd like to be seen.

You can help to break the beauty myth that has been used "to separate the haves from the have nots and thereby to divide women," says author Rita Freedman. "The narrow boundaries of beauty can be stretched to make room for the stouter, older, plainer, flatter, freckled, and funny-faced among us." To broaden the concept of beauty, she advises that you reinforce others (and yourself) for nonconventional beauty choices. That way, you'll help to change the norm and increase the possibility of self-acceptance for yourself as well as others.[21]

2. Think of your body as presenting a whole picture to others. You may concentrate in the mirror on what you consider are your "big thighs" but other people are most likely to see the *entire* you. They are not likely to notice the parts of you that you consider flawed. Practice looking in the mirror and seeing — as other people do — the Total You. If you notice yourself loathing one of your body features, give yourself a command: "Cut it out, Self! Now is the time to develop more compassion for your face, your hips, and all those other fragmented parts that you've found unacceptable. They've suffered long enough."

Quit dwelling on the minutiae of your body parts so you'll be free of self-consciousness.

3. Give yourself permission to have body flaws. "If we saw the same models that appear in *Vogue* in the grocery store without their make-up and all their trappings, they would look just like us," says a woman. And, if we looked closely enough, we would see flaws. With the use of make-up artists, creative

lighting, and sensitive camera lenses, the media models present an inflated norm against which the average woman can't compete.

4. Interrupt negative self-talk. Remember, when you have what Marney called the "uglies," you are playing out messages in your head that were recorded perhaps fifteen, twenty, or thirty years ago.

One woman still remembers the pain of a comment made by the boy next door who said to her when she was thirteen, "I feel sorry for your parents because they're stuck with you forever. You're so ugly nobody would ever want to marry you." Never mind that this same male, now a grown adult, saw her twenty years later and told her she looked "like a million dollars." She still discounts that and agonizes over his comment and all the other negative messages she absorbed when she was young, gangling, and sensitive.

5. Value your body for how it works rather than how it looks. Urges Barbara Harris, editor-in-chief of the magazine *Shape:* "Recognize your body for what it is — a precious physical wonder through which you experience life. . . . Your body is not your adversary to be criticized and rebuked for not having the 'right' shape; rather it was meant to serve you."

Therefore, invest in your body and make exercise a fundamental part of your life, she encourages. "Through exercise, you will begin to relate to your body at a higher level. You will learn to respect it. You will hear its needs, feel its limits, and know the importance of resting and nurturing it. You will begin to see that your body is designed to fit *you* and no one else. You'll discover that your body responds to exercise in its own unique way, too — according to *your* genetics. . . . [And] you'll realize that your ideal body should never be found by looking in a mirror but by feeling and appreciating what your body does for you when it's in motion."[22]

Endorsing Yourself

As you fill in the self, it is vital that you embrace yourself for *who you are.* Walt Whitman aptly captured the essence of coming to terms with the self when he wrote: "Do I contradict myself? Very well, then, I contradict myself." Essentially, he is saying: "I am who I am, who I am, who I am. . . . And I embrace *all* that I am."

Endorsing yourself thus means accepting your fallibilities and limitations, without apology, as an innate and acceptable part of you.

This concept is captured in one woman's response: "I've been a poor speller since childhood, and I've accepted that I'll always have this problem. I've also come to love what Mark Twain says: that a person who doesn't know how to spell a word more than two ways is not very creative. I used to avoid writing letters because I never could catch all my spelling errors. Now I write letters and I simply say to my correspondents, 'Please just use your creativity to figure out what I'm saying.' "

Endorsing yourself also means accepting yourself as a being who has preferences that you need not defend. Illustrating this, a woman relates: "When we travel, my husband just throws everything in the suitcase and he's ready to go. But I'm different. It's important for me to plan out a trip in great detail, which usually takes me about three days. As I was preparing for our last trip, my husband kept criticizing my style. I finally said to him: 'I *like* planning trips and taking care of details. It's okay for me to be deliberate — I enjoy the trip more this way.' "

Endorsing yourself further means accrediting yourself for strengths rather than diminishing yourself for limitations or for growth not yet achieved. Says one woman: "I've made a list of things I can do, talents I have, resources I have to draw from, that I keep on my refrigerator. When I'm discouraged, I go to that list and remind myself of assets that can help me through the moment."

Endorsing yourself also means to affirm that self. Behavioral research indicates that as much as 77 percent of everything a person thinks is negative, counterproductive, and works against the self, says Shad Helmstetter, author of *The Self-Talk Solution*. He emphasizes that you have countless unnoticed but very potent patterned thoughts and phrases that constantly go through your mind. And, he asks, how can you possibly expect the best from your *self* when you tell that self things like these:

- I'm going nowhere at work.
- I have a problem with my weight.
- I just can't seem to get caught up.
- I have the worst memory.
- I'm no good at . . .
- I never seem to get a break!

How much better if the things you said worked for, rather than against, you, observes Helmstetter, who turns around the preceding phrases to demonstrate the contrast:

- I'm making progress at work.
- I'm getting in control of my weight.
- I'm getting caught up on everything.
- I have an excellent memory.
- I'm good at . . . .
- I'm fortunate that things go my way.[23]

The input or instructions you give yourself, of course, affect your choices and your self-esteem. Typically, many of your thoughts aren't within your conscious awareness or your control. But you can bring them to the fore for inspection by becoming an observer of what you're thinking. When you find negative thoughts about yourself, deliberately edit them out and insert positive thoughts in their stead. Adopting affirming statements will open for you a whole new vision of yourself and a greater appreciation of your inner strengths.

Finally, endorsing yourself involves the challenge of fully loving that self. Most people don't achieve this end "because they have learned all their lives that self-love is akin to conceit and selfishness, a personal quality to be held under strict control," says Harold Bloomfield, author of *Inner Joy*. This misguided belief is responsible for untold self-forfeiting behavior and self-made unhappiness.

Learning to love yourself means adopting a number of affirming behaviors, says Bloomfield. These may include:

- Giving yourself approval.
- Talking to yourself gently, with affection.
- Trusting your inner voice and intuition.
- Developing your full potential and creativity.
- Giving yourself the benefit of the doubt.
- Forgiving yourself.
- Having fun — lots of it!
- Being free and easy.
- Taking responsibility for yourself.
- Developing your own values and rules.
- Rewarding yourself when you deserve it.
- Taking risks for your own advancement.
- Feeling pleasure fully, knowing you deserve it.
- Liking your body.
- Taking care to look your best.
- Giving yourself permission to pursue your dreams.
- Providing yourself with life-supporting and enriching people.
- Surrounding yourself with beauty.
- Accepting freely the affection and compliments of others.[24]

Using these nurturing behaviors to endorse yourself will

aid you in achieving your full potential. The story is told of the Hasidic rabbi Zusya, who, on his deathbed, was asked about what he thought the kingdom of God would be like. "I don't know," he replied. "But one thing I *do* know. When I get there I am not going to be asked, 'Why weren't you Moses? Why weren't you David?' I am only going to be asked, 'Why weren't you Zusya? Why weren't you fully you?' "[25]

Chapter 10

Investing in Your "Self"

For a woman, a vital part of filling in the self involves investing in that self. Some women might say, "Whoa! I've tried to be open-minded and patient with this somewhat disconcerting 'new era' approach, but this is just too much. I can't invest in myself because (and here are the top four reasons) I'm—

—too busy.

—too tired.

—too preoccupied with taking care of other people. (*"They* need me more than *I* need me!" says one woman.)

—not deserving.

Now, if you're a too-tired/too-busy woman, you'll be happy to know that there is a new, improved approach for investing in yourself. Some women report taking mental health days, but now it is even possible to take mental health minutes! Even a too-tired/too-busy woman can use what Spencer Johnson calls the "One Minute" method for investing in the self. Johnson, the author of *The One Minute Manager* and an article entitled "Why Don't Women Take Care of Themselves?," observes: "Can you imagine what would happen if you raced your car across town without stopping at any of the stop signs — the injuries you would inflict on yourself and anyone unfortunate enough to cross your path?" That's exactly how some women play out their lives, Johnson claims. Essentially, what he is alluding to is that a woman needs to take her foot off the gas pedal and put her foot on the brake — she needs to stop what she is doing to evaluate where she is and what she needs.

There are 1,440 minutes in each day, says Johnson, who emphasizes that it is vital to spare a few of those minutes each day to begin creating balance in your life. Periodically using minutes, you can start tending to the person who most needs your care — you! — with the Stop, Look, and Listen approach.

The first step in this approach is to observe and obey your own mental stop sign, Johnson explains. Whatever you are doing: *Stop!*

Next, *Look!* Look at what you are thinking and doing. "Don't be critical. Don't make value judgments. Just notice what's going on. Observe yourself as if you were observing someone else. Be the witness of your own thoughts," advises Johnson.

After you have a mental picture of what is going on, spend a moment in total silence. Clear your mind and ask yourself: "How can I best nurture myself today?" Or, "How can I best nurture myself right now?" Now, *Listen!* "You may not hear anything at first, but be patient," Johnson says. "Do not analyze. Do not try to figure out the answer. You will only get lost in a maze of complicated thinking. The late Dr. Albert Einstein knew that figuring out is not how answers finally come. 'The answers come,' he reportedly said, 'while you're eating an apple.' "[1]

Turning to the third reason that deters a woman from investing in herself — "I'm too preoccupied with taking care of other people" — consider this question: "Why does *everyone else* come first, before you get anything?"

This question was posed to a woman by her very intuitive husband, a man who recognized his wife's propensity to take care of others at the expense of taking care of herself. The answer to his question is that his wife, like most other caretakers, is programmed to give, not to receive. Whenever she gets into unfamiliar territory—tending to herself (which is a receiving position)—her alarm buttons go off. The word *selfish* pops into her mind, and she tends to beat a hasty retreat.

One tentative woman says, "I try to take time out by leaving my husband with the kids but I always feel guilty, as though I'm inconveniencing him. I make sure everything is just perfect before I leave so things will go smoothly. I should be able to do what he does—just say 'I'm going fishing today' and walk out the door. But I can't. The silly thing is that I feel so grateful to my husband for letting me go anywhere!"

Do you remember a concept introduced earlier: "If you take care of *you,* you'll be in a much better spot to take care of *them"?* The position women need to take is analogous to the instructions passengers receive before an airplane takes off. Stresses one woman: "In event of an emergency, you're told to put on your own oxygen mask—and then help your children with their masks. Most mothers would put their children first—that's the unselfish thing to do—but what good are you to your children if you're dead? You have to take care of yourself first!"

The final reason women give for not investing in themselves—"I'm not deserving"—admittedly is tough to exorcise because many women do truly feel that they are not deserving. Not comfortably investing in themselves is another manifestation of the "I don't deserve it" syndrome discussed in chapter nine. One woman said, "I've always felt I'm only worth the sales rack." And another explains, "I've felt for years that there isn't enough money left over for me. I can buy for the kids, the house, the husband, the dog (the dog gets treats!), but not for myself."

A woman's trouble with investing in herself may not be over even if she has money. "While my children were home, I felt guilty if I spent any money on myself," a woman relates. "Now that my children are grown and I have a good job and discretionary money, I feel guilty because I can have anything I want. My guilt never ends!" This same woman might not think twice about spending seventy dollars on her daughter's prom dress — or buying the material and spending two weeks making it. But there is nothing for her. *If there's money left over, I'll use it,* she thinks. *And if there's time left over, I'll take it.* But there never is. And the woman waits. And she gets angry because no one is tending to her needs. And she doesn't see that the responsibility for taking care of herself rests foremost with her.

If this discussion has been at all convincing, and you want to consider ways of investing in yourself, read on for investment strategies especially designed for you. First of all, it is important to embrace this rather bold position:

"I'm going to invest in me. I'm worth it!"

Reports one well-intentioned woman: "I always say to myself, 'Today I must start exercising. Today I must practice my painting strokes.' Instead of that, I find myself going into the kitchen and making something for dinner that my husband would love."

Essentially, this woman chronically defaults to the position: Other people are worth it — I'm not! A much more viable position would be: Other people are worth it — and so am I.

Moving to the "I'm worth it" position is a long-term struggle for most women. Says one, "When I finished business college and needed an outfit to interview in, I went shopping and found a beautiful dress. It was perfect for me and I just looked spectacular in it. But I agonized over the decision to buy that dress. I felt guilty because I wasn't putting the money into food or my kids' clothes or shoes. I was thinking of getting something for me. After I finally bought the dress, I remember just sitting in the bedroom looking at it. I'd hang it in the closet and then take it out and look at it again. That's when it really hit me—how little I cared about myself. That happened several years ago. Since that time, I've been saying to myself, 'I deserve good treatment. I'm worth it.' But to this day, I still go to the sales rack first."

Feeling a surge of "I am actually worth it!" can be confusing to anyone who chronically operates from the reverse position. Says an evolving caretaker: "I went shopping, intending to pick up some tabs for my weekly planner. But then I got excited about all the things I saw. After I got home, I spread all the items I'd bought out on the bed just to savor them. And then my husband walked into the room. I looked at him and then it hit me: *He's* got a planner too—and I didn't buy these things for him! I was stunned because ordinarily I would have bought the very same things—but they would have been for *him* and for *his* book. I would have waited until some indeterminate 'later' to get accessories for my book. I was shocked because this was a new role for me. I actually hadn't thought about him! I felt as if I had been caught doing something terrible. I resolved the conflict with myself by asking my husband if he would like me to pick up any of the items for him. Then I thought, *My new response is certainly a more balanced one. But am I getting TOO released?*"

Investing in yourself doesn't mean that you give more to yourself than to someone else. It simply means that you give as much. Typically, women have difficulty with this concept— a point illustrated in a story Marcy tells about her mother:

"My mother and I went to a department store and she

started looking at some men's shirts that were on sale. 'Oh, this one would look so nice on your father, and these would look nice on your brothers,' she said, gathering an assortment of shirts together. As she carried the shirts to a cashier, she passed through the women's department, pointed to a dress, and said, 'Oh, Marcy, that is the most gorgeous dress I have ever seen. But I can't buy it—it costs fifty dollars! Besides, I have to buy these shirts for your dad and your brothers.' She purchased the shirts, which came to 115 dollars. As we walked out of the store, she suddenly paused and looked pensively at me. 'You know what?' she said. 'I could have gotten that beautiful dress for less than half the money I spent on these shirts.' 'I know, Mom,' I said. 'And besides, everyone in our family has an overabundance of shirts.' She started walking again. 'You're right,' she said—and she took the shirts home!"

Invariably, when Marcy's mother is confronted with the decision of whether or not she counts, she defaults to this position: *Other people count. I don't.* With regard to investing in herself, she needs to gravitate to this spirited stance: *They count—and I count too!*

You may need to steel yourself to get yourself in the "I count" position. This is no small challenge. One woman describes her struggle to "count" as she tried to get into a routine of walking for half an hour every evening: "For weeks I tried to take that walk, but most of the time I found myself distracted and my plans scuttled by my children, who would say things like, 'But Mommmmmmm, don't go *now!* I need help with my homework' or 'I need to go to the store right away!' And so I would stay home to help until it was too late to take the walk. Finally, I realized I was going to have to clear a very firm space for myself if I was actually going to get into a walking routine. I said to my children, 'You get me almost all evening, but from 6:30 to 7:00 is my time for *me.* It's my sanity time. If you need me, please work around that time.'After that, it wasn't hard to walk. And frequently I would hear my children cautioning each other: 'Don't ask mother right now because she has to take her walk. It's her sanity time.' "

The woman who perseveres in counting in herself despite opposition from the "theys" of this world can count on rewards. One homemaker explains: "I suffered for months over a decision to take an art class because it cost money. When I finally went, it was so illuminating that it was almost like there was a light in the room. I thought I had died and gone to heaven. I looked at the others in the class to see if they were enjoying it as much as I was. When I showed my first drawing to my kids, they were so excited about it that they put it on the refrigerator. To them, now mom wasn't just mom. She had become Mom — The Artist!"

As you invest in yourself, perhaps the most luxurious thing you can do is give yourself permission to enjoy a few hours alone every week. Diedre Laiken, in an article entitled "How to Make Friends with Yourself," speaks of committing time to herself: "It seems like only yesterday that practically my whole life was devoted to loading and unloading the washing machine, the dishwasher, the family car. I've always kept frantically busy, taking care of everyone's needs and rarely considering my own. Then, one spring, I decided to steal a few minutes to check on the tulip bulbs I'd hastily planted in the fall."

Those few minutes changed her life. In experiencing a moment of rare serenity, she began to wonder what life would be like if she scheduled private time on a regular basis. She then committed herself to experience daily small but potent new pleasures — perusals through glossy magazines, walks in the rain, strolls down residential streets, and trips to museums.

She observed, concerning the new world that opened to her, "We all have vast, mysterious, inner worlds, but few of us take the time to explore that terrain. We get so embroiled in our fast-paced lives and in nurturing and supporting others that we lose touch with an important part of ourselves. True, it takes a bit of courage to begin, but if you're like me, you'll come to treasure your prime time. You might even discover an exciting old friend you've missed for a long time — yourself!"[2]

Assume Responsibility for Your Growth and Maintenance

One challenge in investing in yourself is that of taking full responsibility for your own growth and maintenance. Sometimes that may mean representing your growth needs to other people.

If you are married, you may be fortunate to have a husband who supports your growth. One woman recalls, "A music teacher encouraged me to take voice lessons when I was thirty years old. I thought thirty was too late — but my husband said, 'How old will you be if you don't take lessons?' I took the lessons."

Whether single or married, you may be fortunate to have others — parents, relatives, or friends — who clap and cheer when they see you doing something for yourself.

But what if you don't readily receive the support you want for expanding that self? What will you do? Will you cave in and use someone else's resistance as an excuse not to grow? Or will you represent yourself?

One woman admits: "I do cave in. I back-pedal fast when something I want to do is inconvenient for someone else or makes that person unhappy. I have to have a pretty clear go-ahead from someone else in order not to feel guilty about doing something for myself." Waiting for permission, or caving in, is a way of "de-selfing" — of abnegating responsibility for your own guardianship and for your own growth.

*"We have a lot in common—
my best years are ahead of me, too!"*

To take charge of you and to represent yourself, you must first view yourself as a being with legitimate needs. That's a tough issue for most women. Says one, "The only way I allow myself to take time out, even when I'm deeply exhausted, is if I'm sick. Sometimes I've even wished I could be ill enough to enter the hospital for a while so I could have a real excuse to rest." Another one says, "I can meet a need of mine only if I have a good reason."

Many women feel that they aren't supposed to have needs, and, if one inadvertently surfaces, they often feel guilty and consequently set that need aside and resort to self-denial. But there are decided psychological costs to this behavior. In an article entitled "Confessions of an Unfit Mother," author Andrea Thompson writes that women have always "lopped off the purely private pleasures when the hours can't stretch anymore, and regarded the amputation with feelings running from anger to wistfulness to self-righteousness." There is a movement in the offing, however, that tells women their needs are important

too, she says. This undeniable, wonderful, life-giving message — one that women have needed to give themselves for too
long — conveys the idea that "along with getting to work on
time and seeing that the kids eat breakfast, and planning birthday parties, and seeing that your husband has fresh shirts in
the drawer, it's fit and proper and good for everybody that you
take a leisurely bath or a long walk or read Jane Austen or
study the guitar."[3]

Take a moment to ask yourself: What kind of needs do you,
as a separate self, have? You may ache for more nurturance or
fulfillment in a number of areas. Do you need, for example,

• more private time?

• more time alone with a spouse; or, if you're single, with
a male friend; or simply with other adults?

• more appreciation?

• more affection?

• more sexual or nonsexual intimacy?

• more fun and recreation in your life?

• more time to rest or relax?

• more time to develop a talent or interest?

• more access to decision-making that affects your life?

• more sharing of ideas or thoughts with others?

• more emotional or spiritual intimacy?

• more support for personal needs and goals?

• more influence in financial affairs?

• more help with household tasks or with children?

• more opportunities for low-risk, nurturing communication?

• more time for taking personal care of yourself — for
grooming, for styling, for learning, for updating, for physical
and emotional upkeep?

You, as a forever evolving and growing being, need a self-
maintenance, repair, and enhancement program. And you need

to be the one to develop that program. No one else can consistently keep in touch with your needs or consistently represent those needs to others. You're the one who is elected to acknowledge and clarify the needs you have. That is good news because it means you no longer need to wait for someone else to do the job for you.

Assume Responsibility for Your Own Happiness

Another challenge in investing in yourself is that of taking responsibility for your own happiness. Think for a moment. Who makes you happy or unhappy? Your husband? Your parents? Your children? Maybe your friends or boss?

In your head, you'd probably acknowledge: "I'm the one who makes myself happy or unhappy." Though intellectually you believe you are responsible for your own happiness, in your heart you may still hold other people responsible.

If you are like most people (men are included in this category, too!), you have been tricked into thinking that it's the job of other people to fill you up or to make you happy—and you may attribute your unhappiness to others failing in their duty.

Consider Lynn. After an exhausting day with the children, she expects her husband (who has had an exhausting day at work) to make her happy in the evenings. She is continually disappointed there isn't more conversation, more companionship, more cuddling. And so she complains. She is angry and hurt. *Randy makes me so unhappy,* she thinks. But what her husband, Randy, wants is less pressure, less talk, less aggravation, so he typically doesn't respond to her complaints.

Tracy has a similar problem. Despite enduring twenty-five years of her mother's favoring her brother over her, Tracy still expects her mother to respond to her overtures and give her equal attention — so she is constantly disappointed. "My mother always hurts me," she laments.

Both Lynn and Tracy are making the same mistake: setting themselves up for pain by expecting behaviors that others aren't providing. In essence, both women are making themselves unhappy and blaming others for their distress.

Fortunately, you — not others — are the one in charge of whether or not you will be happy. You have the power to control your mental world. Author Wayne Dyer suggests that if someone says to you, "Think of a pink antelope," you yourself "can turn it green or make it an aardvark or simply think of something else if you choose. You alone control what enters your head and if you don't believe this, just answer the question, 'If you don't control your thoughts, who does?' "[4] You can think differently by operating from the premise that the locus of control for your happiness or your unhappiness resides in your head and not in other people or things.

Recognizing that she causes her own feelings, Lynn might say, for example, "I continually upset myself when Randy doesn't respond to me the way I'd like. What I'm doing is blaming Randy for angry and hurt feelings I generate in myself. I need to alter my thoughts and feelings so I don't wound myself over his behavior. And I need to initiate action to get my needs met by appealing to him in positive ways that might influence him to respond to those needs."

Likewise, Tracy might say: "I continually distress myself and leave myself vulnerable by expecting my mother to respond in positive ways that she is either not able or not willing to do. I need to quit expecting anything from her so I don't continually hurt myself. I have to change — my mother's not going to. And if I want something from her, I need to ask for what I want."

As you work at taking charge of you, notice the kinds of

expectations you have of others. Do you always expect those close to you to do what you want? to understand you or know what you need? to keep you from being lonely? to make you feel good about yourself? Try releasing others from such unrealistic expectations. Remember, making yourself happy is your job.

Assess also if you chronically blame people or things for what is going wrong in your life, thus putting the focus outside of yourself. To move, focus inward on your own thoughts, feelings, choices, and possibilities, and take the position that you are in charge. Your life will change when *you* decide to change and refuse to let any person or situation become an excuse for becoming inert or defining your life as outside your control.

Because of embedded cultural programming, guess whom women are most likely to blame for their unhappiness. If the word *men* popped into your mind, you're right on the money. Women are notorious for failing to see themselves in charge of their choices, their own development, or their own futures when they are in relationships with men.

Too often, says Julia Cameron, a woman may enter a relationship as her own person, only to find that the man she loves soon thinks of her as an extension of his own personality. Worse yet, so does she. "The trap that so many of us tumble into begins in the traditional language of love," says Cameron. "You're my own true love, my woman, my wife, the mother of my children. . . . It's true that a woman may be all those things—and happily—for the man she loves. The trap lies in forgetting she is also someone else—herself." Keeping themselves intact once they have married remains a considerable challenge for many women. Observes Cameron: "Too often when a woman says, 'I do,' what evolves is 'I don't'—I don't do any of the things I used to do, see any of the friends I used to see; in fact, I don't see myself anymore. I do not recognize the woman I have become . . . and I barely remember the woman I was."[5]

Unfortunately, a woman can sabotage herself and set herself up for a life of disillusionment when she submerges herself in her husband's personality and buys into the myth that he, as a magical protector, will always take care of her and make her unfailingly happy. In fact, burdening her husband with the entire responsibility for her happiness puts an impossible burden on the relationship.

One woman says: "Over a period of years I became chronically disillusioned with my marriage and angry at my husband. I was empty, and I expected him to fill me up. But he was invested in his work and just wasn't there for me very often. We lived out his life-style, relating to his friends, always doing what he wanted. And I lived on the sidelines of his life, supporting him, being his cheerleader, paving the way, and making his life easier. My value resided in being his wife, not in being myself. Gradually, however, I began to confront the deep sense of emptiness and lack of focus within myself that had always nagged at me. I realized there was very little of me left—that I didn't really even know who I was anymore. Finally, I decided it was not my husband who was the problem. *I* was the one who had kept myself from growing, not him. From that moment on, I decided to stop blaming him and to carve out a life and a self for me within our marriage."

For many women, defining a "self" means taking back power over their own lives that they have assigned to others and acting to find interests and activities of their own. Roger Gould, in his book *Transformations,* writes: "For women who've lived in a traditional marriage until their mid-life decade, going back to work or starting a career is only one way to support and affirm their new sense of who they are. A woman does not need to go back to work to take back her power. She can use her self-determined freedom as she will. Some women pursue interests in politics, or in social, cultural or artistic endeavors. It matters only that women use their powers without reservation to pursue *something*."[6]

To take charge of your life, you need to think of yourself as in the process of becoming. A fixed image of self is the kiss of death to growth. Daniel J. Levinson, the author of *The Seasons of a Man's Life,* says, "My view is that there is a kind of growing up to do in each season of the life cycle. No matter how much growing up we do, there is always more to do after a while."[7]

Assume Responsibility for Growing Up and Out

Everyone incurs some growth and maturity in this life simply by happenstance — that is, simply by riding out various life crises and by growing older. The question is, of course, whether you want to leave your growth to chance or, as the guardian of yourself, to plan systematically for the development of that self.

You come into this life an empty vessel and you spend the rest of your life filling that vessel — sometimes through experiences you choose, sometimes through experiences not within your own control. You, of course, can increase the probability of growth by creating more opportunities of your own making. According to new and extensive research, diversifying yourself is good for your health.

In earlier decades, opportunities for a woman to grow were limited and her choices were restricted to the home, says Nela S. Schwartzberg, author of the article "Call Me Supermom." Conventional wisdom dictated that assuming any role beyond taking care of her husband and children was too taxing for her. Her supply of emotional stamina and energy was viewed as limited, and it was thought that she would overtax her resources by taking on a strong commitment to anything else. She would end up burned-out, overwrought, and suffering from psychological and physical problems. However, times have changed. Reviewing research studies, Schwartzberg reports: "Women with multiple roles report better health, less psychological distress, and a greater sense of self-esteem and satisfaction with their lives." These results apply not only to women in the workplace but also to women with multiple societal roles who do not hold paying jobs. "Busier is better," she says decisively.[8]

Why are multiple roles better for women? One reason is the manner in which having more roles affects a woman's self-esteem. Paula Piertromonaco, who helped conduct one of the studies referred to earlier, observes: "The more roles you have, the more likely you are to interact with different people and get feedback about yourself. This allows you to define yourself in different ways — competent and creative at work, supportive and loving at home, intelligent at school." The roles a woman holds give her purpose and meaning, tell her who she is, and give her a more positive, complex, and differentiated view of herself, she continues: "Adding roles adds to our sense of identity, while losing a role diminishes it."[9]

Multiple roles also offer a form of protection from unfortunate events and problems, points out Schwartzberg: "A woman who is not involved in outside activities has, in a sense, put all her emotional eggs into one basket. Death, divorce, or separation can leave such a woman without a sense of meaning or purpose."[10]

Assume Responsibility for Your Own Welfare

As you consider ways of investing in yourself, it is vital to look at today's woman and the profound cultural changes that have an impact on her. If you are a younger woman, one implication of these cultural changes is this: *Whether or not you choose to be in the workplace, investing in education and/ or marketable skills represents an asset and an insurance policy in today's society.*

Consider what has happened to women over the past few decades. It used to be that the question of where a woman should be was clear: Her place was in the home. Consistent with the cultural message, then, that is where most women were twenty or thirty years ago. Today they are not. Sixty percent of women today are in the workplace. By the year 2000 the projection is 75 percent. And predictions regarding women and the workplace are startling. Says one source: "Today's young women are likely to spend thirty or more years in the paid work force. A married woman with no children will work an estimated thirty-five years. A mother of two will work twenty-two years. Even a woman with four or more children will spend seventeen years in paid jobs. Only one out of ten women will never work outside the home."[11]

What has caused the dramatic shift of women from the home to the workplace? For one thing, sweeping cultural changes over the past several decades have brought great stress to bear on families. Forces such as double-digit inflation, soaring divorce rates, and skyrocketing housing, medical, and educational costs have caused an accelerating economic burden on families. "No one quite bargained for the Middle-Class Squeeze . . . [the phenomenon of] falling behind while getting ahead," says a *Time* article. As a result of these changes, it now often takes two paychecks to fund what many have imagined is a middle-class life.[12]

The shift of women to the workplace has occurred for yet another important reason. Though many changes over the past several decades have been positive for women, others have not been good to them. Dramatic cultural shifts, some related

*"I've come back to school to study carpentry
and mechanics. I'm rebuilding my life."*

to the women's movement, have "pulled the rug" out from beneath many and, in a sense, betrayed them.

Three or so decades ago a woman felt secure if she but lived to be married and, once married, dedicated herself to merging with a man and raising their children. Her investment was to be in others, not in herself. Her man would take care of her and make her happy.

But times have changed. In essence, today's cultural message is that, in addition to others, a woman must also take care of herself. She must be prepared to sustain both herself and her children in the eventuality of divorce. She can no longer count on the traditional position of "being saved" by a man. The laws that once supported and protected women in that position are gone.

The goal in changing traditional family laws has been to achieve justice by treating husbands and wives as equals, but the inadvertent result has been to put women at a disadvantage. A divorced woman today can expect her standard of living in the first year after her divorce to fall by an average of 73 percent, while the divorced man can expect his standard to increase an average of 42 percent, says Leonore J. Weitzman, author of *The Divorce Revolution.* "Traditional family law established a clear moral framework for a lifetime commitment. The required grounds and the need to prove fault made divorce difficult—and expensive. If she was 'innocent,' the wife of a propertied man could expect lifetime alimony and the family home. The law gave the spouse who wanted to remain married considerable bargaining power." However, new sex-neutral laws have "redefined marriage as a time-limited, contingent arrangement rather than a lifelong commitment. They shifted the state from protecting marriage to facilitating divorce. Family responsibilities can now be terminated soon after divorce."[13]

As a result, in today's world an award of alimony is out of the question for all but the most senior of homemakers, and transitional support to women is provided for shorter and shorter periods. The support awards for children are minimal (the average award is $126 a month for one child and $195 for two or more) and, in over half the cases, full child support is not paid.[14]

One outcome of changed laws has been to create conditions of poverty for staggering numbers of women and children. ("Many women are just one man away from poverty," says one woman.) Another outcome has been to thrust millions of displaced homemakers—women who trusted the cultural message that they would be taken care of—out into the workplace without the skills to command an adequate wage.

Observes Colette Dowling, author of *The Cinderella Complex:* "Women today are caught in a crossfire between old and radically new social ideas, but the truth is, we cannot fall back on the old 'role' anymore. It's not functional; it's not a true option. 'The prince' has vanished."[15]

We must recognize, Dowling stresses, "the connection between the false security we connect with being wives and the loneliness and poverty of older, often widowed women. You begin . . . making the connection . . . once you look at the economic plight of older women in this country. While everyone's talking about choice, we might more profitably ask ourselves, 'Who takes care of women once they get old?' The answer is, of course, no one. By the time women's hair has turned gray, the old 'women-and-children' support system has long since fallen away. Reality hits hard when the men die off. More than one out of two women can expect to be a widow by the age of sixty-five. And even those women who spend their adult lives working are not protected in old age; one out of four of them will be poor — much poorer than men the same age."[16]

The implication of these sobering statistics is different for different women, depending on such factors as their age, financial assets, number of children, marital status, and the stability of their marriages. As far as your own situation is concerned, only you can make judgments regarding ways in which to invest in yourself. *You* know your situation. *You* know what is best for you.

Regardless of how you invest in yourself and further your growth, it will take time and commitment to develop *you*. In expanding yourself — in growing up and in growing out — you may find helpful the philosophy espoused by Jo Coudert, author of the article "Help for Your Hardest Decisions." When Coudert told her painting-workshop instructor that she might go to art school in the fall, he merely remarked: "The next five years will go by anyway." At that, Coudert thought, "What's that supposed to mean?" After considerable contemplation, she understood. The next five years were going to go by anyway, whether she did something or nothing. Now, whenever faced with an important choice, she tells herself, "The next five years will go by anyway." This, she relates, "clarifies choices in a wonderful way." She concludes: "Your life isn't a practice run, a warm-up for the real thing. This is *it*. Don't let life get away from you by default. Remember that all the years you have will go by anyway and only by making good choices can you truly say you have lived those years."[17]

Chapter 11

The Woman and Work

Preliminary to a discussion of women and work, consider this proverb by Hester Mundis:[1] *"There is no such thing as a nonworking mother."*

In question is not *whether* a woman is working, but *where* she is working, because all women have twenty-four-hour-a-day, seven-day-a-week jobs. And whether a woman chooses a career exclusively at home or splits her time between work in the workplace and work at home, she is plagued with issues. Consider first the woman who stays home. This woman has to cope with job conditions you would never find in a formal office.

"In an office, someone tells you that Thing One has to be out of here by noon, but we don't need Thing Two until Tuesday, and there you are. The work is vertical," writes author Barbara Holland. However, there is nothing vertical about housework, no reasonable arrangements of jobs in order of their importance in the *home* workplace. Rather, housework is horizontal: "It all has to be done all the time, and nothing is on top, and most of the time you have to do the first thing again before you've even gotten to the third thing. And other things keep clamoring for their turn so you can't concentrate and you burn the potatoes or leave out something major like picking up Billie after band practice."[2]

Who would like to have a job like that?

"I would," say many homemakers. But the going is tough in an era that offers women many competing choices. Consider this group discussion among today's homemakers about the typical dilemmas they experience:

"I like staying home, doing my job, but every time I read another article about a successful heroine juggling family and career, I feel pangs of inadequacy."[3]

"Me, too! When you come right down to it, it's still embarrassing to say, when people ask you what you do, 'I'm a homemaker.' It doesn't feel like it's enough to say."[4]

"The job of homemaker is simply whited out. A typical example occurred at a luncheon recently. 'Meet Linda. She's an accountant.' Then, 'Meet _____ (introducing me). Her husband teaches at the college.' No wonder my sense of identity periodically goes into crisis."[5]

"Child raising has also gotten bad press. Instead of 'How are the kids,' I hear, 'What's a smart woman like you doing at home?'"

"I get the 'no-paycheck blues.' To me, a paycheck is an absolute standard, an indicator of performance and achievement, a medal. Without a paycheck, there's no objective standard indicating that I've done enough and that not only can I relax — I can also feel good about myself. That leaves me searching. 'Am I doing okay today?' 'Where does my job end?' I never achieve a sense of completion."

"I've lost confidence in my abilities. Even if the principal of my school was waiting for me with open arms, I'd be scared at first. You're out of the work routine and it's hard to get back in. It's like suddenly lifting a hundred-pound weight with muscles you haven't used in years."[6]

"I worry about going back into the workforce. My skills are getting rusty, and I know I'll have to start from the bottom again. That's hard to take."

"Since I quit work, I wake up every morning and realize I'm in charge of filling my own time. There are no coworkers, no clearcut routines, no praise for accomplishments, no reason to dress for success, no superior to answer to, no one to notice if you hang out in a bathrobe all day. That's kind of a shock."[7]

"Now that I'm home, I miss talking to adults and dressing up, and I especially miss compliments. At home, no one ever says to me: 'You did a good job vacuuming' or 'My shirts look so good!' "

Homemakers are in a tough position, and they aren't getting any support, concludes one woman. "Absolutely no woman's magazine is addressing our needs," she says. "The articles on stress and the beauty makeovers are for women in the office. The sexy, glamorous lady is the lady on the job. The housewife looks harassed and dowdy. The mother at home has been edited out—abandoned."[8]

Can you feel the discontent and disillusionment—even puzzlement—of these homemakers who are experiencing a bias against staying home?

To what do women owe this disconcerting state of affairs?

Susan Jacoby, author of the article "In Praise of Imperfect Women," expounds on this question: "As women's choices have expanded, so have the varieties of their defensiveness and guilt. Women of my mother's generation, who raised families in the fifties, expected to be full-time homemakers and felt assured of social approval in that role. . . . Today, just about any choice is likely to make a woman feel she ought to apologize." Times have changed for homemakers, who can no longer expect unqualified approval for staying home with their children, she adds. "Those glossy images of women in dress-for-success suits convey to many housewives, not an invitation but a command, rather like those old Army recruiting posters saying, 'Uncle Sam Wants YOU.' They feel it is somehow antisocial not to enlist in the work force—that they are denying themselves the personal satisfaction of a paying job and their families the economic advantages of a second income."[9]

"I know just what's she's saying," one woman responds. "I don't feel I can win either way, and it's hard to decide what to do. I stay home for a while, and then people say to me, 'Oh, you don't work? That's too bad. What do you do all day? Is it sofa and bon-bons?' So then I decide to go to work, and they say, 'Oh, you leave your family and go out and work. That's too bad. Aren't you cheating your children?' "

And how do women feel who have made the plunge and are out in the workforce? Here is a representative sample of such work-at-work/work-at-home women discussing their unique struggles. Says each in turn:

"I'm a woman who wants to work, but it does cause problems. I learned long ago that it's impossible to be a super housekeeper if I am to do my chosen work. But when I visit someone else's beautiful home, I think with a pang how mine *might* look and acknowledge to myself that I like housework— that I honestly enjoy cooking a meal at leisure, making a room shine, cleaning out drawers and closets."[10]

"I'm a woman who doesn't want to work outside my home, but I don't have a choice. So I often feel resentful and then I feel guilty about that because I've got a good life."

"It's tough to be in the workplace. I brood about all of those hours in my child's day when I'm not there. Does she get enough of me, evenings and weekends? If I'd been home, would she know how to print her name by now? Would she be less of a bully in the playground? Would she remember to say please when she asks for apple juice and thank you when she gets it?"[11]

"I wonder if my children can get from day-care what they get from me? Even if they are well cared for, mightn't they come out sort of homogenized? I want my special print on my children—not someone else's."[12]

"The worst days for me are those days when my son is home sick and I have to go to the office. Of course, I always make sure someone is home with him but shouldn't I be the one taking care of him?"[13]

"No matter how much we need the money, no matter how important our jobs are to our sense of ourselves as adults, a prim little inner voice says, 'Selfish, selfish. This is the only childhood they'll ever have, and it seems you're blowing it.' "[14]

"Although I'm sometimes relieved to be away from my children, that causes major guilt. What kind of a woman doesn't see her child all day and then is happy to continue not seeing her into the evening? Is this a fit mother? Even the Wicked Witch of the West, if she had children, probably looked forward to her time with them after a hard day riding on her broomstick and scaring the Munchkins."[15]

"On the other hand, I'm a better parent because I'm working. I don't lose my temper as often, and since I don't have to spend every minute of my day changing diapers or getting my child more juice, these chores now seem more like privileges."[16]

"I'm always playing 'catch-up' at work and then I go home and play 'catch-up' at home. I don't dare stop pushing myself to get things done because everything comes crashing down on my head."

"I feel guilty leaving work when other people are toiling

overtime, but I feel worse if I don't make it home in time to make dinner."

"But at least you're making your family a home-cooked meal. I'm always feeling guilty because my family has to eat so much pizza."

Reporting on the guilt that the work-at-work/work-at-home woman experiences, Jacoby observes that such a woman is "certainly hands down the winner in the defensiveness sweep-stakes. The possibilities for guilt are endless. An attack can be triggered by anything from feeding the kids fast food more than once a week to sending a child off to school with the sniffles. The divorced mother has it especially hard. She has the added burden of trying to explain why she is divorced—to herself and the rest of the world."[17]

"That's just the tip of the iceberg," responds a divorced woman who knows. "I always feel guilty about my children and here's a perfect example: I tried to sign up Jennifer for dance classes. But because I work on Wednesdays, she can't have the class she needs. And it just breaks my heart to take my children to day-care. So I try to overcompensate. I buy them things and take them places rather than sitting down and reading stories and watching a movie. Add to that a divorce, and not a day goes by that I don't hurt about the divorce for their sake. I look at them and think, 'They don't deserve this.' I'm envious of couples who are still married. My best friend just had her second baby, and she and her husband are a wonderful couple—and I am angry!"

Karen Levine, author of an article entitled "The Satisfaction Factor," points to the work dilemma today's women are ex-periencing. Citing findings from a study indicating that 40 per-cent of the mothers surveyed who work outside the home would rather be at home with their children, and 40 percent of the mothers at home with their children would rather work outside the home, Levine observes: "When I first encountered this finding, I thought about the proverbial grass that's always greener elsewhere.... 'What's wrong with women?' I wondered. 'Why can't we be satisfied with what we've got?' Then I realized that the source of widespread marital dissatisfaction might have little to do with women personally. Rather it may be the result of living and working in a culture that is unresponsive to the needs of families with children."

Continuing, she says: "Women who work outside the home might manage to avoid the economic stress of being a single income family, but they pay for it with concern about who watches their children. And women who stay home with their children, thereby avoiding the problems associated with child care, pay for their decision by suffering the economic stress of maintaining a family on one income. It is, to be sure, a no-win situation."[18]

The sad fact is that mother guilt of one sort or another is unavoidable, observes Elizabeth Crow, editor-in-chief of *Parents Magazine*. As "the best educated generation of parents in our country's history . . . we were raised to find satisfaction in work, as well as in our family life. We're a transitional generation, too, struggling to find new ways of living and working."[19]

In the writings of many female authors is this repeated theme: There is no way a woman can do it all—or have it all! Jacoby, for example, observes: "Some decisions that bring greater satisfaction in one part of a woman's life are bound to cause a degree of dislocation in other areas. A woman with pre-school children may have to pass up a promotion if it demands too much of her time. A mother with a full-time job will certainly miss some of the special moments with children that a mother at home enjoys. And a mother at home will probably feel she is missing something in the world outside—

even if she is firmly convinced that full-time motherhood is best for her and her family. It is impossible to 'have it all' without some conflicts, compromises, or losses."[20]

These same writers emphasize that women will have to make choices. Declares one: "Choices abound and the manner in which a woman's life is divided between work and home, between her own needs and the needs of those she loves should be as individual as her fingerprints."[21]

Another adds: "Maybe the pressing question isn't really whether or not we should work. Rather, it's how can we achieve a balance between work and the responsibility of parenting. When a baby is on one end of the metaphorical seesaw, a mere ten pounds can feel like a ton. Working and mothering may be at odds in a woman's life but to achieve peace of mind we must somehow make our working world fit in sync with the world of our children."[22]

Reformulated slightly, perhaps the pressing question is this: How can we achieve a healthy balance in the mix of three aspects of our lives: parenting, our own personal care and development (whether or not this includes paid work), and our own relationships, including a possible one with a spouse?

The Woman and Her Options

Once the question of a woman's working is posed in terms of needs — her children's needs, her needs, her husband's needs — a host of creative possibilities and solutions that suit a woman's unique circumstances, interests, talents, convictions, and family needs are available. Choosing what fits best for her and her family will help to alleviate guilt. When a woman puts herself in the actor role and actively moves to create conditions that conform to her needs and those of her family, she is in charge of the course of her life and will feel more content with any decision she makes.

Believing that whatever you are doing is by choice will enhance your self-esteem, says Mary Howell, a physician and author of the article "The Best Kind of Mother." After extensive review of research regarding women and work choices, she stresses: "It is clear that mothers who want to hold paid jobs and do so—and mothers who want to stay home with their children and do so—are, comparatively speaking, happier with themselves and function better as mothers than those who wish they were at home but feel they must hold a paid job, and those who wish they were working at a paid job, but can't for whatever reason."[23]

Unfortunately, often women don't have a choice. Many have to work to help support their families, whether they like it or not, and many others are the sole support of their families. Almost one family in four is headed by a woman these days, and the number is steadily increasing. Thus, for many women the choice is not whether they work but how well they adjust to working and whether they feel guilty about it. Emphasizes Howell: "Ten years ago, when the great working-mother debate began, it heated up quickly because the issue was believed to involve an element of choice; women could stay home if they chose to."

At that time, she continues, "We were discussing the pleasures of an extra paycheck, but those days are gone. Now we are almost always talking about a no-choice situation—in many instances it is not the extra paycheck but the *only* paycheck that is in question. In greater numbers than anyone is acknowledging, women are *the* breadwinners for their families in this country today."[24]

Though today's woman may have no choice regarding employment, she may have choices regarding a creative work schedule that meets more of her needs than today's traditional nine-to-five job. Alternative job schedules are becoming a more accepted possibility in today's business world. Points out Wendy Lowe, author of an article entitled "Working My Way Back to You, Babe," "more and more women (and a small but growing number of men) are quietly finding ways to minimize the conflict between their roles as parents and employees. They reevaluate their goals, deciding where they want to spend what seems to be an ever-shrinking pool of time. They stick by their priorities, negotiating with employers, caregivers, and spouses for the help they need. Most important, they work hard to strike a delicate balance between meeting the needs of their children and the demands of a career." Creating the "rational life" may be "as sticky as working a jigsaw puzzle covered with peanut butter," she says, but it is possible.[25]

One option women are choosing is that of sequencing. The woman who can't do it all at once can do it in smaller, more manageable pieces. Says Lois Wyse, an author who has written about her own experience with sequencing: "It truly is possible to arrange one's life in segments: a time for wiving, a time for careering, a time for mothering." Wyse suggests that women create their own ten- or twelve-year plans. "I believe women will have to decide not only what to give and what to keep—but *when*, she says. "We're going to have to decide what part of our lives we'll sacrifice now to make other parts work. But—I don't think these decisions have to be made once for a lifetime, and that's what's different about choices now from those of a generation ago. We assumed that each choice was forever."[26]

Another option gaining in popularity is that of working part-time. This option, for millions of women, is "the greatest thing since sliced bread," observes an expert, who continues: "What's really new about this growth in the part-time labor market is that companies are starting to realize they can save time and money and gain flexibility by paying workers only when they're needed."

And women may increase their mental health by working part-time. Recent research findings revealed that mothers who worked part-time were generally better adjusted than mothers who stayed at home or who worked full-time.[27]

Another option is beginning to develop and may in the not-too-distant future be readily accessible to women. The option? "Telecommuting." Says a forecaster: "About two million Americans now 'telecommute' to work each day, and experts say that the number could more than double by the mid-1990s. Telecommuting via computer, fax machine and other electronic links will increase job satisfaction. Another benefit: Skills will be much more transferrable. . . . If you lose your job in Butte, Montana, you might be able to get another one, telecommuting to New York City, without even having to move."[28]

Other options available to women are flextime, an arrangement that allows full-time employees to work nontraditional hours; job-sharing, which allows two employees to share a fulltime position, and V-time — voluntary, temporary reduction in working hours sometimes taken by women after childbirth.

In thinking about full-time versus part-time work and a traditional versus a flexible work schedule, you may also be contemplating another choice: a fast-track (an intense focus on moving up in a company, which has the benefit of consistent raises and promotions and the limitation of little flexibility for family life) versus what has come to be known as a "mommy track" (a nontraditional track that has the benefit of special accommodations for family and the limitation of reduced opportunities).

A third choice for women — a choice that is currently in an embryonic stage — is developing. Author Betty Holcomb observes that a growing number of companies are creating new

"Welcome to the mommy track!"

options for women that will provide flexibility without serious penalty to careers. But, she warns, these opportunities are just now emerging in the workplace and "scaling back at work entails some risk" to the woman who wants to focus intently on both career and family.[29] Thus, it is important to analyze carefully both job-related and family goals in view of company opportunities, in order to make an informed choice about your future.

To increase the possibility that a flexible arrangement will work for both your career and your family, Holcomb recommends the following:

• Make your goals known. "Tell your boss, 'I want to advance. What would that require?' "

• Be available for important meetings to show that you're a team player.

• Keep in touch by phone, even on your day off.

• Hang on to high-profile jobs. Don't give up any plum assignment.

• Keep abreast of office politics. Check with friends to keep on top of changes that could affect your status or duties.

• Document your value through memos and informal conversations with management.

"With these precautions," notes Holcomb, "you can make sure that a temporary lull in your momentum doesn't turn into a permanent derailment."[30] Speaking to women who plan to stay in the workforce, even if they take time out for a maternity leave or a period of raising children, Lori B. Andrews, author of an article entitled "The Working Mommy's Game," also recommends moving-ahead strategies: "Keeping on top of your field is especially important. . . . Staying in contact with co-workers, retaining a minimal involvement in your professional organization, or even using your particular skills in a volunteer activity can keep your talents up-to-date."[31]

Women, Work Choices, Kids, and Guilt

Most women, whether or not they're in the workplace, struggle somewhat over their decision of where to work. A woman may ask herself, "Did I do my very best for my kids? Did my work choice make a difference?" Luckily, scientific studies point to the answer to these questions. Today's big news is that work choices don't make the difference.

Researchers and experts in child development have converged over the past few decades to convey one message: It is not the variable of employment that determines how children fare. In fact, says one expert who has extensively reviewed current literature regarding women's employment and its effects on children, "The more closely the children of employed mothers are studied, the more they appear just like the children of mothers who are not employed."[32] Another expert comments, "The consensus among social scientists, after years of research dating back to the 1930s, is that a mother's working outside the home has no predictable effect on children."[33]

"What matters most is a stimulating, nurturing home environment, and working mothers are just as likely to provide that as women who don't work," says still another expert, who adds: "Mothers don't come in two categories: good and bad, nonworking and working. There is no right way to be a good mother. Women today should realize that they have options and that they can have a life outside the home and bright, well-adjusted children."[34]

While employment per se is not a critical variable in child development, another variable is critical: a woman's satisfaction with what she is doing, regardless of her employment status. "Most experts believe that what affects a child is not whether a mother stays home or goes to work, but whether she feels good about her choice," says Kim Brown, author of the article "Do Working Mothers Cheat Their Kids?" The impact of choice in determining a woman's physical and emotional well-being (and, therefore, her children's physical and emotional well-being) cannot be overstated. In a study of more than six hundred women, for example, the crucial element affecting the women's adjustment was whether they were doing what they wanted to do. The women who seemed to be most depressed were those who wanted to work outside the home but did not. And those who were not happy with their roles — whatever they were — were physically less healthy than their more satisfied counterparts.[35]

Women, Work, and the Examined Life

Margaret Brownley, a homemaker, has written of herself and her friend Carol, who worked outside the home, and poses this question: "Given what we know now, would we make the same choices?"

"Yes," says Carol, "but I would definitely take more time off. Looking back, I doubt that an afternoon stolen once in a while to attend a ballgame or school play would have seriously damaged my career."

"Yes," echoes Brownley, who, however, reports that she would also make some alterations. "I would stay home all over again, but I'd attend some classes in preparation for reentering the work force, and I would do more freelance work at home."[36]

In retrospect, these two women are having some regrets: Brownley, because she didn't invest more in herself; Carol, because she didn't invest more in her family.

Most women are caught—frantically racing on a treadmill, blinders in place—trying to just make it through every day. Most women don't lead the examined life or take time out to review whether they are allocating time to meet the needs of both family and self. Any woman—whether or not she "stays home"—needs to have a self. A mistake many make, however, is that of being a mother at the expense of being a person.

Says Judy Abbott, a homemaker and author of an article entitled "Mom Is A Person, Too": "I'm glad my kids think of me as the ideal mother, but I hope they understand that I am more than a mother of nine children. I am a person, too. And since they happen to have me for a mother, they have been exposed to some unique experiences and points of view because, like every other mother in the world, I am an individual first."[37]

"That there's more to me than being a mother" is a stance seconded by Sanford Matthews, a physician and author of *Through the Motherhood Maze*. Matthews, who has attended to more than twenty-five hundred mothers in his pediatric practice over a period of fifteen years, says that often the most telling question he asks mothers is, "Who is the most important person in your life?" Usually, he says, the answer the mother offers is self-effacing, apologetic, self-denying: "The most important person in my life is my child."

Matthews emphasizes that the only viable, health-sustaining answer is this: "In the context of your responsibilities to your husband and your children, the most important person in your life is, and must be, you. . . . Your own life must burn brightly before you can illuminate anything or anyone: your two-week-old infant, your family of five, your whole community or the world at large. And this love implies a trust in your own abilities to do, to be and to act as an independent person."

If you throw all your mothering resources into one gamble — your child — that child's inconsistencies, temper tantrums, and personality flaws will become yours, he claims. "You may lose all sense of adult proportion when you are living for and through your children. You can't be rational or objective when you are pouring all your life into them. And eventually your own identity will ebb away ever so easily while no one benefits from your sacrifice — neither you nor your children." Prepare for the day your children will grow up, he urges. "At that point, when you are forced to stand alone and ask yourself, 'Who am I?' you can easily answer, 'I am a fulfilled person. Besides being myself, I have raised marvelous children who are independent individuals in their own right.' "[38]

In contrast to a woman's intensely submerging herself in a "mother" role, she may likewise submerge that same self in a "work" role, bringing to her employment traditional women's programming that drives her elsewhere to push to succeed perfectly at every moment in every aspect of her life.

Herself ensnared by such unconscious cultural conditioning, Donna Carty, author of an article entitled "Yes, I Was Doing More and Enjoying It Less," describes her journey to find an appropriate balance between family and employment. Carty, who had a challenging career, a loving and supportive husband, well-adjusted children, and a picture-perfect home, wondered why she felt so empty. After contemplation, the answer was

"I'm afraid your mother has to work late again tonight. We do, however, have this videotape of her eating dinner with us last week."

simple, she says. "I was too tired to enjoy the things I had worked so hard for because that's just what everything entailed — work."

Carty finally met her Waterloo one early morning when she shoveled snow after a heavy snowfall and ruptured a lower disk in her back. She subsequently spent three painful months in the hospital and at home, which time-out allowed her to reevaluate her priorities, her do-it-all approach, and the fact that she always put herself last.

Realizing she needed time to relax and enjoy those things she had earned, she faced the fact that the life-style she chose — career woman, wife, and mother — required setting priorities for her time. There were compromises to be made in all areas, she says, but when she was working eighty hours a week on a regular basis, she was compromising everything — most of all, herself. Consequently, she changed to a job in which the work hours better reflected her real priorities.

As Carty sums up her experience in achieving a better balance in distributing her time between work and home, she offers a truism to her readers. Remember, she says, that it's not your job that keeps you warm at night — it's your friends and family that do.[39]

Carty's quest to realign her priorities is similar, although much less dramatic, to that of another person — a much sobered man who, facing the possibility of his own death, called into question his ardent preoccupation with work: "Nobody on his deathbed ever said, 'I wish I had spent more time at the office.' "

These are the poignant words of former Senator Paul Tsonga of Massachusetts, who, a few years ago a rising star in politics, found at age forty-three that he had a form of lymph-node cancer. Although the cancer proved ultimately treatable, Tsonga's first confrontation with mortality forced him to assess his priorities and to realize he would not be around long enough to do everything he'd like to do.

At the top of his list was not running for high office or shaping the nation's laws, but helping his young children grow up. So he decided not to run for reelection in 1984 and instead went home to Massachusetts to be with his family.

Harold S. Kushner, a rabbi and author of such popular books as *When Bad Things Happen to Good People* and *When All You Ever Wanted Isn't Enough,* relates Tsonga's story in an article that chronicles his own reevaluation of life priorities. Kushner himself has a poignant observation that we as women can wisely keep in mind as we come to terms with our own priorities.

"Sooner or later," Kushner explains, "we all learn that our immortality is rooted not in our professional involvement and achievement but in our families. In time, all of our wins and losses in the workplace will be forgotten. If our memories endure, it will be because of the people we have known and touched."[40]

My Self and the Examined Life

It's been a long and arduous task conceiving and writing this book—somewhat like piecing together a 100,000-piece jigsaw puzzle. However, as the pieces have converged to clarify the issues and dilemmas of the '90s woman (and thus my own), I've concluded that the task has been well worth the price.

Through writing this book, I've gained increasing ability to observe my own caretaking and juggling and to make conscious choices regarding expenditure of my time, energy, and resources. That, in turn, has given me greater control over my well-being. I quoted a woman earlier in the text as observing, "If you don't take care of yourself gracefully, you *will* take care of yourself ungracefully." I've dedicated myself to the positive choice of taking care of myself gracefully—keeping myself in good physical and emotional repair—the rest of my life. That means from now on I'll take care of *me* as well as I take care of *them*.

I've waited until the book's ending to write about me because I've wanted you to understand my view of the world before I spoke of myself. I do so now because it may be of some benefit to you—and because we need to take chemical depression out of the closet.

There was a time when I took care of myself ungracefully. Under the tremendous pressure of supporting more things and people than was humanly possible, I became a depleted woman, and I fell into a depression. Depression's grip often closes gradually, taking a silent and insidious toll on one's well-being. It did so on me.

I'm candid about this because I want you to realize that as for taking care of yourself, the stakes are high and the penalties serious if you don't maintain a self-repair and maintenance program. Your body just simply won't run very far on fumes, and anytime you chronically overstress that body physically or emotionally, you run the risk of depression, just as you risk the possibility of many other physical disorders. Remember that depression can wreak havoc on anyone—even you. *No one* is exempt, not even a therapist with twenty-five years experience!

Many causes for depression are not within our conscious management. That is so of a woman's typical cultural characteristics—the caretaker, juggler, guilt sponge, pleaser, and perfectionist—when they go unrecognized. You have an opportunity now to take charge of these characteristics, to bring them into conscious control, and to make the native skills embodied in them work for, rather than against, you. And you have an opportunity to take care of yourself gracefully.

I leave you to that possibility as I wish you well and turn now, as a '90s woman, to implementing—seriously—all my own advice. If you spot me anywhere, you'll find me doing the very best I can. But if I inadvertently make a mistake or miss a step, or simply can't stretch far enough to juggle one more thing, you may hear me saying to myself: "I know I'm a day late and a dollar short—but, for my own emotional survival, it just has to be okay."

Jo Ann Larsen
Aspiring Conscious Caretaker

Notes

Introduction

1. Karen Levine, "Survival Tips for Working Mothers," *Parents Magazine,* November 1988, 69.

2. Nicholas von Hoffman, "American Woman of the '90s," *Self,* January 1990, 94.

3. "Self Survey: 1,100 Women's Answers to Work, Love, Money, Fitness and Health," *Self,* September 1989, 165.

4. Barbara J. Berg, "Working Mother Overload," *Redbook,* March 1989, 93.

5. Janet Murphy, quoted in Nancy Fasciano, "Guilt Trip: Guess Who's Taking a Ride?," *Working Mother,* April 1985, 56.

6. Susan Jacoby, "In Praise of Imperfect Women," *Woman's Day,* November 24, 1981, 66.

7. Maggie Strong, "More Power to You," *Redbook,* September 1983, 174.

8. Ibid.

9. Berg, "Working Mother Overload."

10. Arlie Hochschild, *The Second Shift: Working Parents and the Revolution at Home* (New York: Viking Penguin, 1989), 11–12, 205.

11. Judith Viorst, "Domestic Tranquillity," *Redbook,* April 19, 1980, 75.

Chapter 1: The Caretaker

1. Herbert J. Freudenberger and Gail North, *Women's Burnout* (New York: Penguin Books), 1985, 80.

2. Linda Tschirhart Sanford and Mary Ellen Donovan, *Women & Self-Esteem* (New York: Penguin Books, 1984), 5–6.

Chapter 2: The Juggler

1. Karen Levine, "Survival Tips for Working Mothers," *Parents Magazine,* November 1988, 69.

2. Nancy Gibbs, "How America Has Run Out of Time," *Time*, April 24, 1989, 58.

3. A. Hamer Reiser, "Did You Sleep Through the Lecture on 'Tryna'?," *Postgraduate Medicine*, July 1989, 27.

4. Sally Wendkos Olds and Diane E. Papalia, "Are Kids Growing Up Too Fast?," *Redbook*, March 1990, 91–100.

5. Carolyn Jabs, "Relax: Seven Ways to Be a Happy Stress-free Parent," *Working Mother*, January 1990, 57.

6. Kent Griffiths, "A Potpourri of Stress Management" (unpublished manuscript), 8.

7. Sherod Miller, Daniel Wackman, Elam Nunnally, and Carol Saline, *Straight Talk* (New York: Signet, 1981), 243–45.

8. Carol Osborn, *Enough Is Enough* (New York: Pocket Books, 1988), 76–79.

9. Clyde Reid, *Celebrate the Temporary* (New York: Harper & Row, 1972).

10. Judith Viorst, "Why Don't You Stand Up for Yourself?," *Redbook*, April 1988, 188.

Chapter 3: The Guilt Sponge

1. Barbara Holland, "The Phone Is Ringing, A Child Has Just Skinned Its Knee, The Soup Is Boiling Over, The Cat Is Throwing Up and Someone's at The Door. Which Do You Take Care of First?," *McCall's*, July 1983, 20.

2. Mary Z. Gray, "Who Are 'They' To Say?," *New Woman*, June 1984, p. 98.

3. Lynn Caine, "Mother Guilt," *New Woman*, May 1985, 83.

4. Jean Marzollo, "Why Mothers Get a Hard Time," *Parents Magazine*, November 1987, 103.

5. Lynn Caine, *What Did I Do Wrong?* (New York: Arbor House, 1985), 158, 164.

6. Marzollo, "Why Mothers Get a Hard Time," 108.

7. Cathleen Collins Lee, "Mothering My Way," *Parents Magazine*, September 1989, 85.

8. Karen Levine, "Mother vs. Mother," *Parents Magazine*, June 1985, 65.

9. Ellen Switzer, "Are You Their Mother or Their Servant?," *Family Circle*, May 19, 1978, 150.

10. Lee, "Mothering My Way," 88.

11. Levine, "Mother vs. Mother," 66.

12. Antonia Van der Meer, "Free Yourself!," *Redbook*, March 1989, 169.

13. Carolee Lewin-Scheidman, quoted in Karen Levine, "Defending Your Career," *Parents Magazine*, May 1988, 62.

14. Brent Barlow made this statement in a *Deseret News* column titled "When Have Parents Failed in Raising a Child?" (date unknown).

15. Jean Marzollo, "Making It Through the Holidays," *Parents Magazine*, November 1987, 109.

16. Pamela Redmond Satran, "I Always Flunk Christmas," *Working Mother,* December 1989, 133.

17. Kristin M. Tucker and Rebecca Lowe Warren, *Celebrate the Wonder: A Family Christmas Treasury* (New York: Ballantine/Epiphany Book, 1988), 5–21.

18. Jo Robinson and Jean Staheli, "Bring Home the Joy," *Redbook,* December 1986, 100.

Chapter 4: The Pleaser

1. George Bach and Ronald M. Dentsch, *Stop! You're Driving Me Crazy* (New York: Berkley Books, 1979), 152.

2. Celia Halas and Roberta Matteson, *I've Done So Well — Why Do I Feel So Bad?* (New York: Ballantine Books, 1978), 25.

3. Sam Keen, "Coping with Anxiety and Guilt," *Family Circle,* January 1977, 30.

4. Idea adapted from Robert Conklin, *How to Get People to Do Things* (New York: Ballantine Books, 1979), 76–77.

5. Sidney J. Harris, *The Best of Sidney J. Harris* (Boston: Houghton Mifflin Company, 1975), 94–95.

6. Will Durant, author of *The Story of Civilization,* quoted in Jennifer James, *You Know I Wouldn't Say This If I Didn't Love You* (New York: Newmarket Press, 1990), frontispiece.

7. Natalie Shainess, "Are You Too Good for Your Own Good?," *Redbook,* June 1984, 99.

8. Betsy Hilbert, "How to Stop Being So Tough on Yourself," *Ladies' Home Journal,* May 1987, 155.

9. Andrea Williams, *Making Decisions* (New York: Kensington Publishing Corporation, 1985), 13–14.

10. Mary Ellen Donovan, "This Is DEFINITELY What I Want — I THINK!," *New Woman,* March 1987, 39.

11. Harriet Lerner, *Dance of Anger* (New York: Harper & Row, 1985), 9.

12. Henrie Weisinger, *Dr. Weisinger's Anger Workout Book* (New York: Quill, 1985), 39–40.

13. Lerner, *Dance of Anger,* 102–7.

14. Neil Clark Warren, *Make Anger Your Ally* (New York: Doubleday, 1983), 170–71.

Chapter 5: The Perfectionist

1. Ellen Sue Stern, "The Indispensable Woman," *New Woman,* April 1989, 75.

2. David Burns, *Feeling Good: The New Mood Therapy* (New York: William Morrow and Company, Inc., 1980), 300–301.

3. Dorothy Briggs, *Celebrate Your Self* (New York: Doubleday, 1971), 67.

4. Burns, *Feeling Good: The New Mood Therapy,* 67.

5. Wayne Dyer, *Your Erroneous Zones* (New York: Funk and Wagnalls, 1976), 126.

6. Briggs, *Celebrate Your Self,* 191.

7. Ibid., 65.

8. Carl Rogers, quoted in Alan Lay McGinnis, "How to Weather Marital Storms," *Reader's Digest,* April 1983, 53.

9. John Bradshaw, author of *Bradshaw On: The Family.* Quotation taken from seminar in the Salt Palace, Salt Lake City, Utah, fall 1988.

10. William Gaylin, author of *Feelings,* quoted in Susan Jacoby, "I Feel Used," *McCall's,* May 1985, 26.

11. Ellen Sue Stern, *The Indispensable Woman* (New York: Bantam Books, 1988), 22.

12. Sue Patton Thoele, *The Courage to Be Yourself* (Nevada City, Calif.: Pyramid Press, 1988), 106.

13. Elizabeth Berg, "Giving Up the God Role," *Parents Magazine,* March 1989, 138–40.

14. Marcia Mihakik, "A Perfect Way to Be Miserable," *Prevention,* August 1986, 52.

15. Joan Libman, "How Close Are You to Motherhood Burnout?," *Family Circle,* July 2, 1985, 66.

16. Margorie Hansen Shaevitz, *The Superwoman Syndrome* (New York: Warner Books, 1984), 160.

17. Barbara Law, "How to Add an Hour to Your Day," *Family Circle,* February 10, 1987, 26.

18. Burns, *Feeling Good: The New Mood Therapy,* 303.

19. Lisa Strick, "What's So Bad about Being So-So?," *Woman's Day,* April 3, 1984, 136.

Chapter 6: The Depleted Woman

1. Carol Tannenhauser, "Motherhood Stress," *Woman's Day,* December 26, 1985, 57.

2. Herbert J. Freudenberger and Gail North, *Women's Burnout: How to Spot It, How to Reverse it and How to Prevent It* (New York: Viking Penguin, 1985), 9.

3. Ibid., 10.

4. Ibid., xvii.

5. Maggie Strong, "More Power to You," *Redbook,* September 1983, 103.

6. Kathryn E. Livingston, "When It's Time to Let Go," *Parenting,* September 1989, 76.

7. Hester Mundis, "So You Think You'd Like to Stay Home . . . ," *Working Woman,* October 1983, 84–86.

8. Joseph Procaccini, author of *Parent Burnout,* quoted in Tannenhauser, "Motherhood Stress," 54.

9. Cynthia Lynch and Maurine Ward, "Doing the Fizzle," *This People,* Holiday 1987, 25.

10. Tannenhauser, "Motherhood Stress," 61.

11. Freudenberger and North, *Women's Burnout,* 78–116.

12. "Majority of Women Feel Stressed, Many Say They're Chronically Tired," *Deseret News,* August 23, 1987.

13. Procaccini, in Tannenhauser, "Motherhood Stress," 54.

14. Holly Atkinson, author of *Women and Fatigue,* quoted in Dianne Hales and Jennifer Cook, "The Newest 'Disease' of American Women: Exhaustion," *Self,* June 1988, 123.

15. Hales and Cook, Ibid.

16. Charles Tkacz, quoted in Emrika Padus, *The Complete Guide to Your Emotions and Your Health* (Emmaus, Penn.: Rodale Press, 1985), 14.

17. Laraine C. Abbey, R.N., quoted in Padus, *The Complete Guide to Your Emotions and Your Health,* 14.

18. Padus, Ibid., 15.

19. Ibid., 1.

20. Erica E. Goode, "Beating Depression," *U. S. News & World Report,* March 5, 1990, 48.

21. David Gelman, "Depression," *Newsweek,* May 4, 1987, 48.

22. Winifred Gallagher, "The DD's: Blues Without End," *American Health,* April 1988, 80.

23. Goode, "Beating Depression," 50.

24. Patrick Young, "Chemical Links to Depression May Someday Help Prevent Suicide," *Salt Lake Tribune,* April 20, 1986, A-5.

25. Gelman, "Depression," 49.

26. Susan Mirow, M.D., quoted in "Chemical Depression," *Deseret News,* September 2, 1988.

27. Earl Ubell, "They're Closing In on Mental Illness," *Parade,* December 3, 1989, 13.

28. Abigail Trafford, "New Hope for the Depressed," *U. S. News & World Report,* January 24, 1982, 40.

29. Thomas L. Schwenk and James C. Coyne, "Recognition and Treatment of the Depressed Patient: An Effective Office Approach," *Modern Medicine,* February 1990, 82.

Chapter 7: The Woman and Her House

1. Jean Fitzpatrick, "The Dirty Truth About Housework," *Parents Magazine,* January 1984, 52.

2. Aaron T. Beck, *Love Is Never Enough* (New York: Harper & Row, 1988), 13.

3. "Life in These United States," *Reader's Digest,* May 1989, 83.

4. Linda Essig, "I'm a Lousy Housekeeper So Sue Me," *Woman's Day,* October 1987, 48.

5. Telephone interview with Dorothy Leeds, author of *Smart Questions: A New Strategy for Successful Managers* (New York: Berkley Books, 1987).

Chapter 8: Women, Husbands, Kids and Houses

1. Arlie Hochschild, *The Second Shift: Working Parents and the Revolution at Home* (New York: Viking Press, 1989), 9.

2. Ellen Goodman, *At Large* (New York: Fawcett Crest, 1981), 107–8.

3. Morton H. Shaevitz, *Sexual Static: How Men Are Confusing the Women They Love* (Boston: Little, Brown, and Company, 1987), 18–19.

4. Ibid., 8.

5. Erica Abeel, "The Hurting Husband," *Ladies' Home Journal,* January 1981, 32–40.

6. Niki Scott, "If Your Husband Is The Sitter—It's Hard to Complain," *Working Mother,* March 1983, 96.

7. Patricia Volk, "The Flip Side: The Helpless-Husband Syndrome," *Family Circle,* November 7, 1989, 56.

8. Arlie Hochschild, *Families Without Villains* (Lexington, Mass.: Lexington Books, 1984), 41–51.

9. Charlotte Whitney, *Win–Win Negotiations for Couples: A Personal Guide to Joint Decision-Making* (Gloucester, Mass.: Para Research, 1986), 106.

10. Caryl Waller Krueger, *1001 Things to Do with Your Kids* (Nashville: Abingdon Press, 1988), 299.

11. Gary Emery, *Own Your Own Life* (New York: Signet, 1982), 68–70.

12. Thomas Lickona, *Raising Good Children from Birth Through the Teen Years* (New York: Bantam Books, 1983), 18.

13. Kathy Schubert, quoted in "Check Out," *Redbook,* May 1988, 186.

14. Sherry Ferguson and Lawrence E. Mazin, *Parent Power: A Program to Help Your Child Succeed in School* (New York: Clarkson N. Potter, 1989), 75–78.

15. Christie Hyde, "Confessions of a Nonspanker," *Parents Magazine,* October 1980, 87.

Chapter 9: Filling in the Woman

1. Linda Tschirhart Sanford and Mary Ellen Donovan, *Woman's Self-Esteem* (New York: Penguin Books, 1984), 304.

2. Jean Marzollo, "Don't Call Me Supermom," *Parents Magazine,* April 1984, 63.

3. Sanford and Donovan, *Woman's Self-Esteem,* 16.

4. Caryl Rivers, "The Luck Illusion," *Woman's Day,* May 22, 1984, 190.

5. Jeannie Ralston, "I'm a Fake!," *McCalls,* April 1985, 89.

6. Annie Gottlieb, "Body Hatred," *McCalls,* April 1985, 83.

7. Marcia Germaine Hutchinson, "Transforming Body Image: Your Body,

Friend or Foe," *Women and Therapy,* quoted in Rita Freedman, *Beauty Bound* (Lexington, Mass.: Lexington Books, 1986), 24.

8. Hutchinson, quoted in Gottlieb, "Body Hatred," 83.

9. Sanford and Donovan, *Woman's Self-Esteem,* 370.

10. Freedman, *Beauty Bound,* 1.

11. Ibid., 37.

12. Una Stannard, "The Mask of Beauty," essay in L. Rubin, *Women of a Certain Age* (New York: Harper & Row), quoted in Freedman, *Beauty Bound,* 44.

13. Steven Levenkron, author of *Treating and Overcoming Anorexia Nervosa* (New York: Charles Scribner's), quoted in Dalma Heyne, "Why We Are Never Satisfied with Our Bodies," *McCalls,* May 1982, 116.

14. Sanford and Donovan, *Woman's Self-Esteem,* 371.

15. Carol Travis, "Is Thin Still In?," *Woman's Day,* March 3, 1987, 32.

16. Levenkron, quoted in Heyne, "Why We Are Never Satisfied with Our Own Bodies," 116.

17. Ibid.

18. Susan Brownmiller, "36-26-36: The Outrageous Idea of the Ideal Female Figure," *New Woman,* April 1984, 80.

19. Travis, "Is Thin Still In?," 35.

20. Janice Kaplin, "Slaves to the Scale," *Self,* September 1989, 194–95.

21. Freedman, *Beauty Bound,* 238.

22. Barbara Harris, "One Size Doesn't Fit All," *Shape,* July 1990, 12.

23. Shad Helmstetter, *The Self-Talk Solution* (New York: William Morrow and Company, 1987), 37.

24. Harold Bloomfield, *Inner Joy* (New York: The Berkley Publishing Group, 1980), 118.

25. Alan Loy McGinnis, "How to Get the Most Out of Yourself," *Reader's Digest,* March 1988, 196.

Chapter 10: Investing in Your "Self"

1. Spencer Johnson, "Why Don't Women Take Care of Themselves?," *Redbook,* October 1986, 144–45.

2. Deidre Laiken, "How to Make Friends with Yourself," *McCalls,* October 1988, 95.

3. Andrea Thompson, "Confessions of an Unfit Mother," *Working Mother,* April 1984, 82.

4. Wayne Dyer, *Your Erroneous Zones* (New York: Funk & Wagnalls, 1976), 11.

5. Julia Cameron, quoted in Jo Ann Larsen, "A Message for Women: Invest in Yourselves," *Deseret News,* April 26, 1987, C-3.

6. Roger Gould, *Transformations* (New York: Simon & Schuster, 1978).

7. Daniel J. Levinson, *The Seasons of a Man's Life* (New York: Ballantine Books, 1978).

8. Nela S. Schwartzberg, "Call Me Supermom," *Parents Magazine,* March 1986, 80.

9. Paula Piertromonaco, quoted in Schwartzberg, "Call Me Supermom," 82.

10. Schwartzberg, "Call Me Supermom," 82.

11. Margorie Shaevitz, *The Superwoman Syndrome,* 182.

12. Nancy Gibbs, "How America Has Run Out of Time," 60.

13. Leonore J. Weitzman, *The Divorce Revolution* (New York: The Free Press, 1985).

14. Claire Safran, "Women and Children Adrift: The Divorce Revolution," *Reader's Digest,* September 1986, 92.

15. Colette Dowling, *The Cinderella Complex* (New York: Pocket Books, 1981), 16.

16. Ibid., 41.

17. Jo Coudert, "Help for Your Hardest Decisions," *Reader's Digest,* March 1984, 149–54.

Chapter 11: The Woman and Work

1. Hester Mundis, *Powermom* (New York: Congdon & Weed, 1984), 13.

2. Holland, "The Phone Is Ringing . . . ," 20.

3. Ellen Garey, "How I Rediscovered My Kids," *Parents Magazine,* April 1986, 93.

4. Elizabeth Berg, "Why I'm at Home," *Parents Magazine,* April 1987, 123.

5. Pamela Hobbs Hoffecker, "Will the Real Working Mother Please Stand Up?," *Parents Magazine,* April 1985, 78.

6. Arlene Fischer, "I Want To Stay Home—Where I Belong," *Redbook,* April 1986, 157.

7. Ibid., 97.

8. Marguerite Michaels, "Why More Mothers Stay Home," *Parade Magazine,* October 13, 1985, 25.

9. Susan Jacoby, "In Praise of Imperfect Women," *Women's Day,* November 24, 1981, 66.

10. Artis Whitman, "What Women Won't Trade for Independence," *Women's Day,* May 19, 1978, 108.

11. Angie Thompson, "Why Am I So Happy in the Absence of My Child?," *Working Mother,* August 1983, 55.

12. Whitman, "What Women Won't Trade for Independence."

13. Barbara J. Berg, "Working Mother Overload," *Redbook,* March 1989, 91.

14. Crow, "Feeling Guilty," *Parents Magazine,* August 1987, 8.

15. Thompson, "Why Am I So Happy in the Absence of My Child?"

16. Kathryn E. Livingston, "When It's Time to Let Go," *Parenting,* September 1989, 67.

17. Jacoby, "In Praise of Imperfect Women."

18. Karen Levine, "The Satisfaction Factor," *Parents Magazine*, September 1988, 83.

19. Crow, "Feeling Guilty."

20. Jacoby, "In Praise of Imperfect Women," 71.

21. Whitman, "What Women Won't Trade for Independence," 204.

22. Livingston, "When It's Time to Let Go."

23. Mary Howell, "The Best Kind of Mother," *Working Mother*, November 1983, 124.

24. Ibid., 127.

25. Wendy Lowe, "Working My Way Back to You, Babe," *Parenting*, October 1989, 83.

26. Lois Wyse, "So Long, Supermom," *Good Housekeeping*, November 1981, 106.

27. Linda Stern, "Work," *Self*, January 1990, 70.

28. Mary Ellen Schoonmaker, "The New Decade: What's in Your Future?," *Family Circle*, January 9, 1990, 42.

29. Betty Holcomb, "Is the Mommy Track a Trap?," *Working Mother*, July 1989, 86–90.

30. Ibid., 90.

31. Lori B. Andrews, "The Working Mommy's Game," *Parents Magazine*, April 1985, 75–76.

32. Mary Howell, "The Best Kind of Mother," *op. cit.*

33. Kim Brown, "Do Working Mothers Cheat Their Kids?," *Redbook*, April 1985, 76.

34. Adele Gottfried, quoted in Dianne Hales, "Are Working Moms Good Mothers?," *Redbook*, March 1987, 73.

35. Brown, "Do Working Mothers Cheat Their Kids?"

36. Margaret Brownley, "A Tale of Two Mothers," *Working Mothers*, September 1987, 111.

37. Judy Abbott, "Mom Is a Person, Too," *Parents Magazine*, December 1988, 230.

38. Sanford Mathews and Maryann Bucknum Brenley, in "The Biggest Mistake a Mother Can Make," *Redbook*, October 1982, 40–42.

39. Donna Carty, "Yes, I Was Doing More and Enjoying It Less...," *Working Woman*, February 1986, 18–87.

40. Harold S. Kushner, "Family Time," *Redbook*, January 1990, 92-93.

Index

Abbott, Judy, 303
Abeel, Erica, 206
ACT formula, 224
Andrews, Lori B., 301
Anger, 17; appropriate responses to, 95–96; expressing, continuum of, 107–9; strategies for dealing with, 109–12; physiological components of, 111; of parents and children, controlling, 231–33
"Approvalitis," 80–81; strategies for combatting, 98–103
Asking directly for what one wants, 211, 213. *See also* Help, asking for
Atkinson, Holly, 158
Average, daring to be, 145–46. *See also* Perfectionism

Bach, George, 80–81
Balance, 296
Barlow, Brent, 74
Beauty: equating self-worth with, 254; impossibility of perfection in, 255; conflicting standards of, 255–56; broadening personal concept of, 262
Beck, Aaron T., 176
Behavior: shaping, through positive messages, 227–28; unacceptable, dealing with, 229–31
Berg, Barbara J., 2–3, 5
Berg, Elizabeth, 140
Blame: and mothers, 69–70; assigning, 131
Bloomfield, Harold, 266
Body image, 252–53, 261–63
Boundary Box, 19–23, 26
Breast cancer, 162–64
Briggs, Dorothy, 121, 126, 127–28
Brown, Kim, 302
Brownley, Margaret, 302–3
Buber, Martin, 24
Buddha, 98
Burnout: physical symptoms of, 151; vulnerability to, 151–53; role of change in, 153–55;

twelve phases of, 155–56; combatting, with exercise, 157–58; combatting, with nutrition, 159–61; avoiding, with preventative health care, 161–64
Burns, David, 120, 145, 176

Caine, Lynn, 69–70
Cameron, Julia, 280–81
Caretaking: unconscious versus conscious, 9, 12–13, 136; as woman's foremost strength, 12; self-recriminations in, 16–17; unconscious, anger accompanying, 17–18; conscious, moving toward, 18–19, 22–23; by workaholics, 32–33; and guilt, 54–55; example of, in *Peter Pan*, 82–83
Carty, Donna, 304–6
Centered-in-self versus being self-centered, 23–24
Change: accepting possibility of, 123; and burnout, 153–55
Chemical short-circuiting in depression, 167
Children: time pressures of, 37–38; connecting with, 38–39; accepting imperfections of, 72–74, 224–25; getting help of, with housework, 221–24; are not short adults, 224; misbehavior of, is not personal, 225–26; avoiding nagging, 226–27; effect of mothers' employment on, 301–2
Choices: guilt accompanying, 2–3; making your own, 23, 59–60, 136–37; regarding time allotment, 41; myriad of, 155; conscious, regarding housework, 192–94; of chores, offering, 222;

regarding outside employment, 296–301
Chores. *See* Housework
Christmas and guilt, 74–79
Communication, 115–16
Comparisons: guilt accompanying, 66; women's tendency to make, 242–44; fruitlessness of, 244–45
Compliments: deflecting, reasons behind, 246–50; learning to accept, 250–52
Conflict, family, strategies for avoiding, 234–38
Control, and perfectionist, 133–35
Coudert, Jo, 287–88
Crow, Elizabeth, 295
Cultural programming, 8, 33; and burnout, 152; and housework, 202–3

Day off, taking, 25–26
Decision making, 103–7
Depleted Woman, 5; characteristics of, 150–51. *See also* Burnout
Depression, clinical or chemical: long-term nature of, 164–65; impossibility of "snapping out of," 165–66; biological base of, 166–67; description of effects of, 167–69; susceptibility to, 169–70; often goes untreated, 170–71; symptoms of, 171–73; bipolar, 173–74; seeking treatment for, 174–76
Disapproval: vulnerability to, 85–88; limited power of, 88–89; depends on others' choices, not yours, 89–91, 94–96; developing explanations for, 91–92; defusing, by listening and inquiring, 96–97; declining to accept, 97–98, 189–90

Divorce laws, changes in, 285–86
Donovan, Mary Ellen, 107, 243–44, 248, 253, 255
Dowling, Colette, 286–87
Dyer, Wayne, 124, 279

Education, importance of, 284
Egos, fragility of, 130–31
Einstein, Albert, 269
Emery, Gary, 223–24
Endorsing yourself, 264–67
Essig, Linda, 194
Excuses, making, for chaotic house, 177–79
Exercise, benefits of, 157–58, 263
Expectations, unrealistic, releasing others from, 280

Family: traditional concept of, 5–6; ideal, myth of, 42–43; avoiding conflict in, strategies for, 234–38
Fatigue, 156
Feelings: expressing, with "I" messages, 112–13; learning to express effectively, 113–16
Ferguson, Sherry, 228–29
Finiteness, recognizing one's own, 141–43
Fitzpatrick, Jean, 182
Freedman, Rita, 254, 262
Freudenberger, Herbert J., 151–52, 155–56
Funt, Allen, 238–39
Full-time homemakers, challenges of, 289-92

"Good-enough" mothers, 70–74
Goodman, Ellen, 203
Gould, Roger, 281–82
Gray, Mary Z., 58–59
Growth, personal, assuming responsibility for, 275–78, 282–83

Guilt: due to increased choices, 2–4; over relaxing, 31; and caretaker role, 54–55; from tyrannical "shoulds," 55–60; earned versus unearned, 61; felt by mothers, 65–69; and holidays, 74–79; over housework, setting aside, 194; feeling, when asking for help, 210; and working mothers, 294
Guilt Sponge: woman as, 4, 53–54, 150; overcoming tendencies of, 60–63; and decision making, 104

Happiness, personal, assuming responsibility for, 278–82
Harris, Barbara, 263
Harris, Sidney, 93–94
Health care, preventative, 161–64
Helmstetter, Shad, 265
Help, asking for: guilt feelings over, 210; roadblocks to, 214–15; contrasted with nagging, 216; in task-centered manner, 216–18
"Helpless-husband syndrome," 207–8
Hochschild, Arlie, 6, 7, 202
Holcomb, Betty, 299–301
Holiday guilt, giving up, 74–79
Holland, Barbara, 56, 289–90
Homemakers, full-time, challenges of, 289–92
House: making excuses for condition of, 177–79; self-esteem linked to, 180–84; "perfect," myth of, 184–86; releasing yourself from, 187–200; taking relaxed attitude toward, 194–96; responsibility for, seems to fall on women, 203
Housework: cultural perspective to,

186–87; is not a "fault" issue, 187–88; changing self-talk about, 188–89; setting one's own standards for, 190–92; determining priorities in, 192–94; monetary value of, 196; placing people ahead of, 196–97; hiring help with, 199; disputes over, between spouses, 201–2, 206; men's attitudes toward, contrasted with women's, 202–6; tendency to re-do, 208; criticizing husband's methods of doing, 208–9; sense of indispensability in, 210; task-centered approach to, 218–19; developing mutual philosophy of, 219–20; dividing, 220; getting children to help with, 221–24; horizontal nature of, 289–90

Howell, Mary, 297

Hutchinson, Marcia, 252–53

Hyde, Christie, 238

"I" messages, 110, 112–13

Imposter phenomenon, 249–50

Independence: allowing, in others, 137–40; physical, encouraging, 222–23

Initiating, getting needs filled by, 213

Invincible Woman syndrome, 142

Jabs, Carolyn, 38

Jacoby, Susan, 291, 294, 295–96

Johnson, Spencer, 268–69

Judgment: toward others, suspending, 63–65; trusting your own, 101–2; toward change, 116

Juggler: woman as, 4, 27–28, 150; reasons for being, 28–29; in

workplace, 29–31; overcoming tendencies of, 39–42

Kaplin, Janice, 257–58

Keen, Sam, 88

Kushner, Harold S., 306

Labels, perfectionistic, 122–23; overcoming habit of using, 123–25

Laiken, Diedre, 274

Lee, Cathleen Collins, 71, 72

Leeds, Dorothy, 196

Lein, Laura, 219, 220

Lerner, Harriet, 108

Levine, Karen, 71, 72, 294–95

Levinson, Daniel J., 282

Lewin-Scheidman, Carolee, 73–74

Lickona, Thomas, 224

Listening: to defuse anger, 96–97; and expressing feelings, 116

Logsdon, Valerie, 161–64

Lowe, Wendy, 298

Luck Illusion, 248–49

Lynch, Cynthia, 154–55

Martyrdom, 135–37, 209

Marzollo, Jean, 69, 70, 75

Matthews, Sanford, 303–4

Mazin, Lawrence, 228–29

Men: cultural programming of, regarding housework, 202–6; eliciting help from, 207

Miller, Sherod, 39

Mind reading: avoiding, 189; expecting, of husband, 211–13

Mirow, Susan, 166–67

Mistakes: advertising, 101; fear of making, 125–26; growing from, 126–27; mislabeled, 127; letting go of, 127–29; letting others make, 129–33

Moods, taking charge of, 93–94

Mothers: guilt felt by, 65–69; "bashing" of, 69–70; being "good-enough," 70–74. *See also* Children
Mundis, Hester, 153, 289
Murphy, Janet, 3–4

Nagging, 216, 226–27
Needs, personal, recognizing, 276–77
No, learning to say, 46–52
North, Gail, 151–52, 155–56
Nutrition, importance of, 159–61

Osborn, Carol, 40
Over-apologizing, 98–99

Padus, Emrika, 160
Perfectionism: continuum of, 118–20; ultimate illusion in, 120–21; and fear of making mistakes, 125–26; releasing others from, 129–33; and martyrdom, 135–37; dependence fostered by, 137–40; releasing self from, 141–49
Perfectionist: woman as, 4–5; and decision making, 104; example of, 117–18; all-or-nothing thinking of, 121–22; labels used by, 122–23; desire of, for control, 133–35
Peter Pan, 82
PHS (preholiday syndrome), 75–76
Piertromonaco, Paula, 283
Pleaser: woman as, 4, 150; suffers from "approvalitis," 81–82; identifying characteristics of, 84; egocentricity of, 87; overcoming tendencies of, 98–103; and decision making, 104
Positive messages: shaping children's behavior through, 227–

28; focusing on, 228–29; to deal with misbehavior, 229–31; building self-esteem through, 238–39; keys to using, 239–41; learning to accept, 250–52; in self-talk, 265–66
Preholiday syndrome, 75–76
Present, living in, 44–46
Priorities and housework, 192–94
Procaccini, Joseph, 153–54, 156

Ralston, Jeannie, 249–50
Reid, Clyde, 45–46
Reiser, A. Hamer, Jr., 36–37
Relaxing: difficulty in, 31; defusing anger through, 111
Responsibilities, juggling, 4
Risks, taking, 101
Rivers, Caryl, 248–49
Robinson, Jo, 77–78
Rogers, Carl, 129
Roles: changing, of women, 2, 6; traditional, of family members, 5–6; juggling a multitude of, 13; related to housework, 181–82; multiple, advantages of, 283

Sanford, Linda, 243–44, 248, 253, 255
Satran, Pamela Redmond, 75–76
Schwartzberg, Nela S., 282–83
Self: caring for, 9, 23–26, 307–8; healthy sense of, 83–84; endorsing, 264–67; investing in, roadblocks to, 268–71; acknowledging worth of, 271–72; always putting others ahead of, 272–73; taking time for, 273–75; assuming responsibility for growth of, 275–78, 282–83; happiness comes from within, 278–82; as most important person, 303–4

Self-centered versus centered-in-self, 23–24

Self-esteem: crumbling, causes of, 8–9; taking charge of, 10; tied to productivity, 28–29; and saying no, 48; and "approvalitis," 81, 86; linked to house, 180–84; and positive messages, 238–39; and accepting compliments, 250–52; basing, on beauty, 254; and endorsing yourself, 264–67; tied to husband, 281–82

Self-talk, positive, 265–66

Shaevitz, Margorie, 145

Shaevitz, Morton, 203–4, 205

"Shoulds": tyranny of, 55–60; tracking and evaluating, 60–61; releasing others from, 63–65

Staheli, Jean, 77–78

Stannard, Una, 255

Stern, Ellen Sue, 137

Stop, look, and listen approach to self-investment, 269

Stress: modern causes of, 1–2, 6–7; article about, 14–15; feelings accompanying, 15–16; due to time pressures, 34; strategies for relieving, 34–37; accepting responsibility for, 39; assessing reactions to, 43–44. *See also* Burnout

Strick, Lisa, 147

Strong, Maggie, 4

Success: "illusion of," 1

Switzer, Ellen, 71–72

Tannenhauser, Carol, 155

Temper tantrums, 231–33

Thompson, Andrea, 276–77

Time out, taking, 211, 273–75

Time pressures, 34–38

Toffler, Alvin, 154

Travis, Carol, 255–56, 257

Tsonga, Paul, 306

Twain, Mark, 264

Usefulness versus being used, 136

Van der Meer, Antonia, 72–73

Volk, Patricia, 207

Von Hoffman, Nicholas, 2

Ward, Maurine, 154–55

Warren, Neil Clark, 111–12

Weight: obsession with, 256–57; coming to terms with, 257–59; focusing on health instead of, 259–61

Weisinger, Henrie, 109

Weitzman, Leonore J., 285–86

Whitman, Walt, 264

Whitney, Charlotte, 220

Williams, Andrea, 105

Women: changing roles of, 2, 6, 284–85; characteristics of, 5; traditional role of, 5–6; as caretakers, 7–8; importance of education for, 284

Workaholics, 32–33

Workplace: juggler in, 29–31; increasing percentage of women in, 284–85; women in, challenges of, 292–94; options available in, 297–301

Wyse, Lois, 298

Zusya, Hasidic rabbi, 267